BILLY THE KID

Also by Richard W. Etulain (*a selective listing*)

AUTHOR

Owen Wister
Ernest Haycox
Re-imagining the Modern American West: A Century of Fiction, History, and Art
Telling Western Stories: From Buffalo Bill to Larry McMurtry
Beyond the Missouri: The Story of the American West
Seeking First the Kingdom: Northwest Nazarene University, A Centennial History
Abraham Lincoln and Oregon Country Politics in the Civil War Era
The Life and Legends of Calamity Jane
Calamity Jane: A Reader's Guide
Ernest Haycox and the Western
Thunder in the West: The Life and Legends of Billy the Kid

COAUTHOR

Conversations with Wallace Stegner on Western History and Literature
The American West: A Twentieth-Century History
Presidents Who Shaped the American West

EDITOR

Jack London on the Road: The Tramp Diary and Other Hobo Writings
Writing Western History: Essays on Major Western Historians
Basques of the Pacific Northwest: A Collection of Essays
Contemporary New Mexico, 1940–1990
Does the Frontier Experience Make America Exceptional?
César Chávez: A Brief Biography with Documents
New Mexican Lives: Profiles and Historical Stories
Western Lives: A Biographical History of the American West
Lincoln Looks West: From the Mississippi to the Pacific

COEDITOR

The Popular Western: Essays toward a Definition
The Idaho Heritage
The Frontier and American West
Basque Americans
Fifty Western Writers: A Bio-Bibliographical Guide
A Bibliographical Guide to the Study of Western American Literature
Faith and Imagination: Essays on Evangelicals and Literature
The Twentieth-Century West: Historical Interpretations
Religion and Culture
The American West in the Twentieth Century: A Bibliography
Researching Western History: Topics in the Twentieth Century
Religion in Modern New Mexico
By Grit and Grace: Eleven Women Who Shaped the American West
Portraits of Basques in the New World
With Badges and Bullets: Lawmen and Outlaws in the Old West
The Hollywood West
The American West in 2000: Essays in Honor of Gerald D. Nash
Wild Women of the Old West
Chiefs and Generals

BILLY THE KID

A Reader's Guide

Richard W. Etulain

UNIVERSITY OF OKLAHOMA PRESS : NORMAN

Publication of this book is made possible through the generosity of Edith Kinney Gaylord.

Library of Congress Cataloging-in-Publication Data

Names: Etulain, Richard W., author.
Title: Billy the Kid : a reader's guide / Richard W. Etulain.
Description: Norman : University of Oklahoma Press, [2020] | Summary: "A companion book to Richard W. Etulain's Thunder in the West, it summarizes and evaluates more than a century of the interpretations of Billy the Kid, including biographies, histories, novels, and movies, as well as major archival sources and research collections."—Provided by publisher.
Identifiers: LCCN 2020004263 | ISBN 978-0-8061-6627-8 (hardcover) ISBN 978-0-8061-9092-1 (paper)
Subjects: LCSH: Billy, the Kid—Bibliography. | Billy, the Kid—In literature. | Southwest,
    New—In popular culture.
Classification: LCC Z8108.81 .E78 2020 786.B54 | DDC 012—dc23
LC record available at https://lccn.loc.gov/2020004263

The paper in this book meets the guidelines for permanence and durability of the Committee on Production Guidelines for Book Longevity of the Council on Library Resources, Inc. ∞

Copyright © 2020 by the University of Oklahoma Press, Norman, Publishing Division of the University. Paperback published 2022. Manufactured in the U.S.A.

All rights reserved. No part of this publication may be reproduced, stored in a retrieval system, or transmitted, in any form or by any means, electronic, mechanical, photocopying, recording, or otherwise—except as permitted under Section 107 or 108 of the United States Copyright Act—without the prior written permission of the University of Oklahoma Press. To request permission to reproduce selections from this book, write to Permissions, University of Oklahoma Press, 2800 Venture Drive, Norman OK 73069, or email rights.oupress@ou.edu.

For

Kathleen Chamberlain
Paul Andrew Hutton
Richard Weddle

Superb researchers and writers
on Lincoln County
and
Billy the Kid

Contents

Preface ix

Manuscript Collections and Manuscripts 1

Bibliographies and Reference Works 4

Newspaper Articles 7

Books and Pamphlets 32

Essays and Book Chapters 108

Novels, Other Literary Works, and Criticism 150

Movies: Films and Criticism 193

Photographs 223

Billy the Kid: Unfinished Business 227

Index 231

Preface

Billy the Kid competes with Jesse James and Gen. George Armstrong Custer for being the most written-about character of the Old West. More than a thousand nonfiction books and essays have been written about Billy and the New Mexico Lincoln County War that engulfed Billy in his last years. Hundreds—even thousands—of newspaper stories have kept his name alive, with novelists and filmmakers continuing to make the Kid a central figure in their fiction and movies. Nearly 140 years after his death, Billy the Kid remains a much-recognized character among readers and movie fans, especially those fascinated with the Old West.

The major purpose of this guide is to introduce readers to the most significant of these written or filmed works. When stating that what follows is commentary on the best books, essays, novels, films, and the most significant newspaper articles, I recognize the arbitrary nature of that assertion. But these comments on individual writings and films will provide instructive summaries and evaluations of approximately eighty books, nearly eighty-five essays, about thirty-five novels, twenty-five films, and more than seventy-five newspaper articles. I have had to be selective in all categories so this book does not explode into twice or three times its present length. Choosing which newspaper stories were to be annotated was particularly daunting because notes on journalistic articles of importance could fill an entire volume. Also, I have not included much on recent newspaper articles treating controversies surrounding projects to exhume Billy's body for comparative DNA studies and possible Billy photographs. Nearly all those stories focus more on the controversies than on Billy himself.

Other items have been excluded largely because of space demands. For instance, I do not treat most self-published books, although the large books of prolific author Gale Cooper are exceptions; I have included comments on those self-published sources central to an understanding of Billy's life and legends about him. Again, there are a few exceptions to these exclusions. In addition, I do not deal with television programs, music about the Kid, or dramatic presentations.

My approach here is primarily that of the historian. I point out the historical contributions of authors, books, and movies but also note their factual inaccuracies. Others might place more emphasis on the literary or artistic contributions of books, essays, and movies—a good, acceptable approach—but that is not the way here. I try to summarize more than evaluate so that readers will be introduced, first of all, to the contents of items discussed.

A few comments on the book's organization. The book is divided into several sections dealing with varied writings and films about Billy the Kid. First to be addressed are manuscript collections and manuscripts, bibliographies and reference works, and newspaper articles. The second group embraces extensive, separate sections devoted to books and pamphlets, essays and books chapters, novels, and films. Abbreviated sections on Billy photographs and research and writing projects on Billy that are still needed close out the volume.

All sections, save for those listing manuscripts and newspapers, are arranged alphabetically. Numbers in parentheses refer either to a source's pages (p.) or provide a cross-reference to other numbered entries.

If this book achieves its major purpose, it can be the first stop for those searching for the best or most useful sources on Billy the Kid. The book should also help searchers sort out the most dependable from the misdirected or legend-ridden sources.

Discerning students of Billy the Kid will realize how much shifting sociocultural trends in the United States have influenced changing interpretations of him. Consider the following shifts in Kid interpretations: a desperado from the Gilded Age up through World War I; a possible hero in the West-appreciating 1920s; a singing Western hero in the 1930s and 1940s; an emerging part villain, part hero from the 1960s forward. These chronological shifts, with resultant changes in the interpretations of Billy, suggest how important evolving milieus are in shaping views about the Kid. Such shifts lead one to realize that it is not just historical facts that shape the Kid's identity but also changing cultural environments. We do not view Billy in 2020 as we saw him a century ago.

A few discerning scholars have made clear this combined importance of history and legend. In 1952, in his *Billy the Kid: The Bibliography of a Legend*

(14), western collector and commentator J. C. Dykes traces the chronological development of Kid interpretations, showing how they began with a desperado and gradually shifted toward more positive views of Billy. Ramon Adams also organizes chronologically his *A Fitting Death for Billy the Kid* (1960). Not much into dealing with the influences of shifting sociocultural contexts, Adams stresses the historical accuracy or lack thereof in historical writings about the Kid. Kathleen P. Chamberlain, in the most extensive listing of books and essays (more than eight hundred items) about Billy and other participants in the Lincoln War, *Billy the Kid and the Lincoln County War: A Bibliography* (1997, #13), provides an unannotated bibliography of immense use to scholars and students. Meanwhile, others are digging deeper into the linkages between changing interpretations of the Kid and their shifting cultural contexts. The pioneering work in this area is Kent Ladd Steckmesser's *The Western Hero in History and Legend* (1965, #170). His analytical volume provides comparative studies of the evolving biographies and legends of four major westerners: Kit Carson, Billy the Kid, Wild Bill Hickok, and George Armstrong Custer. Expanding on this approach is Stephen Tatum in *Inventing Billy the Kid: Visions of the Outlaw in America, 1881–1981* (1982, #171). More than any other writer, Tatum pays close heed to the cultural and social shifts in a century's time and demonstrates how those shifts have influenced changes in interpretations of Billy the Kid. Tatum's work remains a model for this kind of cultural contextual study of evolving legends and interpretations.

The annotations that follow are generally in line with Tatum's approach. The author is convinced that through a careful study of both biographical and historical facts and rising and shifting legends and interpretations, one comes closest to gaining a fuller meaning of Billy the Kid's life and ongoing significance.

This book owes much to several sources. Most important, it is the partner of the jointly published *Thunder in the West: The Life and Legends of Billy the Kid* (2020). *Thunder* is both biographical and historiographical, dealing with the Kid's life as well as the histories, biographies, novels, and films about him. The present work, using some of the words, phrases, paragraphs, and even pages from *Thunder*, is an extensive annotated guide of the writings and films dealing with Billy. The carryover between the two volumes is particularly extensive in the discussion of biographies and historical novels and occurs some in films about Billy. Sections of this book are likewise based on five of my recent essays: "Billy the Kid: Thunder in the West," in Richard W. Etulain and Glenda Riley, *With Badges and Bullets* (1999); "Billy the Kid among the Dime Novelists,"

Outlaw Gazette (2017); "Billy the Kid Among the Novelists," *New Mexico Historical Review* (2018); "The Legendary, Mysterious Kid," *Wild West* (2019); and "Is There Anything Left to Say about Billy the Kid?," *Journal of the Wild West History Association* (2018). Still other sections draw on my other writings: my "Introduction" to a reprint of Walter Noble Burns, *The Saga of Billy the Kid* (1999); *Re-imagining the Modern American West: A Century of Fiction, History, and Art* (1996); and *Telling Western Stories: From Buffalo Bill to Larry McMurtry* (1999). I am grateful to editors and publishers for permission to utilize my previous writings for this project.

Several persons have been instrumental in the shaping of this book. Nearly forty years ago, when I was being introduced to Billy the Kid, the writings and then the encouragements of Frederick Nolan and Robert Utley spurred me on my way. My conclusions in these individual annotations and general comments owe much to the writings of Nolan and Utley. I thankfully admit how much their books, essays, and letters have helped me. Conversations with my colleague Paul Andrew Hutton have also been an inspiration. More recently, the writings of Steve Tatum, Kathleen Chamberlain, Jerry (Richard) Weddle, and John Wilson have also added to and influenced my thinking. Graduate student and then tour guide Dan Carnett offered me the opportunity to lead an enjoyable Billy the Kid tour. Over time, librarians and researchers Nancy Brown Martinez, Tomas Jaehn, Cathy Smith, Dennis Daily, and Lisa Wilson provided me with access to needed materials. I greatly appreciate how much help these persons have been.

THANKS TO EDITOR AND PUBLISHER

Manuscript Collections and Manuscripts

MAJOR COLLECTIONS

1. Nita Stewart Haley Memorial Library and History Center, Midland, Tex.

   This important library includes the Robert N. Mullin Collection, one of the four most important major research collections on Billy the Kid and Lincoln County. It comprises the large gatherings of manuscripts, letters, and photographs that oil executive Mullin collected over time. The Haley Library also houses the interviews that J. Evetts Haley gathered for a projected biography of Billy the Kid (never completed). The compiled Haley interviews are worthy of book publication.

2. Lincoln County, Lincoln, N.Mex.

   The New Mexico Department of Cultural Affairs administers in Lincoln the Philip J. Rasch Collection, which comprises the research findings, valuable correspondence, and other miscellaneous information that this indefatigable researcher turned up in his fifty-year research career. This is another of the most important four collections of Kid manuscripts and other materials. Also in this collection is the correspondence of W. A. Carrell, an enthusiastic Kid aficionado whose research and opinions remain illuminating. Researchers should check on the accessibility of these collections; at times they have been closed. Also new in Lincoln is an adobe house just outside of town, the Henn-Johnson Library and Local History Archives, which maintains the valuable collections that longtime Lincoln resident and researcher Nora Henn gathered.

3. National Archives, Washington, D.C.

The collections at the National Archives include the following:

Judge Advocate General's Office, Records Relating to the Dudley Court of Inquiry, CQ 1284, RG 153. An edited version of these records appears in R. M. Barron, ed., *Court of Inquiry: Lieutenant Colonel N. A. M. Dudley, Fort Stanton, New Mexico May–June–July 1879* (1995; Edina, Minn.: Beaver's Pond Press, 2003, #98).

The U.S. Department of the Interior, Bureau of Indian Affairs, includes the Inspector E. C. Watkins report entitled "Examination of Charges Against F. C. Godfroy, Indian Agent, Mescalero, N.M., 1878."

U. S. Department of Justice, "In the Matter of the Cause and Circumstances of the Death of J. H. Tunstall, a British Subject" (referred to as the "Angel Report"), RG 60, 44-4-8-3. A full typescript version of this report is in the Victor Westphall Collection in the New Mexico Records and Archives. The Angel Report deserves editing and publication in book form.

U.S. Treasury Department, Secret Service Department, reports of Special Operative Azariah F. Wild, RG 87, microfilm T915, roll 308.

4. Santa Fe Collections, N.Mex.

The Fray Angélico Chávez Library at the Palace of the Governors administers the William Bonney, Lincoln County, and Charles Siringo Collections. Research at this archive is usually by special appointment. Other valuable collections are available at the New Mexico Records Center and Archives, including Billy the Kid files, Lincoln County records, a special Lincoln County War History File, #20, important territorial archives and legal and court records, and WPA files including many revealing interviews.

5. University of Arizona Library, Tucson.

Another of the four most important collections vis-à-vis Billy the Kid and Lincoln County, the Maurice Garland Fulton Collection, is housed here. Fulton gathered enormous amounts of material, including copies of hundreds of newspaper stories, legal documents, photographs, and numerous letters to other researchers and Billy fans. The library also contains a smaller but valuable Walter Noble Burns Collection, which is revealing for that author's comments about his research methods in the writing of his *Saga of Billy the Kid* (103) and his reactions to questioning criticisms of his romantic biography. A small gathering of Taylor F. Ealy and Mary Ealy papers is also housed here.

6. University of New Mexico, Center for Southwest Research, Zimmerman Library, Albuquerque.

    This library and center contain the largest collection of published information about territorial New Mexico. In addition, another of the four most important collections on Billy the Kid and Lincoln County, the William A. Keleher papers, is available here. Another batch of WPA interviews and others by Lou Blachly is on file, and so are smaller collections dealing with the Ealy family, traveler Marshall Bond (including travel notes and photographs from a 1926 trip to Lincoln County); Miguel A. Otero, Jr.; and Pat Garrett's deputy John W. Poe.

SUPPORTING COLLECTIONS

7. Carrizozo, N.Mex., Courthouse.

    County records in the Lincoln County Courthouse.

8. Fort Sumner, N.Mex., Courthouse.

    Houses DeBaca County and Town of Fort Sumner records.

9. Indianapolis, Indiana Historical Society, William Henry Smith Memorial Library.

    Lew Wallace papers (Wallace's New Mexico years are available on microfilm).

10. New Mexico State University, Rio Grande Historical Collections.

    Papers of Herman B. Weisner, a Billy the Kid collector and researcher; Blazer family and Pat Garrett family papers.

11. Silver City, N.Mex., Library.

    Interviews and newspaper stories about the Kid in Silver City (1873–75); formerly housed in the Silver City Museum.

Bibliographies and Reference Works

12. Ball, Larry D. "The Lincoln County War: An Enduring Fascination; A Review Essay." *New Mexico Historical Review* 62 (July 1987): 303–12.

   Intended as a review essay of books from the 1980s about Billy the Kid, the Lincoln County War, and Pat Garrett, this brief piece becomes much more by providing useful historiographical and bibliographical content. Ball, a well-known specialist on western frontier law officers and legal officials, comments on books by Robert M. Utley, Donald R. Lavash, John P. Wilson, Donald Cline, Jon Tuska, and Colin Rickards.

   Ball's abbreviated evaluation of these books, augmented by his own apt observations, enlarges our understandings of the Kid, the war, and Garrett. These useful additions include balanced interpretations of Alex McSween, the Lawrence Murphy–James Dolan combine, and Sheriff William Brady. As the author notes, most of these writers provide both-and interpretations of Billy rather than the usual either-or views that label Billy hero or villain. Especially important, too, are Ball's attempts to rein in the excesses of Lavash in trying to turn Brady into a hero and Cline's unsupported conclusions. Ball also notes the dated quality of Tuska's chronology of Billy's life. Finally, the author points to the significant contributions of Utley and Wilson to balance the Lincoln County story, revising McSween's above-the-fray reputation and modifying some of the excessively negative depictions of Lawrence Murphy and, to a lesser extent, Jimmy Dolan.

   A rewarding evaluation of trends in Kid and Lincoln County historiography.

13. Chamberlain, Kathleen, comp. *Billy the Kid and the Lincoln County War: A Bibliography.* Occasional Papers, Number 13. Albuquerque: Center for the American West, University of New Mexico, 1997.

   In this eighty-page bibliography, Chamberlain lists more than eight hundred unannotated works of nonfiction, fiction, and films about Billy the Kid. Besides sections on bibliographies and reference works and general works on Billy and the Lincoln County War, Chamberlain includes a section entitled "Billy in Popular Culture," which lists fiction, films, and other works of popular culture. She also devotes sections to "Other Participants," a "Military" listing, and a final section dealing with the major archives containing manuscript materials on Billy the Kid and the Lincoln County War.

   The most extensive and helpful recent bibliographical listing. Now needs updating.

14. Dykes, J[eff] C. *Billy the Kid: The Bibliography of a Legend.* Albuquerque: University of New Mexico Press, 1952.

   After more than a half century, this reference guide remains the most extensive annotated bibliography of published works about Billy the Kid. Dykes, an Old West aficionado, annotates 437 items, covering the period from 1881 to 1951. He treats biographies (books and essays), novels and dramas, movies, and ephemera. Importantly, Dykes makes judgments about his sources, pointing out limitations and praising achievements.

   Dykes also clarifies his middle-of-the-road approach to Billy. He mentions, and criticizes, Billy's misdeeds, such as the killing of Sheriff Brady, but also notes Billy's cheerfulness, his friendships, and his gentle treatment of women and most Hispanics.

15. Tuska, Jon. *Billy the Kid: His Life and Legend.* Albuquerque: University of New Mexico Press, 1997. Reprint and update of the original edition: *Billy the Kid: A Bio-Bibliography* (Westport, Conn.: Greenwood Press, 1994).

   Part reference work, part brief biography, and part bibliography, this book attempts something most volumes on Billy do not aim for. Few biographers devote much space to the developing legends of the Kid as they were formulated in histories, novels, and movies; only Stephen Tatum in his *Inventing Billy the Kid* (171) and the volume in hand do that. So, Tuska's useful reference book provides a succinct life story of Billy and also surveys his treatment in histories, works of fiction, movies, and other venues of legend making. The book also includes a brief chronology of the Kid's life.

The most valuable sections of Tuska's work are the chapters on fiction and movies about the Kid. Until recently, we lacked a thorough discussion of Billy's treatment in novels (see Etulain #309 for such a study) and short stories; at this point, Tuska's brief introduction, alongside that in Tatum's volume, will have to suffice. For many of the last years of the twentieth century, Tuska deserved to be saluted as a major authority on Western films. He illustrates that strength in his chapter on movies about the Kid.

Tuska's chapter on the life of the Kid, about a hundred pages in length, or about one-third of this volume, is a handy overview of the Kid's career. This section is largely derivative, relying extensively on the writings of Maurice Garland Fulton, Frederick Nolan, William Keleher, and other well-known biographers and historians.

Tuska's chapter on historians, especially the part on Robert Utley, falls off track. Indeed, throughout his career Tuska has fallen out with several academic historians, such as Utley, whose work on the Kid, along with that by Frederick Nolan, remains the best source we have on Billy the Kid. Tuska is dead wrong in stating that Utley's work has had little impact on writing about Billy.

Tuska salutes the "fact" writers—Ramon Adams and William Keleher—but also praises the work of Nolan. He has trouble, however, with academic writers such as Utley, Tatum, Henry Nash Smith, and John Cawelti. He also includes questionable conclusions: that the Kid was born in Missouri in 1855–1856; that his younger brother, Joe, was older than Billy; that the Kid had little or nothing to do with Jessie Evans in 1877; that he carried no gun when Pat Garrett shot him in July 1881—and assertions on several other topics.

In short, this is a helpful volume, especially in its treatment of novels and movies, but less so in its biographical section and least so in its discussion of historians. See more commentary on Tuska (173).

Newspaper Articles
(chronological)

16. *Wichita* (Kan.) *Tribune*, 15 March 1871.

    A brief account in the newspaper's first issue establishes that "Mrs. [Catherine] McCarty" is in town. The journalist reports that the City Laundry "is kept by Mrs. McCarty, to whom we recommend those who wish to have their linen made clean."

17. (New York) *Pomeroy's Democrat*, 6 January 1872.

    This issue includes a thirty-two-word personal advertisement of much interest to Billy the Kid searchers:

    > Catherine McCarty, at Nevadaville, Colorado Territory, is anxious to hear of her sister, Margaret McCarty, who, when last heard from, was in Amboy, N.J., and her two brothers, Matthew and Barnard.

    Is this our Catherine McCarty, the mother of the young man who became known as Billy the Kid? Writer Wayne Sanderson (252) thinks it might be and builds a new possible interpretation of Catherine as leaving her young son with her sister, Margaret, in New Jersey for nearly a decade, returning to retrieve him, and now possibly being with him and William Antrim in a mining boomtown about thirty miles west of Denver. Here is a challenge for researchers. Sanderson has examined possible sources for the McCarty origins in New Jersey, but he leaves for others the still-unknown facts of whether this is *the* Catherine McCarty and anything about her and her family in Colorado in 1872.

18. *Silver City* (N.Mex.) *Mining Life*, 19 September 1874.

This article contains the obituary of Catherine McCarty Antrim. She is listed as forty-five years old. The writer states that Catherine and William Antrim and their family came to Silver City "about one year and a half ago," suggesting they came south from Santa Fe soon after their marriage there on 1 March 1873. Since that time, her health had increasingly declined as she was suffering "from an affliction of the lungs." During her last four months she was bedridden. She was smitten with tuberculosis. Some wonder whether her failing health was the reason she and Antrim left Wichita, Kansas, in 1871 or 1872, looking for a warmer, drier climate for Catherine's malady. Information on Catherine's death also appears in the *Silver City Enterprise*, 18 September 1874.

19. (Silver City, N.Mex.) *Grant County Herald*, 26 September 1875.

Henry McCarty was arrested and jailed for "stealing clothes" but broke out of jail. His victims were Charley Sun and Sam Chung, "celestials, sans cue, sans Joss sticks." But McCarty escaped, up through the chimney. The reporter adds, "It's believed that Henry was simply the tool of 'Sombrero Jack,' who done the stealing whilst Henry done the hiding. Jack has skinned out." This piece makes it clear that following his mother's death, Billy had gotten into trouble, and then, about a year later, left Silver City, fleeing punishment. Other information tells us he spent most of the next two years in Arizona.

20. (Tucson) *Arizona Weekly Star*, 23 August 1877.

Francis P. "Windy" Cahill's deathbed statement includes information on how and why Kid Antrim shot him on 17 August 1877. "I had some trouble with Henry Antrem [sic], otherwise known as Kid," Cahill told the reporter, "during which he shot me. I had called him a pimp, and he called me a son of a bitch; we then took hold of one another. I did not hit him, I think; saw him go for his pistol and tried to get hold of it, but could not, and he shot me in the belly." Contrary to Windy's statement, others say the bully blacksmith repeatedly pummeled the Kid before the shooting took place.

21. (Tucson) *Arizona Citizen*, 25 August 1877.

This report opens with the statement that "Austin Antrim [sic] shot F. P. Cahill near Camp Grant on 17th instant, and the latter died on the 18th." Most of the piece deals with Cahill's background, but it also states that Cahill mentioned "some trouble with Antrim during which the shooting was done.

Bad names were applied to each other." The coroner's jury concluded that since Billy's shooting "was criminal and unjustifiable," he was "guilty thereof" of murder. How he was known as "Austin" Antrim is not clear.

22. *Mesilla Valley* (N.Mex.) *Independent*, 13 October 1877.

   C. A. Carpenter of Silver City, traveling through Cooke's Canyon between Silver City and Mesilla, identifies one of the nine outlaws he saw as Henry Antrim. Riding with the group were Jessie Evans and Frank Baker, both of whom Henry/Billy would meet again later in Lincoln County. Not all authorities agree that the Kid was with the Evans group. Some of the same information appears in (Silver City, N.Mex.) *Grant County Herald*, 6 October 1877.

23. (Las Cruces, N.Mex.) *Eco del Rio Grande*, 10 January 1878.

   Responding extensively to an earlier letter in the same newspaper about the Fritz life insurance controversy, lawyer Alex McSween provides a point-by-point answer to those earlier negative charges and, in contrast, advances assertive points substantiating his position. He lists the amount he received ($7,148.94) from the eastern insurance company holding the $10,000 insurance policy for the now-deceased Col. Emil Fritz. He adds that $280 was paid to J. B. Patron and J. B. Wilson for claims they had against the Fritz estate. On the other hand, McSween does not explain why the final settlement was so small, why he refused to make that settlement when he was court ordered to do so, and perhaps why he may have used some of the remaining estate funds for his own purposes. The conflict over the Fritz insurance inheritance was a major cause of the Lincoln County War. Some of this story is expanded on in the 24 January issue of *Eco del Rio Grande* and repeated in the Santa Fe *New Mexican*, 19 January 1878.

24. *Mesilla Valley* (N.Mex.) *Independent*, 26 January 1878.

   Here is John Tunstall's rather naive and negative letter attacking Sheriff William Brady for not paying the Lincoln County taxes (sheriffs were the tax collectors) and allowing Dolan and Co. to use the undelivered money for their purposes. Dolan exploded in anger and soon challenged Tunstall to a gunfight. An important, dramatic source that helped lead to Tunstall's murder about three weeks later at the hands of Brady and Dolan henchmen.

25. (Silver City, N.Mex.) *Grant County Herald*, 9 February 1878.

   Here is another explanation of why McSween was arrested for alleged embezzlement. Summarizing the facts that McSween presented in his defense and some of the points by the prosecutors, the newspaper does not take sides. Better on facts than conclusions.

26. *Mesilla Valley* (N.Mex.) *Independent,* 13 April 1878.

Billy was much involved, as a Regulator, in chasing down and then murdering William Morton and Frank Baker, henchmen of Jimmy Dolan and Sheriff William Brady who had been involved in the killing of John Tunstall nearly two months earlier. This story details the pursuit, capture, and killing of Morton and Baker "as they were trying to escape." Billy, it is rumored, wanted to kill the two fleeing gunman, but Regulator chief Dick Brewer wished to take them into Lincoln and to jail. Clearly, Billy was involved in the shooting of the Dolan men.

27. *Las Vegas* (N.Mex.) *Gazette,* 28 April 1878.

Although written over the name of M[arion] Turner, it is believed by historian Will Keleher that the letter writer was Ash Upson, who later ghostwrote Pat Garrett's biography of Billy the Kid in 1882. The letter to the *Gazette* summarizes the decisions of the recent grand jury and advances several conclusions. Turner/Upson tries to remain evenhanded, speaking of the Lincoln County fighters as the "Murphy Party" and the "McSween Party." They both were accused of murder, but their killings were in war, the act of "killing their enemies," or a "contest for 'the best of the fight.'" And then the writer concludes his attempt at being neutral by reminding readers of the biblical admonition: "Let him who is without sin cast the first stone."

28. "Lincoln County." *Cimarron* (N.Mex.) *News and Press,* 2 May 1878.

In a summing-up of the recent grand jury meeting and its decisions, this reporter clearly demonstrates his support for Alex McSween and his followers and his disgust with Judge Warren Bristol, District Attorney William Rynerson, and businessman Jimmy Dolan. For the reporter, the grand jury's decisions show how little Bristol stood for the people of the county and how much he spoke for the crooks of the county. According to the writer, McSween was exonerated, as he should have been, but the jury did not deal with the killers of John Tunstall. They should have.

29. *Las Vegas* (N.Mex.) *Gazette,* 20 July 1878.

This newspaper story gives an update on the events of early July, leading up to the Big Kill days of 15–19 July. In the previous month, the *Gazette* had told its readers not to pay any attention to the news about possible impending violence in Lincoln County; if they turned the other ear, they would "see how quickly the troubled waters will sink." Now the reporter has to admit that tensions and gathering forces on two sides were probably moving toward a showdown.

30. *Cimarron* (N.Mex.) *News and Press*, 25 July 1878.

Although published on 25 July, this letter is dated 11 July—four days before the outbreak of the Big Kill. It is signed by "Lincoln," but historian Maurice Garland Fulton is convinced the author was Alex McSween. The writer accuses Jimmy Dolan supporters of a recent ransack of San Patricio, which included animal theft, attacks on those supportive of the Regulators, and verbal assaults with vile language. Murphy and Dolan riders, in conjunction with crooked Sheriff Peppin, were controlling and destroying property.

31. *Las Vegas* (N.Mex.) *Gazette*, 16 August 1878.

The aftereffects of the Five-Day Battle in Lincoln were now engulfing the entire county. The disruptions and killings were leading to dozens of people leaving, taking their livestock, and moving on to safer locations. Some were abandoning fully stocked houses, growing gardens, and fields needing harvesting. The reporter concluded, "No new country can well afford to lose so industrious and law abiding class of people."

32. (Santa Fe, N.Mex.) *Rocky Mountain Sentinel*, 30 April 1879.

An early account of Billy's links to Santa Fe, this newspaper story states that the "William Bonny [sic], who has figured so conspicuously in the Lincoln county troubles in this Territory, was once a resident of your City [Santa Fe]." Billy, it is stated further, came from New York, his stepfather's name is Antrim, and he "is known here by the name of 'The Kid.'"

33. *Mesilla Valley* (N.Mex.) *Independent*, 5 July 1879.

Here is a sketchy account of the murder of Sue McSween's lawyer, Huston Chapman. The emphases are on the mounting tensions between gunman Billy Campbell and the stand-up-to-everyone Chapman. After Campbell shot Chapman close up, instantly killed him, and set his clothes on fire, Jimmy Dolan wanted to plant a pistol in the hand of the unarmed, now deceased lawyer. When another participant refused to do this, Billy offered to, marched out of the saloon where they were standing, and quickly got out of town. Probably the Kid realized he had better get off the scene as soon as possible. Some of these same details appear in *Las Cruces* (N.Mex.) *Thirty Four*, 5 March 1879.

34. (Santa Fe) *Weekly New Mexican*, 17 January 1880.

   Not much is known about Billy's shooting of Joe Grant in a Fort Sumner saloon in January 1880. This article includes a brief comment: "Billy Bonney, more extensively known as 'the Kid,' shot and killed Joe Grant. The origin of the difficulty was not learned."

35. *Las Vegas* (N.Mex.) *Gazette*, 3 December 1880.

   Editor J. H. Koogler advanced opinions that Billy would later deny in his 12 December letter to Gov. Lew Wallace (printed next). Koogler asserted that Billy was the leader of a gang of outlaws "harassing the stockmen" and "terrorizing people." They were a gang of "forty or fifty men, all hard characters, the off-scourings of society, fugitive from justice, and desperadoes by profession. . . ." And Billy, their captain, was the worst of the lot, "a desperate cuss." Giving the henceforth-to-be-used "Billy the Kid" sobriquet and accusing him of numerous misdeeds, Koogler placed a target on the Kid's back and urged "the people of San Miguel county" to do something about the rascals down south. Two days later, Governor Wallace announced a reward of $500 for the capture of "Billy the Kid."

36. *Las Vegas* (N.Mex.) *Gazette*, 22 December 1880.

   Printed here is Billy's 12 December 1880 letter to Gov. Lew Wallace, explaining a number of details from his viewpoint. He was not the "Captian [*sic*] of a Band of Outlaws," so the writer of the earlier story in the 3 December *Gazette* "must have drawn very heavily on his Imagination." Billy had gone to White Oaks to see his lawyer, Ira Leonard, but when his horse was killed, he and others went to the Greathouse station. And later Jimmy Carlyle was killed, not by Billy and his riders but by the friendly fire of a posse pursuing Billy. John Chisum, the Kid asserted, was the source of his problems: "If some impartial Party were to investigate this matter they would find it far Different from the impression put out by Chisum and his Tools." Revealing for Billy's self-defense, his attack on Chisum, and his hope to inform the governor "of the truth."

37. "Outlaws of New Mexico: The Exploits of a Band Headed by a New York Youth." (New York) *Sun*, 22 December 1880.

   Drawing on a news story appearing in the Las Vegas *Gazette* on 3 December 1880, this lengthy piece provides backgrounds on Fort Sumner, the rise of illegal and violent actions in eastern New Mexico, and outlaws. The writer, labeling Billy "the leader of the band," provides a capsule biography of him and his followers. While not a "dime-novel fabrication," as one writer claims, the piece is shot through with errors and false information. More important, it shows that the reputation of the newly named "Billy the Kid" had already spread to the East Coast.

38. "The Kid." *Las Vegas* (N.Mex.) *Gazette*, 27 December 1880.

    Beginning with the shock and awe in Las Vegas when Pat Garrett and his riders rode in with captives Billy the Kid and his men, this long piece retreats to cover the events leading up to the deaths of Tom O. Folliard and Charlie Bowdre just a few days earlier. The reporter retrieves a good deal of specific, sound factual material about the shooting in Fort Sumner and the shooting and capture at Stinking Spring. Billy is portrayed as a "notorious outlaw" with a "gang" who have been "destroying" southeastern New Mexico. The capture and entry into Las Vegas, the journalist reports, "ran like wildfire about town and everyone was on the *que vive* for particulars of the capture." The story ends with a salute to Sheriff Garrett "and all of his men for the successful issue of their round-up."

39. "A Big Haul!" (Las Vegas, N.Mex.) *Daily Optic*, 27 December 1880.

    A "gang of daring desperadoes"—"Billy Kid," Dave Rudabaugh, Billy Wilson, and Tom Pickett—were captured. The day before, when the outlaws and the captors came into Las Vegas, the town "was thrown into a fever of excitement." Then the writer returns, retrospectively, to summarize the events leading up to the capture. The deaths of Tom Folliard and Charlie Bowdre and Garrett's success in taking the others at Stinking Spring are described. The writer salutes the "party of men who risked their lives in the attempt to rid the country of this bloodthirsty gang of robbers and murderers."

    The Kid is described as being "about 24 years of age," and having "a bold yet pleasant cast of countenance." He laughed when told newspapers had given him "a reputation second only to that of Victorio." The article ends with the controversies and threats involved in taking the outlaws by train from Las Vegas to Santa Fe.

40. *Las Vegas* (N.Mex.) *Gazette*, 28 December 1880. Reprinted in George Fitzpatrick, "Interview with Billy the Kid." *New Mexico Magazine* 32 (September 1954): 22, 40–41.

    Four days after Pat Garrett captured Billy the Kid and his fellow riders and brought them as captives to Las Vegas, Lucius M. "Lute" Wilcox, the city editor of the *Las Vegas Gazette*, interviewed Billy. The interview was published the next day in the *Gazette*.

Wilcox described Billy as "light and chipper . . . laughing, joking and chatting with the by-standers." When the Kid was asked about his jovial demeanor in light of his situation, he replied, "What's the use of looking on the gloomy side of everything. The laugh's on me this time." Complaining about the condition of the jail and trying to keep warm, he noted the large crowd watching and thought that some would now "think me half a man . . . ; everyone seems to think I was some kind of an animal."

After providing a physical description of Billy, reporter Wilcox asked about some of Billy's recently quoted words. The Kid denounced them, stating he had "never said any such thing" as calling his partners cowards. Billy also wondered why no one would "believe anything good of me." He had not been a gang leader; it was John Chisum who got him into trouble by failing to keep his promises; and too many "men . . . wouldn't let me live in the country." If he had had his trusty Winchester and if a dead horse had not blocked his path, Billy was convinced he could have ridden out of the rock house at Stinking Spring and escaped from Garrett.

An important interview studded with Billy's revealing words describing his attacks on others, bragging about his own actions, and conveying manipulated defenses of his illegal actions.

41. *Las Vegas* (N.Mex.) *Daily Optic*, 21 January 1881.

Biographers have wrestled with whether Billy threatened to kill John Chisum for not paying what the Kid thought the Cattle King had promised for his riding against The House partisans and protecting Chisum's holdings. This newspaper article prints information passed down through the Chisum family. Billy cornered Chisum in Fort Sumner and threatened to shoot Old John if he did not keep his promise. Chisum replied, "Billy, you know as well as I do that I never hired you to fight in the Lincoln County War. I always pay my honest debts. I don't owe you anything, and you can kill me but you won't knock me out of many years. I'm an old man now." Billy stopped a bit and then retorted, "Aw, you ain't worth killing."

Authenticity questionable, but not entirely so.

42. *Las Vegas* (N.Mex.) *Daily Optic*, 22 February 1881.

More than a year after his shooting Joe Grant, Billy answered casually when asked about the happening. "Oh, nothing," he told the inquirer, "it was a game of two and I got there first." Someone who overheard the flippant comment replied, "The daring young rascal seemed to enjoy the telling as well as the killing."

43. (Santa Fe) *Daily New Mexican*, 1 March 1881.

   This story gives an account of Billy and other prisoners attempting to dig their way out of the Santa Fe jail. Evidently, the sheriff thought they might attempt such an escape, so he planted a mole among them to keep track of the skullduggery. At the end of February, the sheriff and his deputies hustled into the cell, threw over the cover-ups, and opened the hole, which was then far along. Afterward, Billy and his fellow prisoners were separated, with the Kid placed in irons and more closely watched.

44. (Las Cruces, N.Mex.) *Newman's Semi-weekly*, 2 April 1881.

   Simeon Newman, owner and editor of this short-lived Las Cruces newspaper, was upset with the delays in Billy's sentencing in the Mesilla courtroom. For Newman, Billy was "a notoriously dangerous character" and had escaped several times previously. It was a threat to society not to push directly ahead with his trial. If the Kid escaped again, there were "a hundred good citizens of Lincoln who would not sleep soundly in their beds did they know that he were at large." Besides, Newman urged, other indictments could be made, so they should push ahead with the process.

45. *Las Vegas* (N.Mex.) *Gazette*, 5 April 1881.

   When Billy, Billie Wilson, and the Kid's lawyer were on their way to trials for the two Billys, they had a brief train stop in Las Cruces before the trial in Mesilla. What happened next is often cited as an illustration of the Kid's inviting sense of humor even in the most stressing situations. A crowd of curiosity seekers gathered at the train stop, and one shouted out, "Who is Billy the Kid?" Billy placed his hand on lawyer Leonard's shoulder and chuckled. "This is the man."

46. *Mesilla* (N.Mex.) *News*, 16 April 1881.

   When Billy was asked whether he thought Gov. Lew Wallace would follow through on his promised pardon, the Kid replied, "Considering the active part Governor Wallace took on our side, and the friendly relations that existed between him and me, and the promise he made, I think he ought to pardon me." But Billy did not know whether "he will do that." And then added, "Think it hard I should be the only one to suffer the extreme penalties of the law."

47. "Gov. Wallace." *Las Vegas* (N.Mex.) *Gazette*, 28 April 1881.

On the day Billy escaped, but before Governor Wallace learned of the dramatic event, a reporter asked the chief executive about the Kid. "It looks as though he would hang," the journalist said to the governor, and added, "He appears to look to you to save his neck." Wallace's response, if entirely correct, is illuminating. The governor told the reporter, "Yes . . . but I can't see how a fellow like him should expect clemency from me." The reporter concluded that the Kid "had undertaken to bulldoze the governor, which has not helped his chances in the slightest."

Provocative observation.

48. *Las Vegas* (N.Mex.) *Daily Optic*, 2–4 May 1881.

These three stories provide details of Billy's escape from the Lincoln jail and the killing of deputies J. W. Bell and Bob Olinger as well as decidedly negative comments about the Kid. The reporter says Billy used his freed handcuff to stun Bell, grab his gun, and kill him—and soon thereafter he shot a returning Olinger. The 4 May piece is headlined "The Dare Devil Desperado" and is an extensive, dark picture of Billy. He is a "young demon" who pays no heed to widows and orphans he has created. Worse, his friends allow his evil ways without criticism. Now the territory, all of it, must "unite in his re-capture."

49. (Santa Fe) *Daily New Mexican*, 3 May 1881.

Historians and biographers differ much on how Billy overpowered Deputy J. W. Bell, got his gun, and killed him in the Lincoln jail escape. This account says Billy slipped out of one handcuff and struck the unaware Bell over the head, and while Bell was stunned, Billy grabbed his gun and shot the deputy when he tried to escape. That point of view also appears in the Silver City *Supplement to the New Southwest and Herald*, 14 May 1881. The latter account also has Billy swearing over the bodies of Bell and Olinger as he left the jail building.

50. *Las Vegas* (N.Mex.) *Daily Optic*, 10 June 1881.

An update on the fleeing Kid, this piece wrongly reports that Billy rode into a Chisum camp and quickly killed three Chisum cowboys because their boss had refused to pay the promised five dollars per day during the Lincoln County War. The Kid was going to kill one man for every five dollars owed him for riding for and supporting Chisum. He was going to stay in the area until he had gotten even with Chisum and "depopulate[d] Lincoln County." This contrived legend continued well into the next century.

51. "'The Kid' Killed." *Las Vegas* (N.Mex.) *Daily Optic*, 18 July 1881.

    Datelined 15 July, this extended story is one of the first reporting Billy's death. The three-part article includes a story from Sunnyside, New Mexico; "A Soldier's Story," from a soldier who was in Fort Sumner when the killing occurred; and "A Talk With Pat Garrett." All three stories contain information about Billy's killing similar to what most acceptable accounts tell us. But the reporter ends his chilling story by stating that Billy, the "terror of not only Lincoln county, but of the whole Territory," was "a bold thief, cold-blooded murderer, having perhaps killed more men than any man of his age in the world." And to make sure, the journalist adds, "All mankind rejoices and the newspapers will now have something else to talk about." The final words are a salute to Pat Garrett. An illuminating example of the early dark newspaper accounts of Billy.

52. "Billy Bonny [sic]." *Albuquerque* (N.Mex.) *Daily Journal*, 18 July 1881.

    A brief summary of Billy's killing, this piece mentions that Billy had probably returned to Fort Sumner "for the purpose of courting [Pete] Maxwell's sister, who had captured his heart." The writer speaks of this as "a very bold and reckless act," for Billy should have fled Lincoln County and probably would not have been killed. Billy is described as a "notorious desperado," in fact "the worst desperado that has ever infested the Territory of New Mexico," who "had become a terror to every family in New Mexico."

53. "The Territory Is Better for His Death." *Las Vegas* (N.Mex.) *Daily Gazette*, 19 July 1881. Reprinted in *Colorado Springs* (Colo.) *Weekly Gazette*, 23 July 1881.

    This journalist's account opens with news of Pat Garrett's killing of Billy and includes details of the shooting that occurred late at night on 14 July in Pete Maxwell's bedroom at Fort Sumner. The content of the article is a mishmash of facts and mistakes. The reporter largely provides a depiction of Billy as a desperado who killed eleven men—if not several more. The writer also speaks of Billy's clear talents, naming him "probably the best shot in the west." He points to Billy's dramatic escape from the burning McSween house in Lincoln in July 1878 as "an index to his dare-devil career" and calls Billy "one of the most fearless of all those who participated" in the Lincoln County War. Generally, after the Kid fled Silver City (nothing is said of his two years in Arizona), his life "kept going from bad to worse."

The author is guilty of several errors. He speaks of a sister Billy never had, claims that the Kid's first killing was of a man who insulted his mother, and says that Billy's "hand [was] against everyone." So, the "territory is the better for his death."

Throughout the story, the journalist praises Pat Garrett, stating that we should all be extraordinarily grateful for his diligent, heroic pursuit and destruction of killer Billy. The Lincoln County sheriff deserves abundant praise for his bravery.

The story fits in well with most of the negative newspaper stories about Billy during the last months of his life and over the next decade or two.

54. (Santa Fe) *Daily New Mexican*, 21 July 1881.

Pat Garrett, a week after shooting Billy, told the reporter that Billy had gone back to the familiar Fort Sumner area rather than to Mexico because "he said he was safer out on the plains, and could always get something to eat among the sheep herders. So he decided to take his chances out there where he was hard to get at." Garrett did not mention, as some others did, that Billy was returning to a sweetheart in Fort Sumner.

When asked why Billy seemed reluctant to shoot Garrett in Pete Maxwell's bedroom late on the night of 14 July, the sheriff said, "I think he was surprised and thrown off guard." Although the Kid was "cool" in difficult situations, here "he was so surprised and startled, that for a second he could not collect himself.... I think Kid would have done so in a second more, if he had had the time."

55. "Obituary." *Santa Fe* (N.Mex.) *Weekly Democrat*, 21 July 1881.

Half humor, half cynical reporting, this brief piece says much about a negative Billy, little about his positive deeds, and includes a macabre description. The writer says the Kid boasted of killing a man for every year of his life, although only sixteen were known for sure. Then a sarcastic, attempt at humor: immediately after Garrett killed Billy, "a strong odor of brimstone in the air, and a dark figure, with wings of a dragon, claws like a tiger, eyes like balls of fire, and horns like a bison, hovered over the corpse, and with a fiendish laugh, said 'Ha, ha! This is my meat.'"

56. (New York) *Sun*, 22 July 1881.

Just a week after Billy's burial, this New York newspaper declared that Billy's "death is hailed with great joy." The relief came because the Kid "had sworn that he would kill several prominent citizens and had already slain fifteen or eighteen men." Donald Cline (107) uses this New York newspaper story as his basis for naming an Edward McCarty as Billy's father; for stating that McCarty never married Billy's mother, Catherine; for saying that he had also fathered Billy's brother, Joe; and, most sensationally of all, for alleging that Billy as a teenager returned to New York from Arizona and famously stabbed a man in a street fight. Nearly all these assertions in Cline's *Alias Billy the Kid* (1986) remain unsupported in other scholarship. Here is more fodder for the "satanic" Billy who arose in the months and years immediately after his death.

57. (Silver City, N.Mex.) *New Southwest and Grant County Herald*, 23 July 1881.

    In a decidedly unfriendly story of Billy's death, this reporter calls the Kid a "vulgar murderer and desperado," a "low-down vulgar cut-throat, with probably not one redeeming quality." The reporter speaks of Billy's first years in Silver City and his jail escape there but denies as "a fabrication" that the Kid killed his first man for insulting his mother. The writer's account of Billy's death in Pete Maxwell's bedroom is a mix of facts and mistakes.

58. (Las Cruces, N.Mex.) *Rio Grande Republican*, 23 July 1881.

    Less than ten days after Pat Garrett shot Billy, this newspaper stated that "the Kid was born in New York State and his true name was McCarthy [sic]. . . . He was 23 years old." This means that well before the publication of the Upson-Garrett biography of Billy the next spring (1882), other sources were stating that Billy was born in New York.

59. *Las Vegas* (N.Mex.) *Daily Gazette*, 29 July 1881.

    Quoting the New York *Sun*, the Las Vegas newspaper claims that the Kid was Michael McCarty, who was born in 1859 and grew up New York. Later he was farmed out west, ran away, and returned to New York City only to be guilty of a stabbing murder. Again, he went west and eventually became Billy the Kid. The account contains too many conflicting facts to fit the life and actions of Henry McCarty–Billy Bonney.

60. *Wichita* (Kans.) *Weekly Eagle*, 18 August 1881.

    Editor Marsh Murdock of the *Weekly Eagle* recalled Henry McCarty, at the time of Billy's death, as a "street gamin in the days of longhorns." He also wondered—and think about Henry/Billy's only being about twelve or thirteen at the time—whether he had not been the shooter who killed a man "in

[a] saloon out on the west end." Murdock questions whether it is "true" that the gun was "fired by 'Billy the Kid.'" But the editor's memory is faulty; the shooting occurred in 1876, about four to five years after the McCartys left Wichita.

61. (London) *Times*, 18 August 1881.

    Repeating information from New Mexico, the *Times* of London was especially fulsome in its praise of Pat Garrett. He was "the mainstay of law and order in Lincoln County, the chief reliance of the people in the dark days when danger lurked on every hand." Billy, of course, was the reason for the "dark days" of "danger." Garrett deserved praise because he had brought down "his fierce and implacable foe single-handed...."

62. Donan, P. "Billy the Kid." (Silver City, N.Mex.) *New Southwest and Grant County Herald*, 20 August 1881.

    One of the longest newspaper stories to appear shortly after the Kid's death, this is also one of the most error-ridden. The author gets many names, dates, and events all mixed up. He has the events of the killing of Sheriff Brady wrong and the details of the Big Killing incorrect, and he jumbles Billy's actions in several other events. The writer dislikes the Kid: he is "a young monster" with a "blood-stained career" who "carried death with him." Yet the writer does have several facts correct about Billy's life in Silver City and Arizona, which many writers at this time had wrong. The piece ends with "Patsy Garrett" as the "hero of the hour." Use caution with any facts.

63. "The Dead Desperado, Adventures of Billy, the Kid, as Narrated by Himself." *Las Vegas* (N.Mex.) *Daily Optic*, 12–23 December 1881. Eleven parts. Reprinted in Bob L'Aloge, *The Code of the West*. Las Cruces, N.Mex.: B and J Publications, 1922, pp. 1–31. Page references to the L'Aloge volume.

    This newspaper serial, more dime novel than biography (although it seems to claim the latter), both does and does not follow the life story of Billy. The nameless author—perhaps the editor or a staff member at the *Las Vegas Daily Optic*—opens the story in a Santa Fe gambling hangout where Billy threatens to kill a gambler who has tricked him in a card game. The narrator of the story, first called Charlie Fresh and then John Antrim, seems to be playing with his names, but Billy takes a liking to him. They ride back to Billy's adobe castle to the south, where the Kid and his gang of a dozen or more outlaws hang out. Billy accedes to the narrator's request to hear Billy's life story.

Billy tells of his birth in Ireland, the poverty of his family, the death of his father, and the immigration of his mother, his two sisters, and himself to Canada. Soon thereafter, his mother marries "an old reprobate named Antrim" (p. 19; this newspaper series depicts Antrim as a drunken, dictatorial stepfather), and they move to Silver City. Quickly, Billy gets into trouble, although he defends himself in arguing that if he had "received proper treatment from others" (p. 19), he would not have set out on a career of violence and murder. He steals two or three items, and when a Chinese man "rats on him," Billy sneaks up on him and cuts his throat. Captured and jailed, Billy escapes through the chimney and heads off to Arizona, where he falls into the clutches of a bully blacksmith. Unable to stand the blacksmith's behavior, Billy shoots him and hies off for New Mexico.

After a two-year hiatus, Billy falls into the Lincoln County War boiling up in the Pecos country. Contrary to fact, he takes the side opposing a man (McSween) administering a $12,000 inheritance and the sheriff, who is supporting the administrator. Billy kills the sheriff and a dozen others in the "tough tussle" (p. 29). All these stories are wrong.

Storyteller Billy zips through the last three years of his life in the eleventh and final installment of the series. His account spins a different version of the Lincoln jail breakout and the killing of two guards. The narrator, in the last four sentences, notes Billy's death but skips over the details.

Billy is depicted here as violent gunman, always ready to take a life. But he is also painted as friendly, caring, and warm, especially to the narrator. The writer's pedestrian style, his lifeless story, and the numerous vague details undoubtedly kept the series from being published in book form early on. Plus, publishers in the area already knew that Pat Garrett had completed a book on the Kid that would appear soon. This dime-novel-like series never attracted much attention in New Mexico—or outside the territory.

64. *Albuquerque* (N.Mex.) *Review*, 2 August 1882.

Many expected that when Billy's brother, Joseph Antrim, met Pat Garrett, he would get even, perhaps violently, with the sheriff for killing his brother. Not so. They met at the Armijo Hotel in Albuquerque on 1 August 1882; several hours of quiet conversation followed, and the two rose, shook hands, and parted amicably. Garrett explained to the reporter the next day that Antrim "merely intended talking over the killing of the Kid with the man who had killed him." Garrett told Joe he had only done his duty. Antrim expressed no animosity toward Garrett.

65. (White Oaks, N.Mex.) *Lincoln County Leader*, 1 March 1890.

Godfrey Gauss knew Billy the Kid well, having served as a cook at the John Tunstall ranch and later as a gardener behind the Lincoln jail. Here he reminisces about his observations of Billy's breakout in late April 1881. He saw Deputy Bell stagger out of the jail's back door after Billy shot him. Gauss remembers that Bell "ran right into my arms [and] expired the same moment, and I laid him down dead." He also tells the reporter that, in coming around the body of Olinger, whom he had just shot, Billy nudged the body and said, "You are not going to round me up again."

66. Whitehill, H. H. "Billy the Kid: The Subject of an Interview with H. H. Whitehill of This City." *Silver City* (N.Mex.) *Enterprise*, 3 January 1902.

This story includes an interview with Harvey Whitehill, earlier a sheriff of Silver City. He states that "early in [Billy's] career he changed his name to Billie Bonney in order to keep the stigma of disgrace from his family. . . . Billie's right name, you know, was Henry McCarty and he was born in Anderson, Indiana." Here was one of the earliest references to the McCarty-Antrim days in Indiana. Perhaps Whitehill, knowing of stepfather William Antrim's birth in Indiana, assumed Billy was also born there. Some biographers speak of Antrim not paying attention to Billy and Joe after Catherine's death in September 1874. Not so according to Whitehill, who says the stepfather "lavished on them almost a mother's care." But Whitehill also speaks of having arrested Billy—perhaps for the first time—for theft, and suggests the Kid was about fifteen at the time.

67. *Indianapolis* (Ind.) *World*, 8 June 1902.

More than twenty years after Billy's letter-writing deluge to Gov. Lew Wallace in the January–March 1881 period, Wallace told a reporter that he recalled these letters and what Billy was trying to do. The Kid's threats, Wallace explained, were an attempt to get Wallace to see him by publishing letters he and the governor had exchanged earlier in Lincoln. "I thwarted his purpose," Wallace added, "by giving a copy of the letter and a narrative of the circumstances connected with it to the paper published in the town." A copy of the paper was sent to the Kid in his cell.

68. Coe, Frank. "A Friend Comes to the Defense of Notorious Billy the Kid." *El Paso* (Tex.) *Times*, 16 September 1923.

Frank Coe, unlike his cousin George Coe, never turned out a memoir, but he did write enthusiastically about his good friend Billy the Kid. Here he speaks about their hunting, especially in the fall and winter of 1877, when the Kid arrived in Lincoln County. He claims Billy "was a fine shot with a rifle; he was handy in camp, a good cook and good-natured and jolly."

Coe also speaks of the early demands that shaped the Kid's character. "He had been thrown on his own resources from early boyhood," Coe notes. Billy never had a usual boyhood because he was on his own, but he "was eager to learn everything and had a most active and fertile mind." Not able to compete physically with larger, studier, and older men, he learned how to use guns to defend himself.

Coe took to the Kid early on. "We became staunch friends. I never enjoyed better company," Coe added. Billy was an entertaining storyteller, loved the laugh; he had "a touch of humor in everything." And Coe wanted people to know that Billy's "disposition was remarkable kind; he rarely thought of his own comfort first."

Obviously, Frank Coe saw a far different person in Billy than those who viewed him as a violent and selfish desperado.

69. (Albuquerque) *New Mexico State Tribune*, 23 July 1928.

In his letter to the Albuquerque newspaper, Billy's friend Frank Coe describes the killing of Buckshot Roberts at Blazer's Mill. His account says he talked to Roberts and tried to get him to surrender to the Regulators. But Roberts replied, "No, never alive. The Kid is with you and will kill me on sight." Shots rang out, with Charlie Bowdre's shot to Roberts's gut eventually proving fatal. Roberts shot at several of the Regulators, but his shot at Billy "just shaved his arm," and the Kid "backed out as if it was too hot in there for him." Billy later saluted Roberts's bravery, saying "he licked our crowd to a finish."

70. Blazer, Almer. "The Fight at Blazer's Mill, in New Mexico." *Alamogordo* (N.Mex.) *Times*, 16 July 1928. Reprinted in *The Billy the Kid Reader*, edited by Frederick Nolan. Norman: University of Oklahoma Press, 2007, pp. 247–56.

A recollection published fifty years after the events transpired by an eyewitness but not a participant furnishes another version of the shootout at Blazer's Mill on 4 April 1878. As a thirteen-year-old, Almer, the son of mill-owner Dr. Joseph Blazer, viewed some of the shootout and was close on the scene for other parts of the incident.

Blazer says that Billy the Kid, not Charlie Bowdre, shot Buckshot Roberts at the mill. He does not mention George Coe's finger being shot off in a glancing shot from Roberts, nor does he speak of the serious injury to John

Middleton. Shortly before relating this story, Almer Blazer had read some of Burns's *Saga of Billy the Kid* (103) and wanted to respond to—and disagree with—parts of Burns's account. Blazer never refers to Roberts as "Buckshot" and disagrees with several small details accepted by most historians and biographers treating the fight. Blazer also concludes, somewhat incongruously, that the events of the Lincoln County War in 1878 "did not end the destruction of the renegades [rustlers]," but they did launch "the 'reign of law' in New Mexico" (p. 256).

A provocative alternative account of the battle at Blazer's Mill.

71. (Albuquerque) *New Mexico State Tribune*, 23 July 1928.

    In this letter to the newspaper and his interviews with J. Evetts Haley (20 March, 14 August 1927), Frank Coe reports that when the Kid saw Tunstall's dead body in the McSween parlor, he swore "I'll get some of them before I die." Coe also provides information on the shooting of Buckshot Roberts at Blazer's Mill.

72. (Albuquerque) *New Mexico State Tribune*, 27 July 1928.

    In terse, revealing comments, George Coe tells a reporter that after the Tunstall murder but before the Big Kill the following July, Billy had not yet come forward as a leader. As Coe put it, "Billy the Kid wasn't known then as a warrior. We just knew him as a smart young lad and we named him the Kid. But he grew bigger and bigger."

73. Denton, J. Fred. "Billy the Kid's Friend Tells for the First Time of Thrilling Incidents." Tucson (Ariz.) *Daily Citizen*, 28 March 1931.

    An interview with Gus Gildea, who knew Billy as Kid Antrim in Arizona and became reacquainted in Lincoln County. Gildea gives near-at-hand information about Billy's dress and his shooting of Windy Cahill in August 1877. His information about the Kid after this killing is harder to sustain, although he obviously was involved with the horrendous killer John Selman in Lincoln County.

74. (Tucson, Ariz.) *Daily Citizen*, 4 February 1932.

    H. E. "Sorghum" Smith, who operated a hay camp in eastern Arizona, remembered more than fifty years later that Billy did not look to be seventeen, as he claimed. "[H]e didn't [even] look to be fourteen." After he had worked only a short time, the Kid asked for money. Smith tried to pay him ten dollars, but the Kid requested all that he was owed—forty dollars.

Immediately he went off "and bought himself a whole outfit; six shooter, belt, scabbard and cartridges."

75. "Billy the Kid Model Youth in Silver City Says Boyhood Chum." *Silver City* (N.Mex.) *Independent*, 22 March 1932.

Here, an interview with Anthony B. Connor, a schoolmate of Billy's, adds further information about Silver City in the mid-1870s. Connor states that stepfather William Antrim "boarded at the Knight home [Mrs. Richard Knight was the married older sister of Connor], and with him was his son Joe Antrim and Billy McCartey [sic], his stepson who afterwards became known as Billy the Kid. Billy sometimes was known as Billy Bonney, his mother's name before she married Mr. Antrim."

76. "Only One Man Living Who Saw 'Billy the Kid' in Both Life and Death." *Clovis* (N.Mex.) *News-Journal*, 13 July 1938.

Not many accounts from Hispanics dealing with Billy's death and the immediate days afterward are available. This story deals with the memories of several Hispanics of these dramatic happenings.

77. *Silver City* (N.Mex.) *Daily Press*, 23 May 1951.

Chauncey O. Truesdell, a friend of Billy's in Silver City, states in an interview here that Billy lived for a time in the Truesdell home. The Truesdells came to Silver City in 1871, and the Antrim-McCarty family shortly afterward. Catherine McCarty "was sickly and died after they had lived there a little while," Truesdell reports. Catherine had told Mrs. Truesdell her name was McCarty before she had married Antrim. Truesdell never heard the name Billy Bonney in Silver City, but others did later, and he was the same person, despite being McCarty and Antrim and later Bonney.

78. McGaw, Bill. "Billy Was Just Another Brat at Silver City." *El Paso* (Tex.) *Herald-Post*, 5 November 1960.

Journalist McGaw wrote a series of newspaper stories about Billy in the 1960s providing good information on the Kid's life in Silver City. This one draws heavily on the interview with Sheriff Harvey Whitehill published in the *Silver City Enterprise*, 3 January 1902 (66). McGaw summarizes Whitehill's reactions to several bits of what he thought to be misinformation being circulated about Kid Antrim/Billy the Kid. Whitehill believed (1) that the Kid's real name was Henry McCarty, not Billy Bonney; (2) that he was born in Anderson, Indiana, not New York City or Brooklyn; and (3) that he was not guilty of murdering a man in Silver City for insulting his mother. McGaw enlarges on these three contributions throughout his story.

79. McGaw, Bill. "Billy the Kid Gets Teacher by Accident." (El Paso, Tex.) *The Southwesterner*, May 1962. "Billy the Kid's Teacher Saw Him as a Fearful 'Sissy.'" (El Paso, Tex.) *The Southwesterner*, June 1962.

This two-part story provides a capsule biography of Mary Richards Chase, one of Henry Antrim's teachers in Silver City. She and Henry bonded quickly and warmly. The story is told through Mrs. Richards Chase's daughter, Patience Glennon, who says her mother recalled facts at odds from what others said about the young man, so mother and daughter had been reluctant to give interviews. The Chase-Glennon story says Billy got into trouble not by stealing clothes from Chinese laundrymen but by dressing up in women's clothes left at his home and prancing down the Silver City main street, thereby breaking a town ordinance about cross-dressing. He left town because of this problem. Later he returned to the area to visit his brother, Joe, for the last time and rode by the Chase home and asked Mary for a gift of money. She gave him all the money she had in the house, and he rode off, never to be seen again. McGaw links this story with other information advancing the often-repeated contention that Billy returned to the Georgetown and Silver City areas for the last time in 1880. Interesting but almost impossible to prove. Some of these ideas had appeared earlier in another two-part story by McGaw: "Out of the West: Mutiny, Fire at Sea, Yellow Fever Combined to Provide Teacher for Billy the Kid," *El Paso* (Tex.) *Herald-Post*, 10 December 1960; "Out of the West: Billy the Kid's Teacher Saw Him as Sensitive, Effeminate and Fearful Youth," *El Paso* (Tex.) *Herald-Post*, 17 December 1960.

80. McGaw, Bill. "Naw, Billy the Kid Didn't Do It!" (El Paso, Tex.) *The Southwesterner*, May 1967.

McGaw uses the research of Robert N. Mullin (151) and W. E. Koop (215) to discuss Billy's early years and to point to photographs of Billy and his mother in Mullin's monograph (151). Then McGaw goes on to argue, in a point not sustained elsewhere, that Billy appears in the 1880 census in the Georgetown area near Silver City working as a dairyman. In a long three-page letter to McGaw (27 May 1967), Philip Rasch dismissed what the journalist said about the photographs and questioned much of the rest of the article's content.

81. McGaw, Bill. "Billy The Kid Still Is Causing Trouble." (El Paso, Tex.) *The Southwesterner*, June 1967.

    McGaw stands by his theory that the 1880 census located the real Billy the Kid in Georgetown, New Mexico. He dismisses Philip Rasch's contention that the 1880 census entry putting the Kid in Fort Sumner with Charlie and Manuela Bowdre is the correct citation. One can argue, with an equally lacking amount of information, that neither of these census entries is correct about Billy the Kid in 1880.

82. Henn, Nora. "Lew Wallace and the Lincoln County War." *Albuquerque* (N.Mex.) *Journal*, Enchantment Section, January–February 1980.

    This two-part overview of Lew Wallace's role in the Lincoln County War helpfully summarizes, for general readers, the governor's actions in the territory from 1878 to 1881. The January section describes Wallace's backgrounds and actions before he took over as New Mexico's chief executive, whereas the second section, in February, deals with Wallace's actions while in the governor's chair. A balanced and informed brief summary. The essence of these two articles appears in Henn's much later book (130).

83. Abarr, James. "The Legacy of an Outlaw." *Albuquerque* (N.Mex.) *Journal*, Impact Magazine, 7 April 1981.

    On the verge of the centennial of Billy the Kid's death, journalist Abarr provides a brief overview for general readers. It is balanced and uses quotes from several western historians. The journalist tries to examine whether Billy was a hero or villain. Printed alongside this newspaper story is another: Debs Smith, "The Battle for Billy's Bones," which describes in abbreviated fashion Lois Telfer's attempt (she claimed to be Billy's "last surviving relative") to remove Billy's remains from the unkempt and cluttered Fort Sumner graveyard to Lincoln, New Mexico. That was in the summer of 1961. The district judge denied her petition, saying the position of Billy's body was not clearly known. Charlie Bowdre's descendants also opposed moving his bones. Interesting stories but too brief.

84. McCutcheon, Chuck. "Is This Man Billy the Kid?" *Albuquerque* (N.Mex.) *Journal*, Sunday, 22 January 1989.

    The reporter McCutcheon focuses on whether John Miller, a resident of Ramah, New Mexico, who died in 1932 or 1933, was Billy the Kid. He was, says Albuquerque grassroots historian Helen Airy and Canadian writer

Daniel Bantine. The evidence of both writers is very slim—no supporting documents; just stories handed down by family members and a gun. Airy later wrote a book on the subject (95).

85. McCutcheon, Chuck. "Computer Enters Hunt for Kid." *Albuquerque* (N.Mex.) *Journal*, 9 April 1989.

    A story covering the computer project to identify authentic Billy photographs, this piece discusses California and New Mexico photographs said to be of the Kid. The New Mexico photograph at the time seemed to have the better support from Kid specialists, but more than twenty-five years later neither photograph is accepted as an authentic portrait of Billy.

86. McCutcheon, Chuck. "Brushy's Not Billy." *Albuquerque* (N.Mex.) *Journal*, 3 March 1990.

    An updated story on whether the Kid was killed in Fort Sumner in July 1881 or whether he lived on in Mexico and then Texas, this piece reports on the investigations of the controversy. Clyde Snow thought the possibility of Billy being Brushy Bill Roberts nearly impossible, whereas Bob Hefner, a gas station owner and judge in Hico, Texas, says Brushy is Billy. The article reports on the study of photographs sponsored by the Lincoln County Heritage Trust in February 1990.

87. Haederle, Michael. "An Elusive Outlaw." *Los Angeles Times*, 30 July 1990.

    Journalist Haederle expertly surveys the unfolding stories about Billy the Kid, especially those among academics. He quotes Paul Andrew Hutton on Billy's character and shifting personality, Robert Utley's solidly factual biography (174), and Richard Hart, then director of the Lincoln County Heritage Trust. He also makes clear the shaping role of books by Pat Garrett and Ash Upson (127) and Walter Noble Burns (103) and speaks of a few films made about Billy the Kid. A brief but very helpful overview for lay readers.

88. Reed, Ollie, Jr. "Much Ado about Billy." *Albuquerque* (N.Mex.) *Journal*, 15 February 2001.

    Veteran Albuquerque journalist Ollie Reed Jr. presents a well-illustrated front-page story about differing reactions of Fort Sumner residents to the possible pardon of Billy the Kid. The journalist finds residents of this town of 1,350 residents in De Baca County rather evenly divided on the issue of whether Billy ought to be pardoned for his part in the killing of Sheriff

William Brady. Some, seeing Billy as a hero, favor the pardon; others, viewing the Kid as a rascal outlaw, reject the idea of a pardon.

The interviewees—as well as journalist Reed—understand the implications of the Kid and his reputation for the livelihood of Fort Sumner. It is estimated that approximately ten thousand tourists drive out to the Fort Sumner State Monument on the eastern outskirts of the town, a site that remembers the heritage of Indian peoples held at old Fort Sumner in the 1860s. Many of these visitors also come to view Billy's grave, located very near the monument. Some think Fort Sumner would collapse economically if Billy and his legends were to disappear and keep tourists from coming. This controversy over the possible pardon raged on in New Mexico and beyond for several more years.

It is revealing to see how the divided opinions of the residents in the place where Billy is buried mimic the much larger group who read and write about the Kid. A well-written and interesting story.

89. **Newspapers and the Exhumation or "Digging Up" Controversy.**

When New Mexico local officials Steve Sederwall and Tom Sullivan announced in 2003 that they were going to, once and for all, find out whether Pat Garrett had killed Billy the Kid and whether the Kid was buried in the Fort Sumner cemetery, they ignited a thunderstorm of mounting publicity. Newspaper and magazine articles, books, and even films set out to capture the fiery dynamics of what it would mean to exhume the bodies of Billy and his mother, Catherine. And as the controversy continued during the next decade, other ingredients were added, including the exhumation of the bodies of Brushy Bill Roberts in Texas and John Miller in Arizona, two men who claimed to be the real Billy the Kid.

It would be impossible here to annotate the large number of these newspaper stories detailing the controversy through the years. But readers should begin with the sources listed below. They provide stories about the origins of the controversy, the persons involved in the conflict, and the outcome.

90. Janofsky, Michael. "122 Years Later, the Lawmen Are Still Chasing Billy the Kid." *New York Times*, 5 June 2003.

91. DellaFlora, Anthony. "State Not Kidding Around: Governor Won't Mind If Probe of the Notorious 19th Century N.M. Outlaw Boosts Tourism." *Albuquerque* (N.Mex.) *Journal*, 11 June 2003.

These two early newspaper stories (90 and 91) provide national and regional coverage of Sederwall and Sullivan and their controversial plans of exhumation. The front-page story in the *New York Times* reveals how the story would capture national attention in the next few years.

92. Miller, Jay. *Billy the Kid Rides Again: Digging for the Truth.* Santa Fe, N.Mex.: Sunstone Press, 2005.

    Miller, a widely read political columnist, pulled together his columns about the exhumation controversy to provide a helpful overview of the origins and first years of the dispute.

93. Cooper, Gale. *Billy the Kid's Pretenders: Brushy Bill and John Miller.* 2d printing. Albuquerque, N.Mex.: Gelcour Books: 2012 (110). And Cooper, *Cracking the Billy the Kid Case Hoax: The Strange Plot to Exhume Billy the Kid, Convict Sheriff Pat Garrett of Murder, and Become President of the United States.* 3d ed. Albuquerque, N.Mex.: Gelcour Books: 2014 (112).

    These two sources provide lengthy discussions of the "digging up" controversy from a pronouncedly one-sided perspective, but both books also furnish lengthy and very helpful lists of sources, including dozens upon dozens of newspaper articles dealing with the conflict. These lists in Cooper's books should be the beginning place for those pursuing newspaper stories on the exhumation topic.

94. **Newspapers and Billy the Kid Photographs.**

    Another subject captured recent newspaper headlines and feature stories: controversies surrounding authentic and bogus photographs of Billy the Kid. Over the decades, collectors and Kid specialists have agreed on the authentic tintype of the Kid made at Fort Sumner in 1879–1880. But other photographs claiming to be of Billy as a boy or preteen and of his mother, Catherine, were largely rejected.

    Then in 2010 a collector bought what he later claimed in 2015 was a photograph showing Billy the Kid with some of the Regulators and women and children playing croquet. When news of his pennies purchase was rumored to be worth millions—if authentic—that story stormed on to the scene. Arguments back and forth on whether it was the second authentic Billy photograph grabbed newspaper and magazine writers and even surged to television in a *National Geographic* special speaking for the authenticity of what was now called the "Croquet Kid."

    While this photograph roiled Kid collectors and Kid specialists, still another photograph surfaced claiming to be the Kid with friends. Purchased in 2011 and displayed in 2015, this one featured several men in a head-and-shoulders portrait depicting Pat Garrett and Billy with three others—at least as the owner claimed. Again a civil war of opinions followed, with collectors largely speaking for authenticity and most academics doubting that it was the real thing. Dozens of newspaper articles followed.

Since these newspaper articles about the contested photographs, like the journalistic stories about the "digging up" debate, rarely centered on Billy himself but on other subjects, those articles are not annotated here. But those interested in this widely written about subject can read further in the later section on photographs (346–54).

Books and Pamphlets

95. Airy, Helen. *Whatever Happened to Billy the Kid?* Santa Fe, N.Mex.: Sunstone Press, 1993.

Airy is convinced that Pat Garrett did not shoot down Billy the Kid on the night of 14 July 1881 but that the Kid survived as John Miller and lived until the early 1930s in southwestern New Mexico and finally in Arizona. The author argues that the supposed Garrett shooting "had been faked" and that Garrett's deputies, McKinney and Poe, "had been telling people that Garrett had shot the wrong man" (p. 13). But the writer provides almost no hard evidence, save for second- or thirdhand stories for these off-center statements. Nor does she say clearly who was killed instead of Billy, how Garrett worked out that subterfuge, or why Garrett shot someone else.

Indeed, Airy faces the same large problems all deniers are confronted with in believing that a John Miller or a Brushy Billy Roberts was the real Billy the Kid and that he was never killed in Fort Sumner. Miller's life is an interesting, catch-as-you-can one, worthy of examination because he claimed to be the real Billy the Kid. But Airy provides no strong, defensible evidence that Garrett did not shoot down Billy, meaning that her story stands on less-than-shaky grounds. And she has several of the known facts of Billy's killing, the coroner's report, and the viewing of Billy's body all wrong.

Airy's book is primarily a sketchy biography of John Miller, the events of his life, the acquaintances he made, and the stories he told of being the real Billy the Kid. Miller was a hardscrabble cowboy, rancher, and farmworker in southwestern New Mexico until, in his final years, moving to Arizona. Nearly all the book deals with Miller's life, not much with the actual Billy the Kid, and contains little of the strong research available on the Kid up to the early 1990s.

More demanding editors would have caught the author's numerous repetitions, reined in her tendency to quote too much, and straightened out writing miscues. Numerous photographs illuminate Miller's life but tell us nothing about Billy the Kid. This book does not provide sufficiently strong evidence to convert a reader to the contention that a southwestern rancher was the authentic Billy the Kid. Unfortunately, not even close. Disappointing read.

96. Anaya, A. P. "Paco." *I Buried Billy.* College Station, Tex.: Creative Publishing, 1991.

We have needed fulsome accounts by Hispanic writers to give us a larger picture of Billy the Kid, especially in Lincoln County. Sadly, although aimed at giving additional information on Billy, this account by A. P. "Paco" Anaya falls far short of its goal. It fails to provide a much-desired, extensive account of the Kid by a Hispanic.

Anaya's story is too garbled, studded with errors, and incomplete to be really useful. The narrative rambles and repeats information. The author gets years and months wrong and is incorrect on several pre-1877 details of Billy's life. He also subscribes to the legend of Billy killing twenty-one persons, one for each year of his brief life.

Despite the book's limitations, Anaya's reactions to Billy, in one of the few accounts in print by a Hispanic, are notable. To Anaya, Billy was not bad; instead, he was a good man. But "if someone wanted trouble with him, he was ready and wasn't afraid of anything." The Kid "was a very good friend of all Hispanics, and also the Anglo Saxons." He "never meant to do harm to any anybody . . . [and] helped a lot of Americans in Fort Sumner without any money. He gave them something to eat, or clothes" (pp. 144–45).

The author's thoughts about Garrett's handling of Billy's death reports in July 1881 are counter to most other accounts. Anaya's convictions on other happenings, he contends, came from Billy himself, but these, too, differ from those given to John P. Meadows (183) and others.

A bit disappointing for those wishing for a full, accurate account by a Hispanic close friend of Billy's.

97. Ball, Eve. *Ma'am Jones of the Pecos.* Tucson: University of Arizona Press, 1969.

Ball's volume mixes facts, contrived conversations, and imagined scenes. Her book is a clear example of what later was termed creative nonfiction. Some of the conversations and the exact dimensions of events, as Ball gives them, may not be entirely proven, but most of the happenings seem authentic. The story focuses on Heiskell Jones's family, especially his wife, Barbara, who was widely known and loved by most residents of the Pecos valley.

Ball has Ma'am Jones displaying her love for Billy the Kid, treating him as if he were one of her sons (she was the mother of nine sons and a daughter). In turn, Billy, as Ball describes him, viewed Ma'am as a reincarnation of his own deeply loved mother, Catharine.

In Ball's account, Billy comes on the scene barefoot and half dead after nearly losing his life to pursuing Indians. Later, he returns frequently to the Jones home for relaxation and refuge from the escalating violence in Lincoln County. Even though the Jones family sided more with the Murphy-Dolan group than with Billy's Tunstall-McSween tribe, Billy remained, for the most part, friends with the Jones family. Still, the Kid narrowly missed killing son John Jones during the frantic shooting while he escaped from the burning McSween home. Ball does little with the Billy-Jones family connections after the Big Killing of July 1878.

An interesting treatment of an admirable woman who played a minor part in the Lincoln County War, which shows her love for Billy the Kid. Yet one must use the imagined conversations and created scenes with caution.

98. Barron, R. M., ed. *Court of Inquiry: Lieutenant Colonel N. A. M. Dudley, Fort Stanton, New Mexico May–June–July 1879.* 4 vols. 1995. Reprinted as 2 vols. Edina, Minn.: Beaver's Pond Press, 2003.

A mammoth source of nearly one thousand pages, these two volumes contain large amounts of information about the Lincoln County War. Especially revealing of the character and actions of Fort Stanton commander Col. N. A. M. Dudley, these books publish for the first time the court testimonies of more than sixty respondents, including Gov. Lew Wallace, Sue McSween, Juan Patrón, Billy the Kid, and many soldiers and townspeople.

The testimonies illuminate, primarily, Colonel Dudley's roles in the conflicts that launched the Five-Day Battle of July 1878 and particularly the hour-by-hour events of the Big Kill on 19 July. The court hearings also record the impact of events before and after those fiery days. Most illuminating are

Dudley's defensive self-appreciation, the pro-Dudley bent of the examiners, and the alternative views of respondents to both events and ideas of the times. The hearing clearly reflects that the contentious viewpoints of 1877–1878 were still alive a year later.

Billy the Kid's testimony (pp. 185–200) is not very illuminating. Sticking close to factual questions asked of him—when he arrived in Lincoln, who was with him in the McSween house, who was killed during his escape—the Kid still ventures one important opinion. More than once he asserts that about three of Dudley's soldiers shot at him as he scurried out the back of the McSween home and precariously fled toward the Rio Bonito. Most other sources do not agree with this Kid assertion. On the other hand, Sue McSween's testimony (pp. 127–53) overflows with revealing comments about Dudley's supercilious attitudes toward her when she tried to gain protection for her husband and her home. The testimonies of Jimmy Dolan (pp. 249–53, 260–61) and Sheriff George Peppin (pp. 300–331, 358–59) are either so vague or pro-Dudley that they tell us too little about the roles of these major actors in Lincoln.

The longest and most pointed testimony is that of Santa Fe lawyer Henry L. Waldo. His acerbic, witty, but even vicious comments illustrate his first-rate talents in attacking the McSween's followers, denigrating Dudley's opponents, and sustaining the colonel's actions and character. None of the comments by the prosecutors—lawyer Ira Leonard and recorder Henry H. Humphreys—come close to the legal acumen exhibited in Waldo's extensive comments (pp. 536–611).

More than one commentator has called the Dudley Court of Inquiry a "whitewash," sweeping away criticism of the colonel, denigrating his opponents, and obscuring the central issues of his unwise decisions in 1878. Yet these pages provide helpful glimpses into the events and attitudes of Lincoln County in 1878–1879. If the volume editor had provided more historical context for this hearing and avoided the typographical, spelling, and layout errors, the volume would have been even stronger. Indeed, so important is this source that one wishes the equally valuable reports of U.S. investigator Frank Warren Angel were similarly available in published form.

99. Bell, Bob Boze. *The Illustrated Life and Times of Billy the Kid.* 1992. 2d ed. Phoenix, Ariz.: Tri Star–Boze Publications, 1996.

A book written more for general readers than scholars, Bell's richly illustrated volume, overflowing with photographs and the author's own artworks placed alongside the life and sociocultural contexts of Billy the Kid's life, has attracted wide attention. The second edition of 196 pages greatly expands the first edition's 120 pages and remains a very attractive volume for lay audiences.

Bell takes a middle-of-the-road approach on Henry Antrim cum Billy the Kid: the author quotes those who see the young man as typical and not a juvenile delinquent but also cites Henry's illegal actions in Silver City. For the most part, Bell is positive toward Billy but admits to his very bad decisions, such as in the killing of Morton and Baker and the murders of Sheriff Brady and Deputy Hindman.

Generally, Bell moves chronologically through Billy's life, making clear the importance of major episodes in Billy's life such as the Five-Day Battle. The important surrounding happenings in southern New Mexico are also emphasized, including the central characters in the Lincoln County imbroglio. In the second part of the book, treating 1879 to 1881, Billy comes into central focus. The author includes Billy's words at the Colonel Dudley hearing, comments on the one authentic photo of Billy, and introduces some of his rumored sweethearts. Billy's actions—and losses—in December 1880 are stressed. Bell sides, too, with those who think Billy carried a pistol with him into his death scene in Pete Maxwell's bedroom. The closing sections of the book trace what happened to major players in the Lincoln County drama and point to Billy's legendary treatments in later films, comics, and novels.

An interesting work for general readers and dependable on most historical information. The appealing panoply of photographs and Bell's artistic renditions of people, events, and places are especially attractive.

100. Bender, Norman, ed. *Missionaries, Outlaws, and Indians: Taylor F. Ealy at Lincoln and Zuni, 1878–1881*. Albuquerque: University of New Mexico Press, 1984.

Even members of the same family differed dramatically on Billy the Kid. Missionary doctor Taylor Ealy did not care for the Kid, thinking him a dangerous, violent character; but his wife, Mary, thought of Billy as "a charming looking chap with splendid manners. He loved to sing in a beautiful tenor voice when he came to Sunday School, as he did when he happened to be in Lincoln" (p. 19).

Mary found other pleasant characteristics in Billy—"his intelligence, his courtesy, his love of beauty, his capacity of leadership, . . . and without complaint of the rough as well as the smooth in life, and his capacity for making friends" (pp. 31–32). But Mrs. Ealy is mistaken, however, in recalling that Billy attended the Tunstall funeral; Sheriff Brady was still holding him in jail.

Although the book's five chapters, along with a brief introduction and extensive notes, provide abundant information, the volume's content is more valuable for context than for the views of a veteran participant in the Lincoln County War. The information on Billy is limited, but it is valuable for outsiders' perspectives.

101. Brent, William. *The Complete and Factual Life of Billy the Kid*. New York: Frederick Fell, 1964.

Dozens of factual and spelling mistakes, an anti-Billy and pro-Garrett partisanship, and very limited, outdated research sink this book. Plus, it is the product of a "how-to" and "self-help" book publisher who dabbled in western subjects to enlarge sales but hired authors who knew far too little about their subjects. Fell's books on the West fell flat, deservedly so.

Author William Brent was the son of James Brent—friend of Pat Garrett and later a New Mexico sheriff—and Carlotta Baca Brent, daughter of the well-known Capt. Saturnino Baca. The Baca family had an emotional falling out with Alex and Susan McSween during the Big Kill, and the captain's brother Bonifacio (Bonnie or Boni) Baca testified against Billy in his Mesilla trial. Brent's partisanship—his calling Billy an "egomaniac" (p. 152) and a "pathological liar" (p. 175) and Garrett "the most noted lawman the West has ever known" (p. 209)—skew this book against the Kid.

Even more important, the book is rife with oversights and errors. Brent dashes past Billy's early years, does almost nothing with his two years in Arizona, and skips over Billy's close relationships with adult women as friends or sweethearts (Brent insists that Billy had no sweethearts; his effeminate character and questionable masculinity kept him, it is suggested, from such relationships). More than a dozen names are misspelled, and several questions that other historians and biographers find unanswerable are clear and closed according to this author.

Brent's created conversations are troubling because too many are not based on solid research. In fact, the author's evidence throughout his book is limited, including mostly negative comments about Ash Upson's distortions in Garrett's biography of the Kid (1882) and the helpful comments Brent encountered in Maurice Garland Fulton's editing of the reprinted Garrett biography (1927, #124). There is no evidence that Brent read the important writings of Philip Rasch and Robert Mullin, which began appearing fifteen years before this book was published.

Generally, then, an anti-Billy account, partisan and limited in research.

102. Brothers, Mary Hudson, a story by Bell Hudson. *Billy the Kid, The Most Hated, the Most Loved Outlaw New Mexico Ever Produced.* Farmington, N.Mex.: Hustler Press, 1949.

The author gives the story that her father, Bell Hudson, left behind in manuscript notes. Regrettably, the fifty-two-page pamphlet opens with too many errors, including "McSwain" for McSween and jumbled chronology, all miscues that undermine what follows. Contrived conversations add to the mounting doubts. Still, Bell Hudson knew Pat Garrett, and his daughter relates details about the sheriff that earlier writers had not used. Generally, the unofficial details on Garrett are the most valuable contribution of this source; conversely, the details on Billy and the events in Lincoln County should be approached with caution.

103. Burns, Walter Noble. *The Saga of Billy the Kid.* 1926. Albuquerque: University of New Mexico Press, 1999. With an introduction by Richard W. Etulain, ix–xvii.

Walter Noble Burns, a Chicago journalist, produced a highly touted immediate bestseller in his *Saga of Billy the Kid.* A reviewer for the *New York Times* book review, Stanley Walker, wrote on 7 March 1926 that Burns's book about the Kid was an "exciting biography," a "stirring" narrative. Another reviewer for *Harper's Magazine* told readers in the May 1926 issue that Burns's *Saga* was "the most elaborate story of an outlaw that . . . [he had] ever read." New Mexico reviewers were equally impressed. A writer for the *Santa Fe New Mexican* called the book "a classic, an epic, one of the most thrilling tales ever written."

Members of the newly launched Book of the Month Club were similarly smitten and chose the *Saga* as a pioneering main selection for the group's offerings. One of the club's judges praised the biography's "vivid reality of the moving pictures without the infusion of false sentiment and the inevitable hoist of the story away from life toward melodrama." Buyers lined up in droves, and the author and publisher enjoyed telling others that, a bit more than a year after publication, the *Saga* had sold thirty thousand copies. Six months later, Metro-Goldwyn-Mayer bought the movie rights for $10,000, divided half-and-half between the author and publisher.

From his opening pages, Burns dramatizes the Lincoln County War and Billy the Kid's story with the fervor of an epic storyteller. His descriptions of the two warring sides are as titanic battles, like Homeric warriors clashing. John Chisum is "the King of the Valley," L. G. Murphy "the Lord of the Mountains." As Burns told one interviewer shortly after the publication of the *Saga*, he believed "history at its best" was "a drama of facts."

Burns's Billy is a marriage of opposites. He exhibits "knightly devotion . . . [accentuated] with a spirit of primitive savagery" (p. 52). In something of a mini-psycho-biography of the Kid, Burns describes him as a split personality, a youth with a "desperado complex" (p. 55). In the violent territorial New Mexico, Billy became a "genius painting his name in flaming colours with a six-shooter across the sky of the Southwest" (p. 56).

In the most probing overview of the shifting interpretations of Billy the Kid in the century following the Kid's death, literary scholar Stephen Tatum (171) concludes that Burns's biography "has generated more controversy than any book in the Kid's bibliography" (p. 102). The controversies arose largely around two topics: Burns's "artistic" approach to his subject and his tendency to introduce false information. Later historians and biographers often dismissed the *Saga* as merely a historical novel to be catalogued in libraries as fiction rather than history. Maurice Garland Fulton, just beginning his career as a diligent and thorough researcher but reluctant publisher, wrote privately to Burns to express his doubts about "errors and inaccuracies" in Burns's writing. Burns defended himself by saying that he was only looking for "authentic facts," that he had "an authority for every statement . . . [he had] made," and that Fulton was "wrong in assuming that . . . [his] attitude is that of a fiction writer." In the next half century and more, many other critics scorned Burns's handling of facts in the Lincoln County story.

One of the most controversial of Burns's assertions is that Sue McSween, even though threatened with the destruction of her Lincoln home and maybe her life and that of her husband, Alex, sat down to play "The Star Spangled Banner" as bullets whizzed around her house and smoke from the fire burning the house drifted in. Burns also declared that Alex cowered in the corner of the burning home, reading his Bible and unable to move into defensive actions. Later, reading Burns's account, Mrs. McSween denounced these assertions as "ridiculous," including her playing the piano, saying it was "the biggest lie [there] ever was." She was "hurt" by these descriptions. Burns tried to soothe Sue's feelings, but he could only lamely admit that he had heard the piano story so often it had become part of Lincoln County's oral history.

One of Burns's conclusions was his largest contribution. He, generally, sent the Billy story in a new direction. If most writers from Billy's death to the early 1920s pictured the Kid negatively, as a desperado and killer, Burns was less damning—in fact, often quite positive in his descriptions of Billy. Burns admitted that outlaws like Billy "were hard-boiled from the first" (p. 31). They were "bold fellows," a remuda of "desperate and lawless men" (p. 85). True enough, but Billy's frontier New Mexico was a dramatic Wild West, with the Kid playing a leading role in a drama with dark hues. Still, Burns has Billy acting not as the violent murderer of the sensational dime novelists but as a young, energetic, and sometimes off-track outlaw trying to find his place in a chaotic society losing its way.

In Burns's second supposition, if Billy's New Mexico is descending into bottomless turmoil and he emerges more and more as the offspring of the older, lawless West, Pat Garrett is bringing law and order to the territory. With Billy on the older side, Pat Garrett, on the newer side, epitomizes what historian Richard Maxwell Brown called the "Western Civil War of Incorporation" in his book *No Duty to Retreat: Violence and Values in American History and Society* (1991). In Burns's and Brown's views, Billy becomes an anachronistic throwback, refusing to recognize and accept the power of incoming institutions and law and order. When Garrett pursues and eventually kills Billy, he is pictured as the destroyer of Billy's outdated world. Actually, Burns's portraits of Billy and Garrett owe much to the dominant climate of opinion concerning the closing frontier from the 1890s to the 1930s. The frontier had closed and disappeared—and Billy the Kid with it. Now railroads, new government oversights and policies, and statehood—with Garrett symbolizing their entry and successes—had replaced the older Wild West.

Burns makes these ideas explicit in the closing pages of *Saga*. Because Garrett ended Billy's ineffective world and brought in much-needed advancements, New Mexico owed him a great deal. For Burns, Garrett "brought law and order west of the Pecos. He stabilized the land, made it safe to live in and build homes in, cleared the way for statehood" (p. 321). "Constructive through destruction," Garrett "had a job to do and he did it; a mission to fulfil and he filled it" (pp. 321, 322).

For the next thirty years, Burns's *Saga of Billy the Kid*, like the earlier Upson-Garrett biography, was *the* book about Billy that authors—historians, biographers, novelists, and scriptwriters—had to deal with. Not until the 1950s did new research appear that proved Burns wrong on many of his conclusions. But the drama and power of his storytelling even lasted beyond that change point.

104. Caldwell, Clifford R. *Dead Right: The Lincoln County War.* 2008. Rev. 2d ed. Mountain Home, Tex.: self-published, 2010.

This brief, self-published account of the Lincoln County War provides a helpful summary of major participants and events involved in this much-written-about subject. Clifford Caldwell does not endeavor to bring new information to readers but strives to furnish a clear, dependable account of the war.

After an abbreviated section on "The Roots of the Conflict," Caldwell contributes several biographical chapters. His treatment of Alexander and Susan McSween is surprisingly short (seven pp.) and not very sympathetic. Then follow an extensive, positive section on John Chisum (twenty-eight pp.) and another on John Tunstall (eighteen pp.). Others covered in briefer vignettes are L. G. Murphy, Jimmy Dolan, Billy the Kid, and additional characters.

The major contribution of Caldwell's book, in addition to his concise overview of the Lincoln County War, is contained in his several closing chapters. He contributes one chapter of biographies of the members of the Regulators, another on the regional lawmen, and then a third on The House participants. A final section furnishes a chronology of dates from 1823 to 1952. The book's notes and bibliography are adequate but not exceptional.

One wishes the book were even stronger. Better proofreading and developmental editing would have caught and corrected typos, grammatical errors, and organizational problems. The author is also guilty of mistakes such as having Billy tried in 1881 in Lincoln rather than in Mesilla and in placing the Kid's killing of deputies J. W. Bell and Bob Olinger before the shooting of Joe Grant.

Billy aficionados might be disappointed in Caldwell's very brief treatment of the Kid. The author explains his point: "In my view, . . . [Billy] was but a small part of the [Lincoln County] story from 1877 to 1879. However, he was pretty much the whole story after 1879 and until the time of his death in 1881" (p. x). Summing up the Kid's significance, Caldwell writes, Billy "was, to be certain, an unlikely and to a large degree undeserving hero of the Lincoln County War" (p. 212).

In brief, a helpful compact overview that one wishes were stronger.

105. Chaffey, David L. *Chasing the Santa Fe Ring: Power and Privilege in Territorial New Mexico.* Albuquerque: University of New Mexico Press, 2014.

After thorough research in published books and essays, newspapers, and pertinent manuscript materials, Professor David Chaffey concludes there was no chartered, well-organized, ongoing, and explicit Santa Fe Ring. Moving beyond the best previous work on the Ring by Howard R. Lamar (143), the author deals explicitly and carefully with the lives and actions of supposed Ring members or those supportive of the Ring, such as Thomas B. Catron, Stephen B. Elkins, and dozens of others. Generally Chaffey quotes, seemingly with approval, many of the criticisms of Ring opponents without himself throwing numerous darts.

Chaffey devotes a chapter to the Lincoln County War and connections between the Ring and such persons as L. G. Murphy and William L. Rynerson. He does not believe the Ring was involved in the murder of Englishman John Tunstall or that Gov. Lew Wallace actually planned to pardon Billy the Kid. Chaffey does point to Catron's involvement, however, in the Fritz insurance controversy and his support for Rynerson and Bristol and The House leaders. In a later chapter, "The Myth of the Ring" (pp. 207–21), the author discusses a few novels and films that deal with the Santa Fe Ring, the Lincoln County War, and Billy the Kid.

Chaffey ends his book with brief biographical profiles of "Alleged Ring Participants" (pp. 241–45), "Secondary Participants" (pp. 245–52), and "Peripheral or Doubtful Participants" (pp. 252–58). He traces the activities of many of these persons from the end of the Civil War to New Mexico statehood in 1912, with special focus on the events of the 1870s and early 1880s.

A cautious, nonassertive, and clearly written study, now the most extensive examination available on the Santa Fe Ring.

106. Chamberlain, Kathleen P. *In the Shadow of Billy the Kid: Susan McSween and the Lincoln County War.* Albuquerque: University of New Mexico Press, 2013.

Historians dealing with the Lincoln County story and biographers of Billy the Kid frequently overlook the important roles of women and Hispanics in these two stories. Now we have the needed book on Susan McSween, the leading woman in the Lincoln County War, and on her role in the evolving legends of that war and the life of Billy the Kid.

Chamberlain's biography of Susan McSween Barber is thoroughly researched and pleasingly written. Diligently working through the sparse information on Susan's life (born December 1845) before she came with her husband, Alex, to New Mexico in March 1875, the author traces the difficulties for Sue in her own early family challenged with so many children and straitened finances. Most of those years, for both Sue and Alex, are barren of details, as Chamberlain makes clear.

More than half of the book focuses, as it should, on the backgrounds and dramatic events of the Lincoln County War, from 1875 to midsummer 1878. Without overlooking the roles of the conflicts and then gun battles between the Murphy-Dolan and Tunstall-McSween partisans, Chamberlain focuses on Sue McSween: what her opinions were, what she did, and what the killing of Alex McSween meant to her future. We get exactly what we have needed: the Lincoln County War through the eyes of the most important woman in the horrendous conflict.

Later chapters deal with Sue's life from 1878 to her death in 1931. These sections show her to be a valiant, hardworking, and intelligent woman making her way, very successfully, in a man's world as it gradually transitioned out of that semicivilized frontier. Chamberlain details McSween's burgeoning role as the Cattle Queen of New Mexico, her life as a woman of social aspirations, and her aging and gradual decline.

This is a sympathetic but balanced portrait. Chamberlain praises Sue McSween's energies, ambitions, and diligence. She also shows, however, that McSween could be vain, salty tongued, and self-righteous. What we are given is a valuable portrait of a complex woman, and that picture provides a fuller, more revealing portrait of the history of Lincoln County and New Mexico. We also see how much the continuing legends of Billy the Kid, first as a rascally desperado and then as a possible hero, overshadowed Sue McSween's important activities—and yet made her famous in Walter Noble Burns's *Saga of Billy the Kid*, which she readily admitted.

A superb work, full and revealing. An appealing model for other such biographies on Alex McSween, L. G. Murphy, Jimmy Dolan, John Chisum, and a group biography of women in the Lincoln County War.

107. Cline, Donald. *Alias Billy the Kid: The Man Behind the Legend.* Santa Fe, N.Mex.: Sunstone Press, 1986.

Donald Cline loved advancing assertive statements, overturning what previous biographers had written about Billy the Kid, and touting his own diligent research. He was convinced that he had found the real—and only— Michael Henry McCarty in New York City's Irish Fourth Ward, born on

20 November 1859. That doubtful assertion, coupled with many others dealing with Billy, gravely limits the value of this brief, scattered biography.

Cline had a negative button he pushed far too often. There are no "good guys" in the author's catalogue of characters, save perhaps for Pat Garrett, who did "exactly what he was paid to do" in killing Billy the Kid (p. 116). Billy, on the other hand, is pictured in the darkest hues. "He was a liar, a thief and a user of persons," Cline writes. He sacrificed "his former comrades to protect his own freedom" and "was a cold-blooded murderer who never risked anything." Billy might be a "personable young man," but he has to be remembered, primarily, as "a coward . . . [and] a petty cattle thief," and a youth who "preferred to live off the labor of honest men because he was unwilling to expend his own energy" (p. 11).

The negativity covers many pages. Billy is a "cowardly, petty outlaw" (p. 103), "born to be bad" (p. 31). Alex McSween is equally base; he is a man whose "greed knew no bounds" (p. 62). Moreover, lawyer McSween and rancher John Chisum obviously contracted with the Regulators to kill Sheriff Brady.

Perhaps Cline's largest faux pas is in his shaky argument that William Antrim sent his stepsons back to their natal New York City after Henry got into trouble in Silver City. Then, nearly a year later, Henry stabbed a young man, a former chum, forcing the biological father of Henry and Joe, Edward McCarty, to travel down the Santa Fe Trail to take his two sons back to the Southwest. In making these arguments, Cline threw over all the excellent research that authors Koop (215), Rasch (161–63), and Mullin (151) turned up about Billy's years before he arrived in Lincoln County. No other biographer since Cline has followed any of his wrongheaded chronology in these matters.

One wishes Cline were less negative, so often stiff-arming the opinions of others and championing his own views. In addition, the author's narrative is jumbled, placing, for example, his coverage of the Joe Grant killing *after* Billy's Lincoln jailbreak. Finally, several chapters contain out-of-order footnotes and excessive misspellings and punctuation errors.

A disappointment for a person who obviously did extensive research but could not turn out a dependable, well-organized, and important biography of Billy.

108. Cline, Don[ald]. *Antrim and Billy.* College Station, Tex.: Creative Publishing, 1990.

The only book-length study of William H. Antrim, the stepfather of Billy the Kid, this volume curiously combines thorough research with some unfortunate, undependable conclusions. The author's diligent work in obscure sources deserves praise, but his tendency to vouch for untenable positions undermines his contributions. For example, he still asserts, as he did in his earlier book (107) that Catherine McCarty never married; that she had two sons by one Edward McCarty in New York City; and that Henry Antrim (Billy) fled back to New York City in 1875, stabbed Thomas Moore there, and then quickly journeyed back to the Southwest. No other well-known biographer or authority on Billy the Kid advances these views.

But this book uncovers more on stepfather William Antrim than on Billy, and in its central focus on the stepfather, Cline tells us much more than any other author. He provides chapters on Antrim's early years in Indiana and Kansas and then devotes more than half the book to Antrim's life after 1873 until his death in 1922.

Cline makes much of Antrim's successful challenge to draft laws in 1863. In fact, he states that Antrim "also changed the course of Union history during the Civil War" (p. 11). He also thinks Henry McCarty went to Wichita as Antrim's foster son and that the Catherine McCarty Antrim known in Indianapolis was not Henry/Billy's mother. Cline states that another Catherine, Billy's mother, "might have engaged in occasional prostitution" (p. 44), and that later her reputation "was poor" in Silver City. No other biographer advances these assertions. Two chapters on Silver City provide bits on young Henry/Billy's life and extensive information on the "Antrim House Mystery": where it was located, when, and its type of construction.

The closing chapters, centering on the stepfather, provide an abundance of information on William Antrim from 1880 until his death. One chapter also deals with Billy's brother, Joe.

Interestingly, Leon C. Metz, the biographer of Pat Garrett, declares in the "Introduction" to this book that William Antrim's "real importance has nothing to do with Billy the Kid" (p. 10). Cline, however, contends that the lives of Billy; his mother, Catherine; and William Antrim each "had a decided impact upon the others" (p. 11). Another example in this book of conflicting unacceptable and acceptable conclusions.

109. Coe, George W. *Frontier Fighter: The Autobiography of George W. Coe, Who Fought and Rode with Billy the Kid.* Boston: Houghton Mifflin, 1934.

Coe might have given us a first-rate book overflowing with insights about Billy the Kid. He knew Billy well, hunted with him in late 1877, rode and fought alongside him in 1878, and had many friendly conversations with the

Kid. Some of these firsthand contacts enrich this volume. Unfortunately, the book contains so many factual errors that it must be used with the greatest of caution on details about the Kid. For example, in the first paragraph of a biographical chapter on Billy, Coe is wrong in stating that "William H. and Kathleen [sic] Bonney . . . came West . . . , settling in Coffeyville [Kansas] in 1862" (p. 36). Also, Catherine did not marry William Antrim in Colorado. When Coe tries to deal with events in which he did not take part, he is nearly always in error.

Coe is clearly a supporter of the Tunstall-McSween faction and even more of Billy the Kid. He writes about Billy: "He was gentlemanly as a college-bred youth. He quickly became acquainted with everybody, and with his humorous and pleasing personality grew to be a community favorite. . . . Billy was so popular there wasn't enough of him to go around" (p. 33). Billy "was a good pal, always happy and pleasant. He helped me with all the chores and domestic work, and I could not have asked for a better friend of companion" (p. 34).

Coe is extraordinarily positive about Billy, but his facts, particularly about the events he did not participate in or observe, are often wide of the mark.

110. Cooper, Gale. *Billy the Kid's Pretenders: Brushy Bill and John Miller.* 2010. 2d printing. Albuquerque, N.Mex.: Gelcour Books, 2012.

The briefest of Cooper's otherwise lengthy books, this work, at only 333 pages, is one of the least noteworthy of Cooper's several books. The author is primarily interested in combating the claims of "pretenders" Brushy Bill Roberts and John Miller and their followers. After a brief overview of what Cooper considers the history of the "real" Billy the Kid (1859–1881)—named Henry McCarty, Henry Antrim, and William Bonney—she takes apart the claims of the two pretenders. Then follow, page by page, strongly worded comments on the works defending Roberts and Miller and attempting to further their claims.

Unfortunately, Cooper devotes nearly all of her book to attacking the characters of the pretenders and their advocates. In her words, they are "clowns" and "liars," they utilize "alien invasion illogic," and they often misrepresent history—and the truth—to make a case of their skewed beliefs. Cooper is particularly hard on C. L. Sonnichsen and William V. Morrison, authors of *Alias Billy the Kid* (169); they, like Brushy Bill, are "eccentrics," even though Sonnichsen was a leading authority on the American West (a professor of literature, not a historian, as Cooper wrongly states). She also attacks *The Return of the Outlaw Billy the Kid* (138) by W. C. Jameson and Frederic Bean as a book by hoaxers who undermined the real Billy, a "freedom fighter," and denigrated Pat Garrett as a lying murderer. Curiously, the author does not deal with Jameson's other writings about Brushy Bill that appeared before the second printing of this volume.

Cooper's assertive, attacking style may alienate more than attract readers. Her negativity about the pretenders, writers supporting them, and such figures as Gov. Bill Richardson and historian Paul Hutton (castigated but unnamed here as he is in Cooper's *Cracking the Billy the Kid Case Hoax* [112]) detract from the clear strengths Cooper has as a diligent, sound researcher. Moreover, she sprinkles her quotes with *"sic"* from the writings of others to indicate their miscues but overlooks the dozens of misspellings, missing words, and awkward sentences in her own book.

111. Cooper, Gale. *Billy the Kid's Writings, Words, and Wit.* Albuquerque, N.Mex.: Gelcour Books, 2011.

A valuable collection of Billy the Kid's writings and testimonies, this book is the most important of Cooper's handful of volumes. But it is for the original documents that it should be touted, not for the author's partisan conclusions.

The book reprints all the Kid's letters, particularly the important ones to Gov. Lew Wallace, his comments at trials, and a handful of other Billy documents. This is the first time all these important sources have been printed in one collection. It also includes several other letters, newspaper stories, and other materials that are important for studying Billy and the Lincoln County War.

Most often, Cooper prints a letter or document followed by her analyses or inserts her comments within the reprinted document.

But Cooper's thinking and writing undermine the value of her book. As usual, she thinks and writes in a melodramatic format, making Billy the Kid a brave and brilliant hero and his opponents, primarily the Santa Fe Ring (and her Ring includes nearly all of Billy's antagonists), arrogant, selfish, if not murderous rascals. One wishes she were less inclined to divide the historical world into white and black hats, which loses the complexity of bifurcated characters like Billy.

Cooper seems not to know much about the writings of Maurice Garland Fulton, Philip Rasch, Joel Jacobsen, and, most obviously, Robert Utley.

Although generally to be trusted in her treatment of facts, she occasionally makes mistakes: Susan McSween did comment on Billy the Kid, Paulita Maxwell was not pregnant with Billy's child at his death, and how can one say a setup ambush was traitorously conceived for killing Billy in Pete Maxwell's bedroom by Pat Garrett and Maxwell unless strong proof is given?

A strong-minded editor would likely call for changes in the book's organization. Why devote nearly forty pages to the Spencerian style of writing and fifty pages to the so-called "Billie" letter of ca. 24 March 1879 that Cooper claims to have authenticated. Plus, the repetition: dozens of pages from Cooper's previous books reappears here, and some documents are reprinted as many as three times.

In short, this volume is a mix of valuable information and provocative assertions with disorganized writing, overly zealous conclusions, and extraneous information.

112. Cooper, Gale. *Cracking the Billy the Kid Case Hoax: The Strange Plot to Exhume Billy the Kid, Convict Sheriff Pat Garrett of Murder, and Become President of the United States.* 3d ed. Albuquerque, N.Mex.: Gelcour Books, 2014.

A mammoth volume of more than one thousand pages, this book illustrates the large, numerous strengths of Gale Cooper and, regrettably, the too-numerous limitations. This huge book adds to, rearranges, and changes the similar contents of the earlier version, *MegaHoax: The Strange Plot to Exhume Billy the Kid and Become President* (2010), and also includes information that appeared previously in *Billy the Kid's Pretenders: Brushy Bill and John Miller* (110). This later, revised version includes more than seven hundred pages of text, an annotated list of sixty-seven appendixes (pp. 727–914), and an extensive annotated bibliography of sources (pp. 917–95).

First of all, and most important, Gale Cooper, a Harvard-trained M.D. psychiatrist with extensive experience in murder-case consultations, knows her Billy the Kid history. On the track of the Kid for nearly fifteen years when this book appeared, Cooper had read widely, researched diligently, and seemed to forget nothing. Her story of Billy follows, for the most part, the traditional and accepted stories that such writers as Frederick Nolan and Robert Utley have provided. No one should dismiss Cooper's expertise on the topics that grab her attention.

This book is not so much about the Kid himself as about what Cooper calls the "Billy the Kid Case hoax." She accuses Gov. Bill Richardson, local sheriffs Steve Sederwall and Tom Sullivan, several lawyers, historians Paul Hutton and David Turk, *True West* editor Bob Boze Bell, and several others of multifaceted hoaxes. The accusations are of writers who assert that Pat Garrett did not shoot Billy the Kid but murdered an innocent man, attempt to dig up the bodies of Billy and his mother, provide false support for Brushy Billy Roberts and Jim Miller as the real Billy the Kid, and foster several other miscarriages of justice.

Unfortunately, Cooper often indulges in character assassination. Governor Richardson and his supporters are "thugs, lugs, losers, loonies, and dubious donors" (p. 171). Paul Hutton is a "bottom-of-the-barrel historian" (p. 185), Hampton Sides "an ignorant but hostile historian" (p. 511), and the governor himself a "historically imbecilic" man (p. 513). Cooper cannot just speak of opponents; she must denigrate their characters. In doing so, she undermines her credibility as a believable historian. Conversely, her self-appreciation as an entirely honest freedom fighter and never-quit justice-seeker with an encyclopedic memory knows no bounds.

More an autobiography and a jumble of documents and first-person comments within those documents than a well-crafted history, this book is nonetheless a valuable source for understanding the controversies circling around Billy early in the twenty-first century.

113. Cooper, Gale. *The Lost Pardon of Billy the Kid: An Analysis.* Albuquerque, N.Mex.: Gelcour Books, 2017.

This 975-page volume replicates the contributions and shortcomings of most of Gale Cooper's recent books. Regrettably, the clear strengths are undermined by the equally evident limitations.

Cooper uncovers more documents than any previous historian or biographer in dealing with the Billy the Kid pardon and Gov. Lew Wallace. She has ransacked the Lew Wallace manuscripts in Indiana and elsewhere; U.S. documents in Washington, D.C.; and Santa Fe letters and manuscripts to provide thorough, extensive documentation for her mammoth account. She also makes very good use of key newspaper stories, reminiscent accounts, and other miscellaneous documents. Cooper deserves high marks for her diligent, valuable research.

But her story is so one-sided—Billy the Kid as hero (and sometimes near saint) and Lew Wallace as lying rascal—that readers will question her account and concluding judgments. True, Billy was sometimes a "freedom fighter" and an opponent of the rascally Santa Fe Ring, but he also, at times, was entirely self-absorbed, looking out for himself (which he himself admitted), and also a liar, thief, and murderer. Cooper has a very difficult time dealing with the negative sides of Billy's character and makes the Santa Fe Ring so tightly knit, all-encompassing, and murderous that everyone, under pressure, bowed down to its threats.

One wishes Cooper would avoid these ideological, structural, and storytelling limitations and make better use of the enormous amounts of research she has clearly carried out in this volume.

114. Cooper, Gale. *The Nun Who Rode on "Billy the Kid."* Albuquerque, N.Mex.: Gelcour Books, 2017.

Amateur historian Cooper achieves her major goal in this thick book: she reveals the incorrect, conjured-up information in Sister Blandina's magazine essays and her later book *At the End of the Santa Fe Trail* (1932, 1948, et al.). The author's thorough research discloses much about the nun's life and personality, especially about her roles as a writer and storyteller.

Cooper demonstrates that even though Sister Blandina wrote about Billy the Kid, she never met him as she claimed to have done. Cooper takes on the difficult task of concluding that the nun, under consideration for sainthood, told stretchers, suggesting that she wanted to enliven her stories and enlarge her influence. Most of all, Cooper is upset that Blandina's "hoaxes" helped launch an ongoing legacy of damage to the real history of Billy Bonney as a "freedom fighter" (p. 415).

Cooper's book deals much more with Sister Blandina than with Billy the Kid. The author summarizes the nun's life; describes her writings, through revisions and additions, which became *At the End of the Santa Fe Trail*; and speculates on the motivations of the sister in telling stories that were not true. Cooper also tries to show how followers and supporters of Sister Blandina, right up to the present, have not been able to question her inaccuracies and falsehoods because they consider her in all ways a saint.

One wishes Cooper could correct her own shortcomings and made the book stronger. The story line rambles, is often repetitious, contains dozens of typos and wrong dates, and employs awkward sentences and structure. Curiously, too, Cooper says she was unable, at first, to obtain copies of the first edition of Sister Blandina's book (1932), but librarians at the Santa Fe Chavez Library and the University of New Mexico Library say copies of the first edition were available to her as she did research for this book.

115. Cramer, T. Dudley. *The Pecos Ranchers in the Lincoln County War.* Oakland, Calif.: Branding Iron Press, 1996.

Cramer provides an inviting story of cattlemen and cowboys whose families and lives paralleled the major events leading up to, through, and after the Lincoln County War. Among the families discussed are the Beckworths; John Chisum, Cattle King of the Pecos River country; the Goodnight-Loving cattle trailers; Heiskell Jones's family; W. R. "Jake" Owen; and John Tunstall. The author situates these families and individuals alongside the central events of the Lincoln County conflicts: the Pecos War, the murder of Tunstall, the Five-Day Battle in Lincoln, and Billy the Kid's capture, escape, and death. The later murder of Pat Garrett is covered in the final chapter.

Most of Cramer's story is well known and can be traced in several recent books by Frederick Nolan and Robert Utley. But the author's information on the rancher-cowboy families and riders adds to the Billy the Kid and Lincoln County stories. The author makes especially good use of manuscripts and other sources at the Haley Library in Midland, Texas.

116. Dworkin, Mark J. *American Mythmaker: Walter Noble Burns and the Legends of Billy the Kid, Wyatt Earp, and Joaquin Murrieta.* Norman: University of Oklahoma Press, 2015.

This valuable study of journalist-historian Walter Noble Burns provides a brief overview of his writings about Billy the Kid, Wyatt Earp, and Joaquin Murrieta. Author Mark Dworkin shows how Burns became a best-selling, first-rate storyteller of frontier legends.

The longest section of Dworkin's book deals with Billy the Kid. The author includes four chapters on the Billy the Kid story: (1) a brief biography of Billy; (2) Burns's research methods and creation of characters; (3) the reactions of critics to Burns's biography; and (4) the uses of Burns's *Saga* in subsequent writings and artistic works.

Generally, Dworkin is balanced in his treatment of Burns. He praises Burns's numerous interviews with participants, his extensive newspaper research, and especially his dramatic, lively writing style. But he also notes Burns's willingness to stretch details, hype the drama of his narrative, and wander away, on a few occasions, from the facts.

Overall, Dworkin helps readers to understand how much Burns's *Saga of Billy the Kid* (1926) influenced later writers and moviemakers in their depictions of Billy the Kid. The author's research in Burns manuscripts and other essays and books dealing with Billy and the Lincoln County War is diligent and thorough.

117. Dykes, Jeff C. *Law on a Wild Frontier: Four Sheriffs of Lincoln County.* The Great Western Series 5. Washington, D.C.: Potomac Corral, 1969.

This twenty-five-page pamphlet treats four sheriffs of Lincoln County: William Brady, Pat Garrett, John W. Poe, and George Curry. The links that connect the quartet are their ties to Billy the Kid. Dykes devotes about six pages of solid, if brief, pages to each of the lawmen. In each of the four sections, Dykes quickly summarizes the known facts, argues against those he considers insubstantial, and pushes to balanced conclusions. Helpful introduction.

118. Dykes, J. C., ed. "Introduction." In *The Authentic Life of Billy, the Kid . . .* , by Pat Garrett. 1882. Norman: University of Oklahoma Press, 1954, pp. xi–xxviii.

Dykes's role in this second of the three major reprints of Garrett's biography of Billy the Kid is much less extensive than Fulton's (124) and Nolan's (157) in their edited reprints of the same book. Still, Dykes offers helpful information, and his comments reveal what a Billy specialist knew in the early 1950s.

Dykes divides his introduction, "Pat Garrett and His Book," into three major parts. First, a biographical section on Garrett, with a few comments on his coauthor, Marshall Ashmun "Ash" Upson. Second, discussion of "The Book" with treatment of Garrett's inaccuracies and the book's organization. Third, the book's printing history, noting its marketing failures and its being pushed aside by Charlie Siringo's *A Texas Cowboy* (1885) as *the* early book for information on the Kid.

Some of Dykes's conclusions are clearly time bound. He seemed to know nothing about Billy's two years in Arizona (1875–1877) and his shooting of "Windy" Cahill. Philip Rasch was turning up the information on the Kid in Arizona in the very year this edition was published. Dykes also thinks Billy killed Bob Beckwith, which more recent researchers reject.

But on other important topics, Dykes agrees with others questioning Garrett's accuracy. He—and they—think a preteen Billy did not stab a man in Silver City who had insulted his mother, he did not travel into Mexico for several months, and he did not kill three Apaches in Arizona and rescue a wagon train.

Dykes's three-part discussion of the organization of Garrett's book is also helpful. He thinks Upson invented nearly all the first chapters, Upson and Garrett partnered in the middle chapters, and the final chapters came from Garrett. But Upson might have done all the writing, thus serving as a ghostwriter.

A helpful introduction, but it lacks the more extensive editorial comments throughout Garrett's book that appear in the Fulton and Nolan editions.

119. Earle, James H., ed. *The Capture of Billy the Kid.* College Station, Tex.: Creative Publishing, 1988.

This brief collection provides more confirming, rather than pathbreaking, stories about the capture of Billy the Kid. The editorial apparatus is limited, however, overlooking the possibilities of placing these accounts in larger context.

The manuscript accounts by Cal Poe, written in 1896, and Louis Bousman, written in 1934, substantiate the findings of later authorities dealing with the events just before and after Billy's capture at Stinking Spring in December 1880. But, unfortunately, Poe's references to "geezers" and Bousman's assertion that Billy killed his first man in Silver City at age fourteen also illustrate the times and limited perspectives of the authors.

The two longest sections of the book are reprinted pages from Charlie Siringo's *History of Billy the Kid* (chapter 8, 1920) and Pat Garrett's *The Authentic Life of Billy, the Kid* (chapters 19–21, 1882). The excerpt from Garrett's book is jumbled when compared to subsequent versions of the book.

Additional sections include maps of Fort Sumner and the Maxwell home by longtime Fort Sumner resident Charles Foor and reprinted Las Vegas newspaper reports about the Kid's capture in 1880–1881.

Overall, the book is a bit disappointing because of the limitations of its contents and the abbreviated contextual editorial comment.

120. Edwards, Harold. *Goodbye Billy the Kid.* College Station, Tex.: Creative Publishing, 1995.

Much more important for what it gathers and reprints than for what it states, this brief book collects a few more than thirty obituaries of Billy the Kid published around the United States shortly after Pat Garrett shot him down on 14–15 July 1881. Edwards uses his first five chapters to overview Billy's life and then devotes the next six chapters to reprinting the obituaries. A final chapter raises and comments on a few questions about the meanings of the obituaries.

One wishes Edwards had researched more widely and raised more searching questions about the valuable information he gathered. His first chapters are narrowly researched, with large reliance on the writings of Philip Rasch, Robert Utley, and Maurice Garland Fulton—and almost no use of the works of Frederick Nolan. Edwards has not utilized manuscript collections, nor has he examined newspapers published during Billy's life.

The discussion of the obituaries is organized regionally—from New Mexico to western subregions, the Deep South, the Northeast, the Midwest, and the West Coast. The New Mexico chapter, stretching more than thirty pages, includes seven obituaries with very few authorial comments. The longest obituary is a huge hoax account appearing in the *Boston Globe*. A brief obituary in the London *Times* is included.

Edwards should have pointed out that these early obituaries were of a piece with the negative early accounts of the Kid in newspapers and dime novels—and were much at odds with treatments of the Kid after the mid-1920s. Readers should have been told, too, more about the mistakes and false information given out in these early newspaper reports. Plus, what did the content and points of view in these obituaries tell us about popular opinions concerning Billy the Kid, violence and outlaws, and the American West? None of that here.

Generally, a bit disappointing because the author does not analyze and evaluate sufficiently the useful information he collected.

121. Etulain, Richard W. *Thunder in the West: The Life and Legends of Billy the Kid*. Norman: University of Oklahoma Press, 2020.

The most recent, up-to-date of the extensive books on the Kid, this volume also offers readers a variant approach from most previous books about Billy. Etulain attempts to furnish a balanced study between biography and interpretation, providing equal attention to both these large subjects.

The author calls for a "bifurcated" Billy the Kid. Avoiding the earliest, dark-hued desperado images of Billy, he also shies away from the too positive later portraits of the Kid. Instead, Etulain paints a more complex, part negative and part positive picture of Billy, which he sees as closest to the truth about the enigmatic frontier figure. Both sections of this book follow this dualistic description of Billy as thief, liar, and killer on one side but also as a cheerful, warm companion and friend of women and Hispanics on the other.

Etulain owes much to the major writings of Frederick Nolan and Robert Utley. He also testifies to the shaping influences of recent works by Stephen

Tatum, Jerry (Richard) Weddle, John Wilson, Kathleen Chamberlain, and Joel Jacobsen. His comments on Billy the Kid films also owe much to the books and essays of Johnny D. Boggs and Paul Andrew Hutton. It is in his comments on historical Kid novels that Etulain marks out new interpretive territory.

The author strives for two balances. First, between the life of Billy the Kid and interpretations and legends about him. Second, in a middle-of-the-road view of Billy—sometimes a villain, sometimes a hero, but often both.

122. Fisher, David, and Bill O'Reilly. *Bill O'Reilly's Legends and Lies: The Real West*. New York: Henry Holt, 2015.

Dramatically presented events, jumbled chronology, and a mishmash of detail mar the brief coverage of Billy the Kid in this popular interpretation of the Old West. O'Reilly and Fisher are not sufficiently acquainted with the early years of the Kid's life, mixing up the facts of his life in Silver City and Arizona. Nor have the authors moved beyond a steady drumbeat of sensational events to ask probing questions about Billy's character, his thoughts, and the possible meanings of his life and the subsequent legends about him. Calling Billy an "escape artist" gets at one side of Billy's brief life, but that approach fails to ask searching queries about his personality and ideas. Finally, and most disappointing, the authors get caught up in the deeply flawed story line that Pat Garrett did not kill Billy the Kid in Fort Sumner in July 1881. Their vague speculations on this controversial subject are off-putting, greatly reducing the value of an already abbreviated and shaky account of Billy.

123. Fulton, Maurice Garland. *History of the Lincoln County War*. Edited by Robert N. Mullin. Tucson: University of Arizona Press, 1968.

Fulton arrived in New Mexico in 1922 to teach English at the New Mexico Military Institute in Roswell, and by 1927, already deep in the history of Lincoln County, he promised a book-length study of the subject the next spring. But the book was still not complete at his death in 1955 and had to be edited and completed by his friend and fellow Billy the Kid specialist Robert N. Mullin. Although the book was somewhat out of date by its publication, it was still the most extensive study of Lincoln to that time.

Fulton tells a fairly balanced story, although he is more sympathetic to the Tunstall-McSween side than to the Murphy-Dolan-Riley partisans. Nor does he care much for a Santa Fe Ring headed up by Thomas Catron and followed by District Attorney William Rynerson and Judge Warren Bristol. Also situated on Fulton's positive side are Susan McSween, Juan Patrón, and Gov. Lew Wallace.

Fulton's Billy the Kid was a conflicted figure, sometimes praiseworthy and otherwise blamable for his actions. The Kid's support for Tunstall and McSween was admirable, but his participation in the killing of Morton, Baker, and Sheriff Brady deserved the criticism fired in his direction. Although Fulton skips over most of Billy's virtually unknown early years, he devotes four chapters to the Kid's life from 1878–1879 to 1881. Fulton accepts the pistol-hidden-in-the-privy interpretation of Billy's jailbreak in spring 1881 but never mentions whether Billy had a pistol in Pete Maxwell's bedroom when Pat Garrett gunned him down. Generally, Billy showed "resourcefulness" and "courage," but he could also be hurried into thoughtless, destructive actions.

Fulton writes better than most of those authoring books about Billy and Lincoln County from the mid-1920s to 1960. His numerous pleasing pen portraits; his short, direct chapters; and his appealing diction and syntax drew readers then—and now. Unfortunately, he could also give far too much space to extensive, full documents, including newspapers, personal letters, and government documents. Too many chapters are cluttered and clotted with these scissors-and-paste pages. One wishes, too, that Fulton included footnotes and bibliography. He does not.

Overall a valuable book, one of the two or three best on Lincoln County.

124. Fulton, Maurice Garland, ed. *The Authentic Life of Billy, the Kid, The Noted Desperado*, by Pat Garrett. 1882. New York: Macmillan, 1927. Norman: University of Oklahoma Press, 1954, 2000.

The first of three edited, reprinted versions of Garrett's biography of the Kid, this edition (1927) was edited and annotated by Maurice Garland Fulton. The pioneering academic to provide comment on the Garrett book, Fulton furnishes an introduction and notes illustrating his evenhanded approach to the Billy the Kid and Lincoln County stories that characterize all his writings on these controversial subjects. Billy was no murderous outlaw, and Pat Garrett was a law-and-order man who helped end disruptions in New Mexico and bring in more civilized and legal history to the shifting territory.

Fulton's notes to several chapters demonstrate that even though he had resided in New Mexico for only five years at the time of writing, he had already learned a great deal about the territory's complex history. He adds information from newspapers, interviews from eyewitnesses concerning events in the 1870s–1880s, and finds Billy's words in several previously uncited documents. Too, he straightens out Garrett's faulty chronology and questions a few of that author's conclusions concerning the number of killings by the Kid. One wishes, however, that he had not chosen to edit some of Garrett's phrasing.

A few minor errors creep into Fulton's comments. He erroneously argues that Billy's first killing was a man in Silver City who insulted his mother and places Billy's shooting of Windy Cahill in the wrong location. Nor does Fulton say anything about Billy's interests in young women and his close ties to several Mexican families.

Later, two other writers, J. C. Dykes (118) and Frederic Nolan (157), edited subsequent editions of the Garrett biography and included very helpful information that came to light as the decades passed. But Fulton's early comments remain useful.

125. Garcia, Elbert A. *Billy the Kid's Kid 1875–1964: The Hispanic Connection*. Santa Rosa, N.Mex.: Los Products Press, 1999.

For a long time we have wanted a full-length, thoroughly researched, and dependable account of Hispanic links with Billy the Kid. Unfortunately, this book is not that much-desired volume. It includes interesting information, particularly about Abrana Garcia, said to be one of the Kid's *novias*, and the Garcia family, but the book fails as an extensive, probing, and persuasive examination of Billy's ties to the Hispanic community.

In this spiral-bound self-published book of about seventy pages, the author asserts that "Abrana Garcia and Patrick Henry McCarty (Billy the Kid) . . . were the parents of my grandfather," Jose Patrocinio Garcia, born in 1875 (n.p.). In addition, he posits that Abrana García (1854–1925) was an Indian girl (but also calls her a Mexican) and that she and her later family hid the identity of her boy to protect him and her honor. Elbert Garcia likewise says Billy fathered another little boy with Celsa Gutiérrez, later named Santiago Bonney. But the soundest evidence tells us that in 1875, Billy was fifteen years of age, just leaving Silver City, headed for Arizona, and did not arrive in Lincoln County, New Mexico, until fall 1877.

Other mistakes threaten the credibility of the author's account. He asserts that Billy arrived in southeastern New Mexico at about age twelve (1871) when, in fact, he was still in Kansas the first part of that year, and his name first emerges in 1873 in Santa Fe. Billy did not learn Spanish from his later close friend Yginio Salazar; he was already fluent in Spanish when he first came to Lincoln County. Finally, Garcia contends that Billy was on his way to see Abrana García in Pete Maxwell's house when Pat Garrett shot him down. All these "facts" lack sufficient proof to be *accepted* although they are worthy of *further consideration.*

Garcia makes a strong point in his observation that nearly all Billy biographers have not been Spanish speakers or literate in written Spanish. Those deficiencies mean they rarely have interviewed Hispanics to hear their family stories about Billy the Kid and the Lincoln County War. True enough. Once hopes that drawback will soon be remedied.

A book deserving of attention but to be used with caution because of the incorrect assertions.

126. Gardner, Mark Lee. *To Hell on a Fast Horse: Billy the Kid, Pat Garrett, and the Epic Chase to Justice in the Old West.* New York: William Morrow, 2010.

The largest appeal of Gardner's book is not so much in new information or sharp analysis but in an engrossing story very well told. In this volume, as well as in his later books, *Shot All to Hell: Jesse James, the Northfield Raid, and the Wild West's Greatest Escape* (2013) and *Rough Riders: Theodore Roosevelt, His Cowboy Regiment, and the Immortal Charge Up San Juan Hill* (2016), Gardner exhibits his talents as a first-rate raconteur. From his catchy titles to lively characters and dramatically told events, the author reveals his attention-gathering storytelling.

Gardner devotes more space to Pat Garrett than to Billy the Kid, understandable since Garrett lived more than twice as long. Picturing Garrett as a determined good ole' boy, diligent cowboy, buffalo hunter, and sometime lawman from the South and Texas, the author counters with a portrait of Billy as a youthful, matter-of-fact gunman who, although motivated in his thievery and violence, was nonetheless without plan or purpose for most of his very brief life. Unfortunately, the final chapters, devoted to Garrett after Billy's death, are less dramatic and interesting than those treating Billy's life before July 1881.

To Hell on a Fast Horse illustrates Gardner's diligent research in published—and sometimes manuscript—sources. He draws thoroughly on the best published materials—including works by Robert Utley, Frederick Nolan, and Marc Simmons—but he also mines more than a few unpublished collections.

The most important ingredient of Gardner's pleasing book is its dual-biography approach. Hundreds of essays and books have been turned out on

Billy and dozens on Pat Garrett, but few provide more than passing coverage on both notable figures. Gardner does just that, and it is one of the few books to furnish extensive treatment of the two characters in the same book.

127. Garrett, Pat F. *The Authentic Life of Billy, the Kid, the Noted Desperado of the Southwest, Whose Deeds of Daring and Blood Made His Name a Terror in New Mexico, Arizona and Northern Mexico.* Santa Fe: New Mexican Printing and Publishing, 1882.

Published less than a year after the death of Billy the Kid, Pat Garrett's pioneering biography immediately became the go-to source in the next decades for journalists, magazine authors, and creative writers who wanted to write about the controversial Kid. It was, after all, the first book-length nonfiction account of Billy and by an eyewitness—at least for the last part of the Kid's life. Authors turned to Garrett "for the facts." The book remained *the source* until the appearance of Walter Noble Burns's *The Saga of Billy the Kid* (1926). And when increasing numbers of readers became disillusioned with the excesses of Burns's romantic biography, they returned to Garrett's book.

Garrett's book never gained the sales the author hoped for. His publisher, the Santa Fe Printing and Publishing Company, which published the *Santa Fe Daily New Mexican*, was a newspaper publisher, not a book publisher. They bungled the book's publication, selling only a few hundred copies and then remaindering it. Three years later, cowboy author Charlie Siringo, basing much of his story on Garrett's biography, published his best-selling *A Texas Cowboy* (1885, #168). Selling in the hundreds of thousands over the years, Siringo's account became the most widely circulated early story of Billy the Kid even though it was largely Garrett's story between new covers.

Wider and deeper research leading to new publications in the 1950s and 1960s showed how faulty the stories in Garrett's book were. No writer himself, Garrett had asked his friend and eventual ghostwriter Marshall Ashmun "Ash" Upson to help with the project. Later Upson claimed he had written every word of the book. If so, he was guilty of stretchers and mistakes by the dozens. The early chapters seem a mix of dime novel sensation, journalistic hyperbole, and false facts. Very little of that beginning section can be proven, but leading Kid specialists are divided on the worth of the second half of the book, rumored to come from Garrett. Robert Utley (174), noting the mistakes, nonetheless found a good deal in Garrett's post-1880 coverage that he could trust and use. On the other side, Frederick Nolan (155) argues that the Garrett chapters, as error-ridden and off track as Upson's, are not to be trusted.

But there is another way to evaluate Garrett's book—in its times. It was much less negative about Billy than most of the newspaper and dime novel accounts that appeared in the 1880s to the early 1920s. True, Garrett and Upson point to Billy's thievery and killings, but they also note his camaraderie, courage, and friendships. In fact, the Garrett perspective is much more forward looking than nearly anything written about the Kid until after 1925.

Finally, even accepting all the errors and mistaken descriptions in Garrett's book, one must not forget its shaping power in the first half century after the Kid's death. One must study and understand legends like those Garrett's book launched and their shaping power over time and not just dismiss them as fabrications—and thus worthless.

128. Hamlin, William Lee. *The True Story of Billy the Kid: A Tale of the Lincoln County War.* Caldwell, Idaho: Caxton Printers, 1959.

Kid aficionados should not buy or read this book among their first on Billy—because of the book's large limitations. Hamlin is guilty of two major mistakes: (1) he misspells more than a few names, mixes up the chronology of key events, and adds several events for which there is no evidence; (2) even more off-putting is the author's bent toward creating dozens of factual changes and imagined conversations that did not occur or for which there is no extant evidence to sustain. The author's assertion that he has written "an account of real people as they lived and of true events as they transpired" (p. xi) is incorrect due to his imagined conversations and flawed narrative.

Hamlin is clearly a fan of the Kid, not one of Billy's opponents. The author's sympathies—written in clear, easy-to-follow prose—are evident when he argues that Billy did not shoot at Sheriff Brady in Lincoln or Jimmy Carlyle at the Greathouse Ranch and did not carry a gun into Pete Maxwell's bedroom. There is no evidence here that Hamlin has considered the writings of others who take other views of these events.

Plus, Hamlin's research was out of date when his book was published in 1959. For more than a decade, such writers as Philip Rasch and Robert Mullin had published numerous essays—Rasch fifty or more—with valuable information that is not in Hamlin's book. Hamlin also places too much stress on the memories of participants, now recalled by their descendants, without checking to see whether these long-ago memories are correct.

Hamlin admits he has "reconstructed . . . many incidents" (p. 310), and therein lies the largest problem of this book. The reconstructions and mistakes undermine its value.

129. Hendron, J. W. *The Story of Billy the Kid: New Mexico's Number One Desperado.* Santa Fe, N.Mex.: Rydal Press, 1948.

A thirty-one-page pamphlet, this source is generally disappointing. The author has most of the facts incorrect in Billy's life before he entered Lincoln County in 1877. He has the wrong dates for Billy's mother, Billy's entry into Kansas, and his mode in getting to New Mexico. The same kind of mistakes mar the Lincoln Country coverage. In addition, the author makes up conversations for which there are no sources. In fact, Hendron does not mention his sources. Not to be trusted.

130. Henn, Nora True. *Lincoln County and Its Wars.* Roswell, N.Mex.: Southwest Printers, 2017.

During the midyears of her life, Nora True Henn (1925–2011) worked to complete her long-promised account of Lincoln County's troubled history. Well known for her encyclopedic knowledge of the area and its traumatic past, she began her research nearly fifty years ago, soon after her husband, Walter Henn, and she moved to the Lincoln, New Mexico, region.

Henn knows her Lincoln County history and tells it smoothly and evenhandedly in this engaging volume. She draws on a variety of primary and secondary manuscript and published sources. After several chapters furnishing New Mexico backgrounds in the post–Mexican War and pre-1875 years, Henn devotes two-thirds of her book to Lincoln County, especially the 1875 to 1879 period. Her generally balanced approach tips only slightly toward the John Tunstall–Alex McSween side. She also makes much of links to Washington, D.C., and shows the Santa Fe Ring influences on the county. Readers will enjoy the many helpful photographs scattered throughout the volume.

The largest drawbacks of this book are the author's outdated research and a missing interpretive framework. Her sources and bibliography stop at 1990, meaning she did not utilize most of the Frederick Nolan and Robert Utley books as well as later works by Joel Jacobsen, Kathleen Chamberlain, and other post-1990 writers. Plus, Henn provides no thesis or conclusions around which to organize her narrative. Nor does she smoothly connect the multiple events and topics covered in individual chapters.

Aficionados of Billy the Kid may be disappointed with Henn's coverage of him. He plays little part in this story and is, in most cases, treated negatively. His warm ties to Hispanics and women are not mentioned, and the author's treatment of the important events of his life after July 1878 are limited to a few paragraphs and the weeks after his jailbreak in April 1881 to about three sentences.

Overall, then, a helpful, balanced account, but flawed with outdated information and narrow perspectives.

131. Hough, Emerson. *The Story of the Cowboy.* New York: D. Appleton, 1897.

Hough's first book on the West, including a chapter commenting on Billy the Kid and the Lincoln County War, clearly reveals his shortcomings as a dependable historian of the region. His account is shot through with huge, mistaken generalizations and, just as shaky if not more so, on specific details. Even though Hough lived in White Oaks briefly after Billy's death and wrote for a local newspaper, he seems not to have done in-depth research on Lincoln County.

In a chapter titled "Wars of the Range," Hough calls the Lincoln County War "the greatest and bloodiest" (302) of the West. The western frontier is painted as a wild, violent, and in all ways dangerous and lawless place. And Billy the Kid is the worst of the gunmen and thieves. He is a "young fiend," a "notorious cutthroat," and a "dangerous and outrageous" man who shoots others who merely appear or threaten to oppose him (pp. 304, 305). In his twenty-three years, he killed twenty-three men and, on one occasion, seven Mexicans "just to see them kick."

Most of Hough's details are off track. He has Billy early on opposing John Chisholm (*sic*), leading the Regulators even before the Big Kill, firing at Pat Garrett in Pete Maxwell's bedroom, and being shot down on his way to Mexico.

Hough wonders how this desperado, despite his killings and other violent acts, could remain in New Mexico. But, Hough notes, the Kid "had many warm friends and adherents" (p. 306).

Another example of how negative and wrong the early accounts of the Kid could be.

132. Hoyt, Henry F. *A Frontier Doctor.* Edited by Doyce B. Nunis Jr. 1929. Chicago: R. R. Donnelley and Sons, 1979.

Dr. Hoyt devotes parts of three chapters and a few other pages to the Kid. Chapter 13 (pp. 143–57) deals with the Hoyt-Billy meeting in Tascosa in the Texas panhandle in fall 1878; chapter 16 (pp. 189–204) discusses the correspondence between Gov. Lew Wallace and Billy; and chapter 23 (pp. 275–81) treats the doctor's fleeting meeting with the Kid on Billy's travel to Mesilla for his murder trial.

Hoyt is decidedly partisan in his treatment of Billy. "Unless angry," Hoyt writes, Billy "always seemed to have a pleasant expression with a ready smile" (p. 147). The doctor never saw Billy take a drink in their days together in Tascosa, but he did see evidences of his leadership qualities: "The Kid rules his gang with a rod of iron," Hoyt writes (p. 150). One night Hoyt and Billy engaged in a footrace, and when the Kid stumbled and fell onto the dance floor, "quicker than a flash his prostrate body was surrounded by his four pals, with a Colt's forty-five in each hand, cocked and ready for business" (p. 153)—even though guns were not allowed at dances. Before they separated, Billy gave his racehorse Dandy Dick to Hoyt with a protective bill of sale, and Hoyt, in turn, gave the Kid a lady's watch, which probably was intended for Billy's "Señorita Lolita" (Paulita Maxwell?) in Fort Sumner.

Hoyt also views the Governor Wallace–Billy correspondence and contact from a variant perspective. He could not believe "the reports of serious trouble between them," although the governor did reply "too late" when Hoyt asked him about a rekindled pardon for Billy (p. 265).

The doctor had one brief final visit with the Kid when the outlaw was on the train going south for his murder trial in Mesilla. The Kid was in "high spirits" (p. 280), though tightly shackled, watched closely, and on his way to a possible death sentence.

Hoyt also claimed that he encountered Billy and Jesse James in a fortuitous meeting at Hot Springs, near Las Vegas. Professor Nunis, the editor of this volume, reviews the evidence and leaves to the reader whether what Hoyt claims is true or mistaken.

Nunis's editorial work adds much value to Hoyt's volume. His "Historical Introduction" (pp. xxi–xlix) provides a brief biography of Hoyt, although it offers little comment on the content of the author's book. But Nunis's "Biographical Notes" (pp. 419–68) and "Place Notes" (pp. 469–77) include biographical sketches of Billy the Kid and others involved in the Lincoln County story.

Taken together, the text of *Frontier Doctor* and the editor's notes and additions combine to make this an illuminating memoir, which adds information and context to the Billy the Kid story.

133. Hunt, Frazier. *The Tragic Days of Billy the Kid.* New York: Hastings House Publishers, 1956.

More than few Kid commentators point to Hunt's smoothly written biography of Billy as what Maurice Garland Fulton would have written had he finished his book on Lincoln County and the Kid before his death (the Fulton book was edited by Robert Mullin and published in 1968, #123). Hunt does owe much to Fulton's diligent research, as he makes clear in his codedication to Fulton, whom he describes as the "unrivaled authority on the Lincoln County War" and to whom he is indebted for "documents, letters and newspaper accounts herein published for the first time." Hunt also follows Fulton's format of skipping quickly over most of Billy's early life before he came to Lincoln County in 1877. Parallels exist, too, in the Hunt and Fulton accounts of the Big Killing in Lincoln in July 1878 and of Billy's obtaining a pistol in the backyard privy to aid in his escape from jail in April 1881. Finally, both authors think Celsa Gutiérrez, not Paulita Maxwell, was Billy's *querida* who drew him back to Fort Sumner after his jail escape.

A few differences between the two books should also be mentioned. Hunt provides a variant account of the killing of Tunstall. He also pictures Billy with a knife and pistol on his way into Pete Maxwell's bedroom on the night he is killed, but Fulton makes no mention of a gun. Both books generally lack footnotes, and Hunt's volume does not contain a bibliography or index.

The largest difference in the two books, however, is style. Hunt, a skilled narrative writer who wrote about a dozen other histories and biographies and several books about the American West, exhibits a storytelling power in his volume that is missing in the Fulton-Mullin volume. Appealing descriptions, strong action verbs, and intriguing pen portraits—these strengths power and enhance the Hunt book. In the late 1950s, before books by Frederick Nolan and Robert Utley appeared, Frazier Hunt furnished a refreshingly written and dramatically told life story of Billy the Kid, the most appealing account since Burns's biography thirty years earlier.

134. Jacobsen, Joel. *Such Men as Billy the Kid: The Lincoln County War Reconsidered.* Lincoln: University of Nebraska Press, 1994.

Exceptionally strong on legal matters and extraordinarily thorough in research in primary unpublished and newspaper sources, this provocatively written monograph deserves more attention as one of the best books on the Lincoln County War and Billy the Kid. A lawyer, Jacobsen ransacked local, territorial, and national documents to piece together a revealing and assertive story. The author judiciously and helpfully enters his narrative—even into the quotes—to thicken the description and contexts of his story. His brief, segmented chapters add to reader interest throughout his work.

In the first chapters, Jacobsen deals much more with the Lincoln County War than with the life of Billy. But in the closing chapters the Kid comes to center stage. Billy is an outlaw, verily, but not a vicious, insensitive desperado, and perhaps not as underhanded as such legal leaders as Thomas Catron, some Lincoln sheriffs, and L. G. Murphy and Jimmy Dolan. In paragraph after paragraph, the author shows how numerous residents of New Mexico Territory, especially in its southeastern reaches, knowingly broke the law—sometimes even flaunted doing so. In these comments, Jacobsen sides more with Tunstall and McSween than with The House partisans.

A few minor mistakes mar this account. Paulita Maxwell was not Pete Maxwell's niece but his younger sister. Robert Utley's name carries the middle initial M. (not S.); the name is misspelled throughout this book. And the author is mistaken in asserting that "there is no evidence of Bonney and Chisum ever meeting" (p. 216).

Overall, then, a major work of large importance. Too often it has been omitted from the list of the very best books on the Lincoln County War and Billy the Kid.

135. Jameson, W. C. *Billy the Kid: Beyond the Grave*. Dallas, Tex.: Taylor Trade Publishing, 2005.

W. C. Jameson is the most prolific writer of those arguing that William Henry Roberts ("Brushy Bill"), not William H. Bonney, was the real Billy the Kid. In Jameson's view, neither Brushy Bill nor Billy fell before the pistol of Sheriff Pat Garrett in the Maxwell house on the evening of 14 July 1881 but instead the little-known Billy Barlow. Author of several other books asserting that Roberts was the actual Kid, Jameson reviews Roberts's life, compares it with the story of Billy the Kid, rehearses Roberts's claims to be the Kid, and points to the many limitations he sees in the traditional historical accounts of Billy and the corresponding strengths of Roberts's story.

A talented writer with dozens of books to his credit, Jameson is entranced with beyond-the-grave tales, including those about Jesse James, Butch Cassidy, John Wilkes Booth—and Billy the Kid. Jameson is also intrigued with buried-treasure and lost-mine yarns. He writes well, smoothly, forcefully, and sometimes combatively. He makes what he thinks to be a strong case for William Henry Roberts as Billy the Kid.

Jameson's case would be much stronger if he answered large questions about Roberts, addressed more missing pieces, and avoided so many errors. If it could be proven, among so many unanswered questions, that Roberts was born in 1859, was part of the McCarty-Antrim family, and resided in Lincoln County from 1877 to 1881—and none of these are proven in Jameson's account—we might be more inclined toward his story. In addition, Jameson skips over what we know to be fairly certain about the Kid's life in Indiana, Kansas, Silver City, New Mexico, and Arizona, probably because most of those facts do not fit Roberts's life. Nor can we follow the Jameson-Roberts story when Brushy Bill said that no one was killed in his escape from the Lincoln jail in late April 1881 and that Paulita Maxwell played no role in his life; moreover, as many as twenty or more identified the Kid's corpse after Garett shot him.

Finally, there are too many miscues in Jameson's account. He has the wrong dates for Henry Antrim's years in Silver City and Arizona, includes nothing on the shooting of Windy Cahill by Roberts or the Kid, and is short-sighted in arguing that a uniform story informs biographies, novels, and movies about the Kid. They widely differ—and have over the decades. Many other small errors dot the author's text and bibliography.

Is there any reason to believe the Brushy Bill story? There is if readers want to make a great deal of the unsolved mysteries, the incongruities, and the missing pieces of the Kid's story. We still know too little about the Kid's early life, the exact details of his jailbreak, his sentence in Mesilla to hang, his death, the coroner's report, and his burial in Fort Sumner. But this W. C. Jameson account of William Henry Roberts is even less satisfactory in answering these and yet other unsolved mysteries surrounding the Kid. It does not provide a believable alternative account.

136. Jameson, W. C. *Billy the Kid: The Lost Interviews.* Clearwater, Fla.: Garlic Press, 2012.

Sections of this abbreviated book replicate Jameson's previous account in his *Billy the Kid: Beyond the Grave* (135). But here Jameson adds the interesting texts of recorded interviews of William V. Morrison, who was a paralegal, and William Henry Roberts, who claimed to be Billy the Kid. These pages are important for understanding Roberts but not so much for Billy the Kid—unless one accepts Roberts's and Jameson's contentions that Roberts was indeed the Kid.

Unfortunately, errors, oversights, and incorrect assertions from Jameson's earlier books are repeated here. He is wrong in asserting that nearly all Billy specialists have denounced Pat Garrett's *The Authentic Life of Billy, the Kid* (1882) as totally unreliable. Instead, they have primarily denounced the earlier chapters written by Garrett's amanuensis Marshall Ash Upson and often praised Garrett's first-person, matter-of-fact later chapters. Nor is Jameson correct in stating that most historians have followed Garrett. Beginning with Maurice Garland Fulton and Will Keleher in the 1920s through the 1960s, and then with Frederick Nolan and Robert Utley in the 1980s and 1990s, and also in the writings of Philip Rasch, Robert Mullin, Joel Jacobson, and Jerry (Richard) Weddle, numerous historians have shown where Garrett can be trusted and where not. Also, three critical editions of *The Authentic Life of Billy, the Kid*—with Fulton as editor in 1927, with J. C. Dykes in 1954, and with Nolan in 2000—furnish balanced comments on the strengths and limitations of Garrett's pioneering book.

An angry tone, perhaps fired by frustration and upset, invades this book. Jameson strikes out at "traditional historians" of the Kid, as the author labels them, because they have refused to work with him on a back-and-forth book and a television program presenting what he considers both sides of the killing of Billy question. Most of these specialists are likely to avoid becoming involved with the assertive, one-sided, and negative author of this volume.

Jameson still has not dealt adequately with several of Roberts's key and wrongheaded contentions. These omissions or inadequacies include the conflicting and airy stories of Roberts about the Kid's years in Silver City and Arizona; about the killing of Windy Cahill; about Billy's being at Tunstall's funeral; about the differences between Roberts's account and what Billy testified at the Colonel Dudley hearing; about the killing and not killing of the two deputies in the escape from the Lincoln jail; about the relationship between Celsa Gutiérrez, her husband, Saval (or Sabal), and Billy; and about the absence of Paulita Maxwell in Roberts's story, including the emotional leave-taking after the Stinking Spring capture. And there are several other unanswered questions as well.

Readers should not dismiss out of hand Jameson's several books pushing for Roberts as the real Billy the Kid; they should read them carefully and evaluatively. But Jameson needs to offer more dependable information, avoid mistakes, and cease attacking those who differ with him if he wants to persuade more to his controversial point of view.

137. Jameson, W. C. *Pat Garrett: The Man Behind the Badge.* Lanham, Md.: Taylor Trade Publishing, 2016.

W. C. Jameson is convinced that he is right and nearly everyone else wrong—especially on what they write about Billy the Kid and Pat Garrett.

He believes, particularly, that Pat Garrett did not shoot William Bonney, whom he names William Henry Roberts, on the night of 14 July 1881. Although said to be about Pat Garrett, the first half of this book is as much about the Kid as about the sheriff. This volume repeats what Jameson has been asserting for nearly twenty years: Pat Garrett shot the wrong man in Pete Maxwell's bedroom, lied about his mistaken murder, and Billy the Kid, alias William Henry Roberts, survived and lived on until December 1950.

One wishes Jameson were less convinced that historians, generally, are lazy researchers when dealing with Billy the Kid and have primarily quoted one another with wrong facts through the years. Conversely, the author exhibits extraordinary self-congratulation; his views are correct and should be followed because his research is outstanding and his analysis clearly exceeds the work of other writers.

Jameson's strengths do deserve touting. He tells an interesting, provocative story, digs up new bits of information, and asks provocative questions about Billy and Pat Garrett. And for those wishing an excessively dark portrait of Pat Garrett, they have it in this book.

But consider the author's errors and omissions. Jameson has long argued that Garrett shot a young man named Billy Barlow instead of Billy the Kid/Roberts and that Garrett lied about his murder and then hurried up phony coroner's reports and quickly buried the body of Barlow, not that of the Kid—all to cover up his mistaken shooting. The careful and thorough research of Professor Robert Stahl, however, turned up thirty or more people who viewed the corpse, and none said he was anyone but Billy. Plus, Billy's body was on view at Beaver Smith's saloon on 15 July before he was buried later that day. Other residents of Fort Sumner certainly viewed the body and did not identify the corpse as that of Barlow. Jameson deals with none of these viewers, instead stating (without naming names) that residents began to question whether Garrett had killed the Kid or someone else.

Jameson also omits much of the Kid's life in Silver City and Arizona, events that contradict what the author says about Roberts's early life. The author also leaves out the role Paulita Maxwell played in the last year or two of Billy's life. Another incident illustrates Jameson's tendency to go off track: he asserts that previous historians did not deal with the misnumbered goats on Garrett's ranch that helped lead to his death in 1908. Strangely, the book Jameson is following most closely, Leon C. Metz's dependable *Pat Garrett: The Story of a Western Lawman* (1974, #149), deals exactly with those details on pp. 285–88. So does Mark Lee Gardner in his more recent dual biography,

To Hell on a Fast Horse: Billy the Kid, Pat Garrett, and the Epic Chase to Justice in the Old West (2010, #126), on pp. 233 and 236. Gardner's work, a very strong book, does not appear in Jameson's bibliography.

In short, this is a flawed volume, wrong in concluding that Garrett did not kill Billy the Kid and less valuable on Pat Garrett than the better-researched books by Metz and Gardner.

138. Jameson, W. C., and Frederic Bean. *The Return of the Outlaw: Billy the Kid.* Plano: Republic of Texas Press, 1998.

This book by W. C. Jameson and Frederic Bean advances the same theory that Jameson put forth in several other later volumes. Their "real" Billy the Kid, named William Henry Roberts (or informally as "Brushy Bill," but not in this book), was not killed by Pat Garrett in Pete Maxwell's bedroom on the night of 14 July 1881. Instead, Garrett shot the wrong person, a mysterious Billy Barlow, and then conspired with numerous others in lying that he had killed Billy and that he was buried the next day in Fort Sumner. According to Jameson, who seems to have been the writer of this authorial duo, Roberts (his Kid) escaped, led a nomadic life, and eventually died at age ninety in December 1950 after failing to gain a pardon from the sitting New Mexico governor.

Jameson lists more sources here in his chapter and book bibliographies than he cites in his subsequent books on the Roberts-Kid story. He primarily utilizes the information English professor C. L. Sonnichsen and paralegal William H. Morrison dredged up in their controversial book *Alias Billy the Kid* (169) and adds to it interviews with Roberts family members, documents from those who claimed to know or to have heard about Roberts, and bits and pieces from other Billy specialists. Jameson's research is neither wide nor deep on Henry McCarty, Kid Antrim, and Billy Bonney but instead focuses on Roberts's story. Close attention to the research of Maurice Garland Fulton, Will Keleher, Robert Mullin, Philip Rasch, Frederick Nolan, and Robert Utley will help readers see the large holes remaining in Jameson's arguments.

Why have so few—almost none, in fact—Kid specialists and others who are versed in his history broken ranks to follow Jameson's alternative path? Probably for two reasons: (1) his comments on Billy are often wrong, ill-conceived, and poorly researched; (2) his attempts to replace Henry McCarty/Kid Antrim/Billy Bonney with William Henry Roberts as the real Billy the Kid contain more inconsistencies and unanswered questions than those in the widely accepted story.

Consider these typical statements of Jameson early on in this book: "Billy the Kid was born illegitimate . . . and he had an older brother Joseph. Their father was believed to be a man named Edward McCarty, a peddler who already had a wife. . . . When Henry was about fourteen, he was sent by the New York Children's Aid Society to live with William E. Antrim" (p. 18). All of these statements are unconfirmed by strong evidence, mistaken, or still up for grabs. Repeatedly James writes like this, with too many unsupported assertions and errors. (His books contain no footnotes.)

Second, Jameson tries to get readers to believe that Garrett, an unstoppable liar (Jameson suggests) and murderer, killed the wrong man and tried to get others to accept his mistake and support him—and that Billy the Kid (Roberts) lived for nearly another seventy years. But thirty people—perhaps more—in Fort Sumner saw Billy's body and did not claim that Garrett had killed someone else. Nor did the others who viewed his corpse on display at Beaver Smith's saloon on 15 July. Jameson states that some residents questioned whether Garrett killed the real Billy but fails to mention any—not one—of these doubters.

Jameson devotes most of his book to a brief, scattered biography of Roberts and states that Roberts "knew more than most scholars" (p. 4) about the violent events in Lincoln County. Not so if you begin with the leading specialists on Billy the Kid by 1950—Fulton, Keleher, Rasch, and Mullin—who knew more than Roberts. Jameson is also off track in asserting that most Kid specialists have not moved away from Garrett's biography of the Kid published in 1882 (Jameson wrongly says 1892); after Walter Noble Burns's biography appeared in 1926, Billy authorities more and more abandoned Garrett's book as *the* source on the Kid. Jameson would clearly know that if he read more life stories of the Kid that appeared from the 1950s onward.

The strong opinions of Jameson and Bean, their bombastic style, and their one-sided approach of attacking others and touting their own views has alienated many readers during the past two decades. Even though Jameson has published several other books on this subject—that repeat much of what is in this volume—he has not won over Billy the Kid specialists.

139. Kadlec, Robert F., ed. *They "Knew" Billy the Kid: Interviews with Old-Time New Mexicans.* Santa Fe, N.Mex.: Ancient City Press, 1987.

This brief collection of abbreviated oral interviews and reminiscences of elderly New Mexicans, gathered in the 1930s by members of the New Deal's Federal Writers' Project, brings together the remembrances of persons about events more than a half century in the past. Organized chronologically, the book opens with interviews dealing with Billy's years in Silver City and stretches through until his death at Fort Sumner in July 1881. The stories cover Billy's adventures, the actions of his closest friends (and some enemies), and the complex, shifting events that surrounded him in the 1873 to 1881 period.

The most useful information is in those recollections dealing with generalized attitudes, experiences, and overviews of events. When the interviewees switch to dates, events, or people, they often misremember the specifics. In addition, several of the interviewees seem to have read Pat Garrett and Ash Upson's biography of 1882 and are taking their misinformation from that faulty source. Conversely, the explanatory notes prepared by Professor Marta Weigle are invaluable for adding needed information and correcting mistakes.

Generally, a source to be used with caution because so much of the factual information on dates, names, and places is incorrect.

140. Kaye, E. Donald. *Nathan Augustus Monroe Dudley, 1825–1910: Rogue, Hero, or Both?* Chicago: Outskirts Press, 2007.

A book of fewer than fifty pages of text, this very brief volume is nonetheless the most extensive published account of Colonel Dudley. Author Kaye, himself a military man, traces the nearly fifty-year career of Dudley from his entry into the Massachusetts militia through the Civil War and on through his several stints on the American frontier. Of particular interest here are the years in New Mexico, including his controversial part in the Lincoln County War.

Six chapters deal with the several stages of Dudley's military life. The first two treat his early years in the West and in the Mormon War, then comes a section on his service in the Civil War, followed by two chapters about stations in Arizona and New Mexico and an ending chapter on his final duties up to retirement. Kay briefly summaries Dudley's work at each of these locations.

Dudley's participation in the Lincoln County War, particularly his moves on 19 July 1878, are the most important for the Billy the Kid story. These acts, Kaye asserts, were "undeniably nefarious actions" (p. 1). In Lincoln, Dudley "at best just watched the murders, and at worst had his troops participate" (p. 44). He clearly "acted badly" (p. 45) at the high point of the war. And later, the Dudley Court of Inquiry was a "whitewash." Dudley should have been "tried by Court Martial" (p. 45).

But Kaye is less critical of Dudley than most historians. He believes that despite the colonel's arrogance, unfairness, and combativeness, he deserves better treatment from historians. Dudley, Kay thinks, served well and dutifully and consistently looked after his soldiers, especially the enlisted men.

Although too brief and narrowly researched, Kay's very abbreviated book provides a helpful introduction to a major figure in the Lincoln County War. Still the best account of a person who merits a longer, more complete treatment.

141. Keleher, William A. *Violence in Lincoln County, 1869–1881.* "Introduction" by C. L. Sonnichsen. 1957. Albuquerque: University of New Mexico Press, 1982.

This nonpartisan, document-rich study provided, up to 1957, the most thorough study of the Lincoln County conflicts. Keleher ransacked newspapers, government reports, and personal correspondence to furnish a full account of the conflicts in southeastern New Mexico in the 1870s.

Billy the Kid, only briefly mentioned in the earlier chapters, becomes a major figure in the closing chapters, where Keleher tracks the Kid's actions in 1880–1881. The author's treatment of Billy's pre-1880 actions is abbreviated and scattered. But the closing chapters detail the Kid's journey through his capture by Pat Garrett at Stinking Spring, jailing in Santa Fe, trials in Mesilla, breakout from the Lincoln jail, and death at the hands of Pat Garrett.

Revealingly, Keleher is not so much interested in the Kid as in the history of Lincoln County. But his comments on Billy's personality and actions are remarkably balanced, only briefly mentioning the Kid on one side as an outlaw and on the other as a smart native leader. Where Keleher quotes sources that are negative or positive about Billy, he rarely follows up with comments of his own about these views concerning the Kid.

Taken together with the writings of Maurice Garland Fulton (123) and Philip Rasch (161–63), this book by Keleher, as well as his other books on New Mexico, provides a fact-filled corrective to the excessively romantic account in Walter Noble Burns's *Saga* (103). Still, a good deal of narrative power and reader interest are lost in Keleher's excessive, long quotes from documents. His unwillingness to advance his own opinions also reduces the attractiveness of his narrative. Although dozens were spurred on from reading Burns's lively biography, none testified to such a push from Keleher's work.

A valuable book, well documented and fact-filled, but not a dramatic, personal narrative.

142. Lamar, Howard R. *Charlie Siringo's West: An Interpretive Biography.* Albuquerque: University of New Mexico Press, 2005.

Lamar succinctly covers two Siringo-Billy connections. The first is when Siringo met the Kid in the Texas panhandle at the LX Ranch in fall 1878. Lamar depicts their quick, close friendship as well as their engaging in shooting contests, exchanging presents, and going on visits to nearby sites. Lamar adds that Siringo became "clearly obsessed by Billy's violent career" (p. 82). It was the only time they met in person.

The other Siringo-Kid connection is Lamar's discussion of Siringo's writings about the Kid, first in *A Texas Cowboy* (1885) and later in his book *History of Billy the Kid* (1920). Lamar praises the lively chapter in the first volume but considers the second book "a romantic and inaccurate" work (p. 88). Still, Lamar urges readers to recall that Siringo based his writings about the Kid on firsthand sources and his own experiences as well as his numerous interviews, especially with Ash Upson, Dr. Henry Hoyt, and Jim East. They, too, Lamar reminds us, were entranced with the Kid. A strong biography with brief, important information about the Kid and Charlie Siringo.

143. Lamar, Howard Roberts. *The Far Southwest 1846–1912: A Territorial History.* 1966. New York: W. W. Norton, 1970.

Although published nearly a half century ago, this regional overview remains the best treatment of this subject. Lamar's valuable research, his appealing writing style, and his balanced point of view combine to put this synthesis at the top of southwestern regional histories.

The opening section on New Mexico (pp. 23–201) is followed by other sections on Colorado, Utah, and Arizona. Lamar is particularly helpful in showing how the U.S. government was thoroughly involved in the founding and administering of these four territories. That emphasis is especially important for putting Billy the Kid and Lincoln County in larger territory-wide and national circumferences, rescuing it from excessively narrow stress on local details and showing how regional experiences were shaped by power and politics outside the region.

In the New Mexico section, after four chapters on the period up to the Civil War, Lamar deals with the Civil War to 1900 in three additional chapters. Here he provides backgrounds for Billy the Kid and the Lincoln County War, deals with those two topics, and then closes the section with the 1880 to 1900 period.

The author's comments on Billy and the Lincoln County turmoil are abbreviated. Billy the Kid is succinctly described as a "buck-toothed, left-handed [no!] youth, fond of dancing and a marvelous shot." He was "destined to play the dual role of villain and hero" (p. 158). The Kid became involved in the Lincoln County War, which was "caused by a dispute over a life insurance policy, a business rivalry between two firms—*Tunstall and McSween versus Murphy and Dolan*—and cattle stealing" (pp. 156–57).

Lamar deals more extensively with the Santa Fe Ring—in fact, he devotes an entire chapter to that subject and attendant topics (pp. 136–70). He rightly views the Ring not as an octopus-like, monolithic, well-organized, ongoing coterie of power-hungry and corrupt politicians controlling everything, even though some of that occurred. It was, instead, a loosely aligned in-and-out gaggle of politicians, businessmen, and lawyers who greatly impacted New Mexico politics and economics from Thomas Catron and Stephen Elkins in Santa Fe to William Rynerson and Warren Bristol in regional courts to L. G. Murphy and Jimmy Dolan in Lincoln County.

Altogether, a still-helpful overview of New Mexico politics, economics, and sociocultural history in the time of Billy the Kid and the Lincoln County civil war.

144. Larson, Carole. *Forgotten Frontier: The Story of Southeastern New Mexico.* Albuquerque: University of New Mexico Press, 1993.

Following an organization first by subject and then biographical, Larson narrates the story of southeastern New Mexico during its territorial period from 1850 to 1912. After chapters on landscapes, conquest, Native peoples, and struggles for power and control, the author devotes sections to John Chisum, L. G. Murphy, James Dolan, and John Riley; Alex McSween and John Tunstall; Billy the Kid and Pat Garrett; Joseph C. Lea, Martin Corn, and John Poe; and J. P. White and J. J. Hagerman. A final chapter traces a few frontier legacies into the twentieth century.

Most of Larson's book is based on the strongest books and essays dealing with territorial New Mexico. Such is the case with her chapter on the Kid and Garrett, where she draws heavily on the writings of Maurice Garland Fulton, Robert Utley, William Keleher, and Leon Metz. Larson's approach is narrative rather than analytical and evaluative.

The sections on Billy, which total about twenty to twenty-five pages, are clearly and smoothly written, providing readable, credible stories. Larson concludes that Billy escaped the Lincoln jail by hitting Deputy Bell with one of his loosened handcuffs, snatching the deputy's pistol, and shooting him as Bell tried to run down the stairs. The author also thinks Billy was armed with both a knife and a pistol as he scurried into Maxwell's bedroom and fell before Garrett's gun on the night of 14 July. The most interesting parts of the author's Billy profile are her intriguing speculations about Billy's possible thoughts when facing capture and then hanging.

A valuable, concise account for general readers; less so for Billy and Lincoln County specialists.

145. Lavash, Donald R. *Sheriff William Brady: Tragic Hero of the Lincoln County War.* Santa Fe, N.Mex.: Sunstone Press, 1986.

Lavash moves chronologically through the life of Sheriff William Brady in this concise biography of about one hundred pages of text. After opening chapters on Brady's Irish backgrounds and his stints in the U.S. military, the author deals with Brady's life as a farmer, legislator, and, most extensively, Lincoln County sheriff. Overall, Lavash presents an extraordinarily sympathetic portrait of Brady, labeling him a "tragic hero."

If all humans are made up of strengths and limitations, Lavash chooses to emphasize Brady's strengths without mentioning his limitations. In reverse, the author stresses the limitations but not the strengths of Alexander McSween and John Tunstall. And the limitations and strengths of L. G. Murphy and Jimmy Dolan, which most historians of the Lincoln County conflicts discuss, are not dealt with here. In fact, this account—and Donald Cline's (107) of the same year—is one of the most dark-hued treatments of McSween and Tunstall. The two books also contain the same mistakes and slanted evidence.

Billy the Kid plays a minor role in Lavash's book. But mistakes about the Kid enter the narrative. Billy was not the "self-appointed leader" of the McSween contingent at the time of Brady's death on 1 April 1878. No convincing evidence exists, either, that Rob Windenmann wrote Billy's affidavit for the Angel Report. Plus, Billy's part in the Brady slaying is jumbled.

What Lavash does best is his diligent research on the positive side of William Brady, especially in manuscript sources. But he relies too much on the slanted evidence of Brady's descendants and omits Brady's ties to Murphy and Dolan, his troubles with alcohol, and his willingness to attack opponents like Tunstall and McSween.

William Brady, despite Lavash's subtitle, was not a tragic "hero." A diligent military man, a devoted father, and sometimes a dependable lawman (but not always), he was tragically assassinated by an angry Billy the Kid and his vengeful supporters (for the killing of Tunstall). But to transform Brady into a hero is to whitewash his own limitations and his corrupt ties to the Murphy-Dolan partisans.

146. McCarty, John L. *Maverick Town: The Story of Old Tascosa.* 1946. Enlarged ed. Norman: University of Oklahoma Press, 1988.

Although useful for a brief description of Billy's short stay in Tascosa in the Texas panhandle in 1878 and Texas riders' pursuit of him in New Mexico in 1880–1881, this smoothly written account is rife with errors in dealing with Billy's life. Among the errors are the author's assertion that Billy lived in New Mexico from the 1860s onward, that Billy killed a man for insulting his mother, that he killed a man for every one of his twenty-one years, and that he worked for John Chisum.

But McCarty's helpful descriptions of Tascosa, ranching in the panhandle, and Billy's friendship with Dr. Henry Hoyt add measurably to the context of Billy's life. More than a few historians and biographers of Billy used information from this book and Dr. Hoyt's later memoir (132) to round out Billy's dealings with Texans in the last two to three years of his life.

147. McCright, Grady E., and James H. Powell. *Jessie Evans: Lincoln County Badman.* College Station, Tex.: Creative Publishing, 1983.

These two lay historians furnish opening and closing chapters on the life of noted outlaw Jessie Evans, but most of their book deals with the Lincoln County War and Evans's difficult-to-trace participation in those battles. The brief book draws very heavily on important secondary works by Maurice Garland Fulton and Frederick Nolan and, to a lesser extent, on the writings of William Keleher and Philip Rasch. Little use is made of major manuscript holdings, especially those of Keleher, Rasch, and Fulton.

Without saying so explicitly, the authors suggest that Evans and Billy the Kid were two of a kind, desperados and murderers. They call Billy a "cold-blooded killer" (p. 14) and point to the killings accredited to Evans. They are mistaken, however, in touting Billy as the "top gun" (p. 14) of the Lincoln County War. He did not rise to that position until after mid-July 1878. Nor should the authors term Billy and Jessie "good friends" (pp. 13, 21). Acquaintances they were, but not much more. Even more fanciful is the authors' suggestion that Brushy Bill Roberts, who claimed in 1950 to be the Billy the Kid whom Pat Garrett never shot, might actually have been Jessie Evans.

One wishes the authors had dug deeper and expanded their horizons. This is a very narrowly focused story primarily based on a handful or two of sources. Also, a careful editor should have caught more of the typos, misspellings, and mistaken information.

148. McKee, Irving. *"Ben-Hur" Wallace: The Life of General Lew Wallace.* Berkeley: University of California Press, 1947.

In this full-scale biography of Lew Wallace, the author devotes one extensive chapter, "Governor of New Mexico" (pp. 140–63), to his more than two and a half years in the territory. Generally, the author focuses more attention on military matters dealing with Indians and territorial and national politics than on Lincoln County. He gives a few pages to the Kid-Wallace links: the meeting in Lincoln in March 1879, Billy's subsequent letters to Wallace, and the former governor's comments about the Kid after leaving New Mexico. McKee is neither excessively pro- or anti-Kid, but he does credit the outlaw with more killings than the facts support. He also thinks Wallace was fair to the Kid, with Billy making false statements about his actions and misunderstanding what Wallace could and was willing to do for him. McKee likewise plays up Billy's later threats to kill Wallace. On one occasion, the author calls Billy "the paragon of badmen," but also "obsolescent" (p. 161), being pushed aside by the law-and-order Garrett.

The book is without footnotes, so the author's sources for his writing about Billy the Kid remain unclear.

149. Metz, Leon C. *Pat Garrett: The Story of a Western Lawman.* Norman: University of Oklahoma Press, 1974.

This sturdy, no-nonsense biography of Pat Garrett remains *the* source on the famous sheriff even a half century after its publication. Although Mark Lee Gardner's joint biography, *To Hell on a Fast Horse: Billy the Kid, Pat Garrett, and the Epic Chase to Justice in the Old West* (126), provides bits of new information, a comparative perspective, and an invitingly written narrative, Metz's work continues to be the most thorough account.

Three facets of Metz's biography merit specific comment. First, it provides a full life of Garrett, not limiting the story primarily to Garrett's associations with Billy the Kid. Second, the author is balanced, giving both the positive and less positive sides of Garrett. Third, Metz corrects the emphases in too many Lincoln County accounts that major so extensively on the Kid's actions that the roles of Garrett and others get lost in Billy's huge shadow.

Most of Metz's narrative on the Lincoln County War follows the conclusions of writers like Robert Utley and Frederick Nolan. The depiction of Billy, however, is less positive than in most of these accounts, but neither is Garrett depicted as a saint.

Metz posits that Garrett and Billy were acquaintances but not close friends. He also admits that Garrett's personality often alienated others. The author praises Garrett's diligence in pursuing the Kid and credits the pistol-in-the-privy thesis as the most defensible conclusion about Billy's killing two deputies and escaping the Lincoln County jail. Metz believes that an informer told Garrett that Billy was in Fort Sumner, leading to the sheriff's ride there to attempt to capture the Kid. The author also believes that the Kid's lust for Celsa Gutiérrez, Garrett's sister-in-law, was his downfall, not his attraction to Paulita Maxwell. In Metz's account, Billy was armed with a pistol when Garrett shot him.

The second half of Metz's book details Garrett's life from 1881 to his death on 29 February 1908. The volume details in several chapters Garrett's lack of ongoing success as a lawman, rancher, and government official. Garrett's poor decisions, his gambling, his drinking, and his quirky personality were major reasons for his downfalls. After examining all those who were considered the murderer of Garrett, Metz concludes that Wayne Brazel, as he admitted, was the killer.

In short, this volume should still be the first stop for those wanting a through, dependable biography of Pat Garrett.

150. Morsberger, Robert E., and Katharine M. Morsberger. *Lew Wallace: Militant Romantic.* New York: McGraw-Hill, 1980.

An extensive cradle-to-grave biography of Lew Wallace, this life story contains one lengthy chapter, "Outlaws and Apaches" (pp. 257–96), on Wallace's governorship of New Mexico from 1878 to 1881. The chapter covers the governor's handling of the Lincoln County and Billy the Kid controversies, his Indian policies, and his dealings with territorial political leaders. This chapter—in fact, the entire book—draws heavily on scattered Wallace manuscript collections, standard secondary books and essays, and newspaper accounts.

The husband-and-wife authors provide a balanced account of Billy the Kid. They speak first of the Kid as a "drifter" and "an itinerant worker in Arizona" (p. 260), but also as one of the McSween supporters with "unsavory histories and criminal tendencies" (p. 260). Yet they also quote Susan Wallace, who thought Billy was "a gentlemanly appearing fellow" (p. 178), and mention that he "had tried to keep peace, but Jesse Evans had forced him to watch the [Huston Chapman] killing" (p. 273). Overall, the Morsbergers write that the Kid remained "an administrative nuisance" (p. 292) for Wallace.

A few minor errors creep in. The authors have Colonel Dudley arriving on the wrong day of the Five-Day Battle and are mistaken on a few other details of this horrendous conflict. Jimmy Dolan, as far as we know, did not shoot Huston Chapman on 18 February 1879 but instead fired his gun into the ground or in the air. It is misleading, too, to state baldly that after June 1879 Billy was "the main source of remaining lawlessness" (p. 279) in Lincoln County.

Overall, a thorough and dependable biography of Lew Wallace and his important role in Lincoln County and in dealing with Billy the Kid. More extensive and diligently footnoted than the McKee biography of Wallace (148).

151. Mullin, Robert N. *The Boyhood of Billy the Kid*. Southwestern Studies 5 (No. 1), Monograph No. 17. El Paso: Texas Western Press, 1967.

Mullin's twenty-six-page pamphlet, plus several pages of photographs, treats Billy's life from his birth to the "eve of the Lincoln County War" (p. 2). Drawing heavily on the research of Maurice Garland Fulton, reminiscences of elderly persons who knew the Kid, and contemporary and later newspaper articles, Mullin provides information that most other biographers and historians had not turned up by the 1960s. Mullin's clear, straightforward account parallels the no-nonsense approach of fellow Kid researcher Philip Rasch. Both also clarify how much the Garrett-Upson biography—the first about the Kid in 1882 and so wide of the factual mark—threw subsequent writers and readers off track for several decades.

Mullin readily admits he cannot state with any exactness where and when Billy was born, but he raises the plausible dates and places—and then notes the limitations of each of these assertions. Mullin goes on to fill in the details we can be reasonably certain about: mother Catherine McCarty in Indiana and Kansas, stepfather William Antrim in Indiana and Kansas, and brother Joe (or "Josie," whom Mullin thinks the older brother) in New Mexico. Along the way, the author corrects earlier misleading conclusions and adds new information about Billy's life in Silver City, New Mexico, and Arizona before he surfaced back in New Mexico in early fall 1877. The final paragraphs deal with Billy's friendships and connections just before the Lincoln County War.

Still a valuable source on Billy's pre-1877 years. It corrects false legends that had grown up by the early 1960s.

152. Nolan, Frederick W. *The Life and Death of John Henry Tunstall*. Albuquerque: University of New Mexico Press, 1965.

Nolan's first book on the Lincoln County story, based on years of diligent, cross-Atlantic research (while the author remained in England), provides an extensive account of one of the story's key figures, John H. Tunstall of England. Nolan devotes roughly the first 150 pages to Tunstall's life before he arrived in New Mexico in 1876, the next 130 pages to Tunstall's life in Lincoln County, and the final 160 pages of text to the time from Tunstall's death in 1878 into the 1880s. A very useful "Chronology" (pp. 447–64), a brief bibliography (pp. 465–68), and more than forty photographs complete the volume. Throughout the book, long footnotes add a great deal of interesting contextual information.

Nolan smoothly braids biography and documents, an approach he followed in his subsequent books on Lincoln County and Billy the Kid. Personal letters among the Tunstall family (especially from son John in New Mexico to his parents and siblings in England), diary entries, newspaper stories, and other public documents are interspersed within Nolan's biographical narrative.

Since Tunstall made not one reference to the Kid in his numerous letters, Nolan's comments about Billy consist of backgrounds gathered from other strong sources. The author's approach to Billy is factual and balanced; he does not take sides on most of the youth's actions. In fact, Nolan's comments on the Kid are surprisingly evenhanded.

More than half a century after its publication, this lengthy volume remains the most thorough and best source on John Tunstall. It provides a rich font of information for understanding major Lincoln County issues in Billy's first months in the area in 1877–1878.

153. Nolan, Frederick. *The Lincoln County War: A Documentary History*. Norman: University of Oklahoma Press, 1992. Enlarged ed. Santa Fe, N.Mex.: Sunstone Press, 2009.

When Fred Nolan's oversize, six-hundred-page history of the Lincoln County War appeared in 1992, it immediately became—and still is—the most extensive examination of that dramatic series of events. Exhaustively researched, engagingly written, and full of new information, Nolan's still-definitive documentary history remains all the more amazing since most of the research was conducted from his home in England.

Nolan structures the opening chapters of his extensive volume around the lives and contributions of the major participants on the Lincoln Country War: Billy the Kid, Alex and Susan McSween, John Tunstall, and The House leaders Lawrence Murphy and James Dolan. Once their backgrounds are given and the events previous to 1877 sketched out, Nolan provides a blow-by-blow account of the apex of the war in 1878 and the next three years through to the killing of Billy the Kid in 1881.

The author's research in primary sources—in published works as well as in manuscripts—is particularly thorough. Not only has he dipped into the major collections that Maurice Garland Fulton, J. Evetts Haley, Robert N. Mullin, and Philip J. Rasch gathered in their research on Billy and the war, he has also worked his way through U.S. government and New Mexico territorial records concerning these subjects. In addition, he makes use of all the pertinent local and regional newspapers.

Equally attractive are three other ingredients in Nolan's thick volume. He includes more than eighty photographs of the major and minor participants as well as of scenes important to his story. In one appendix (pp. 442–93) Nolan adds ninety-eight brief biographical entries about major and minor participants in the Lincoln imbroglio, including the backgrounds of these men and women, their roles in the war, and their lives in the aftermath. Another valuable part of Nolan's work is his chronology of the lives, events, and outcomes of the war (pp. 494–520).

A very brief conclusion (pp. 439–41) reveals Nolan's willingness to cast stones in all directions. As he puts it succinctly, "The Lincoln Country War established nothing and proved nothing" (p. 441). It was brought about by dozens of flawed men—and a very few women—who were willing to lie, steal, and kill to achieve their own selfish, arrogant desires. The House operators were the worst, but neither the McSweens nor John Tunstall was much better—if, in fact, they were better. And military leaders and county, territorial, and federal government officials were, for the most part, rascals more driven by their own interests than in solving the huge problems of Lincoln County. Law and order were nonexistent, largely because participants were too motivated by their own greed to look out for the needs and rights of others.

Nolan adds contextual elements to the Lincoln County story that are instructive to other prospective historians and biographers. He shows how the failures of federal and territorial leaders and governments exacerbated rather than ameliorated the problems of southeastern New Mexico. We see the impact of the so-called Santa Fe Ring and the partisanship of county officials undermining rather than helping people living in Lincoln and its environments. Nolan also shows how racism of the time—particularly Anglo negativity toward "Mexicans," sometimes labeled "greasers"—marred local affairs. The author even hints at the roles some women, especially Susan McSween, played in the larger story.

Nolan's invaluable book—one of the two or three most important studies of the Lincoln County War—is rightly subtitled "A Documentary History." On occasion Nolan devotes more than a full page to extensive quotes from important original—usually manuscript—sources. Still, even though these long, thorough quotes add invaluable information, they sometimes slow the author's otherwise lively and sprightly narrative.

No person interested in Billy the Kid and the Lincoln County War can afford to overlook this volume. Indeed, it should be the first book read on this large subject.

154. Nolan, Frederick. *Tascosa: Its Life and Gaudy Times.* Lubbock: Texas Tech University Press, 2007.

Two brief sections—chapter 5, "1878: Billy the Kid Hits Town" (pp. 38–51), and chapter 9, "1880: Hunting Billy the Kid" (pp. 78–86)—focus directly on Billy's connections with the town of Tascosa and Texans from the Texas panhandle. Other chapters include more information on the Kid's actions in Texas and New Mexico. In fact, Nolan brings a good deal of New Mexico into this Texas town's history.

Chapter 5 treats the few weeks to as much as six months that the Kid was in the Tascosa area in fall 1878. Nolan's approach is anecdotal, linking the stories of several persons and events involving Billy. He also discusses the contact and growing friendship of the Kid with Dr. Henry Hoyt, who was then in West Texas. Nolan makes good use of Hoyt's memoir (132) for this chapter.

Chapter 9 summarizes the activities of Texas panhandle riders who attempted to capture Billy in 1880–1881 and to stop his horse and cattle stealing in Texas. This section is primarily a series of long, interesting quotes from obscure sources. Nolan particularly uses, adeptly, sources on James East, a key figure among the Texans looking for stolen cattle and Billy in New Mexico. This chapter also refers to the shooting of Tom O. Folliard in Fort Sumner and the capture of Billy and his men at Stinking Spring.

A good source for understanding the Texas elements involved in Billy's life in the 1878 to 1881 period. More thorough and up-to-date than John L. McCarty's account of Tascosa (146). Excellent photographs of key persons, places, and buildings but, unfortunately, no maps.

155. Nolan, Frederick. *The West of Billy the Kid.* Norman: University of Oklahoma Press, 1998.

Nolan's very appealing biography of Billy the Kid draws thoroughly on his extensive previous works on the western outlaw. Not only does Nolan make use of his books on John Tunstall (152) and Lincoln County (153), he also utilizes his diligent research in manuscripts and published primary and secondary sources. Another contribution of the volume—Nolan's extensive utilization of photographs and information accompanying them—should be emphasized. No one has done a better job than Nolan in picturing the major characters and settings of Billy's life and the Lincoln County War scenes. Alongside nearly all the photographs are helpful captions. These minibiographies explaining most of the Lincoln County notables are especially beneficial.

Nolan's Billy, in all his writings about Lincoln County, appears as a balanced, complex figure. Billy may have had to deal with the rascality of Lawrence Murphy and Jimmy Dolan and the partisan decisions of William Rynerson, Warren Bristol, and the Santa Fe Ring, but, as Nolan makes clear, he could also be a "big man." His role in the assassination of Sheriff William Brady, the killing of William Morton and Frank Baker, and his willingness to wreak havoc on other opponents clearly attest to the dark side of Billy, a human frailty to which Nolan clearly points.

Nolan's approach to Billy and the Lincoln County War differ from those in Robert Utley's equally valuable books (174–77) on these subjects. A novelist and spirited creative writer, Nolan enhances the value of his eminently readable narrative through his obvious gifts of description, strong action verbs, and wry humor. He also utilizes numerous long block quotes to impart the flavor as well as the content of his sources. Altogether, these organizational and descriptive methods add artistic polish and narrative power to Nolan's writings.

This volume and Robert Utley's biography of Billy (174) are the starting places for study of the Kid's life story. Both books are thorough, dependable, balanced, and in all ways pleasurable reading.

156. Nolan, Frederick, ed. *The Billy the Kid Reader.* Norman: University of Oklahoma Press, 2007.

Nolan adds to his notable output on Billy the Kid and the Lincoln Country War with this appealing collection of essays about the magical but enigmatic Billy. The gathering of twenty-six selections is divided in to two parts: (1) "The Legend" of Billy Bonney (nine items) and (2) his "Legend into

History" (seventeen items). Each selection is prefaced with a very helpful one-to-two-page headnote by the editor.

Nolan's purpose for this volume, he tells us, is to provide "a selection of the most seminal, the most influential" of the numerous essays and books published about the Kid (p. xi). This survey "from the first dime novel [1881] ... to the present day" should help readers comprehend "the Kid's life, personality, and legend" (p. xi).

The first section includes a dime novel by Don Jenardo and essays or parts of books by Pat Garrett, Charlie Siringo, Emerson Hough, Harvey Fergusson, and several others. The second section gathers essays by Philip Rasch, Robert N. Mullin, Waldo E. Koop, Lilly Casey Klasner, and Paul Andrew Hutton as well as "In His Own Words" from Billy.

A valuable and entertaining book, this volume achieves its goal of enticing readers to track down the Kid—and more.

157. Nolan, Frederick, ed. "Introduction," "Commentaries," "Postscript." In *The Authentic Life of Billy, the Kid: An Annotated Edition*, by Pat Garrett. 1882. Norman: University of Oklahoma Press, 2000.

Here is the beginning place for anyone wanting to read Garrett's pioneering biography of Billy the Kid—in the context of up-to-date commentaries on the book's contributions and limitations. Not only does this annotated edition include, word for word, the original 1882 version, it also contains the extensive first-rate commentaries and annotations of Frederick Nolan, a top authority on the Kid and Lincoln County. In all, Nolan adds an eight-page "Introduction," eleven "Commentaries" totaling twenty-six pages, a "Postscript" of four pages on Pat Garrett's later life, and a one-page brief list of "Suggested Further Reading." These nearly forty pages, plus all the brief annotations appearing on most pages, add material of first-rate importance for understanding Garrett's book and its handling of Billy the Kid and the Lincoln County conflicts.

Nolan's comments include a few surprises. Perhaps the largest is Nolan's unusual conviction that the final chapters, probably written by Garrett or coming from him, are in some ways as untrustworthy as those agreed-on weak opening chapters from Garrett's friend and ghostwriter Marshall Ashmun "Ash" Upson. The Garrett closing chapters, Nolan asserts, can be considered "almost as unreliable" (p. xvi) as Upson's imagined, sensational ones. In his incomplete and sometimes falsified stories, Garrett was protecting his interests, avoiding criticism and threats from still-living participants, and heightening the challenges and dangers of Billy the Kid so as to heighten further his own achievements. Altogether, Garrett's book was "a farrago of nonsense" (p. xvi).

While admitting "the proposition is impossible to prove" (p. xv), Nolan has a new version of the events leading up to Billy's death. He is convinced that Pete Maxwell wrote to Garrett, told him Billy was in Fort Sumner, and urged the sheriff to come and do something. Pete did not want his younger sister Paulita's reputation to be ruined if she ran away with Billy, a rumor being passed around. Nolan also thinks that Garrett may have been planning an ambush killing of Billy.

With the noteworthy addition of commentaries and annotations from Nolan, we now have a richer, more valuable source in Garrett's *Authentic Life*.

For a helpful review and a revealing brief interview with Nolan about this book, see Dale L. Walker, "Few Know Billy the Kid like the Englishman Behind the Annotated Edition of Pat Garrett's 1882 Book," *Wild West* 13 (April 2001): 66, 68 (265).

158. Otero, Miguel Antonio, Jr. *The Real Billy the Kid: With New Light on the Lincoln County War.* New York: Rufus Rockwell Wilson, 1936. Reprinted with an "Introduction" by John-Michael Rivera. Houston, Tex.: Arte Público Press, 1998, pp. xi–xlv.

In 1926 former territorial governor Miguel A. Otero Jr., joined by photographer and scribe Marshall Bond, traveled through Billy the Kid country interviewing surviving participants in the Lincoln County War. He spoke to, among others, Sue McSween Barber, George Barber, Martín Chávez, Yginio Salazar, Jesús Silva, George Coe, Frank Coe, Francisco Lobato, Paulita Maxwell Jaramillo, Vicente Otero, and Deluvina Maxwell. Earlier, Otero even met Billy the Kid in 1881 when they were both about the same age and the Kid was jailed in Santa Fe. Otero also relied heavily on the Ash Upson–Pat Garrett biography (127), but much less so on biographical accounts by Charlie Siringo, Emerson Hough, and Walter Noble Burns. He did not publish his account until a decade later, in 1936, some think because of the huge, lasting impact of Burns's best-selling biography (103).

Otero made clear contributions to the Kid story. His contacts with and the gathered information from Hispanics who knew and loved Billy are the book's major strength. No one before—and few since—has drawn extensively on these important sources. Conversely, one can make too much of

Otero's own ethnic background since his racial identity was evenly divided between his Anglo and Hispanic heritages and his higher education was clearly at non-Hispanic institutions.

The author's partisan support for Billy and the Tunstall-McSween-Chisum contingent runs strong throughout Otero's book. Billy is courageous, gentlemanly, and fair-minded. Even when Billy killed, he did so to protect himself and because he was "hounded like a mad dog" (p. 63). The Kid was not "half as bad as some of those" (p. 85) who pursued him, including Pat Garrett, who is roundly criticized here by Billy's fans and the author himself. L. G. Murphy, Jimmy Dolan, and John Riley as well as Santa Fe Ring leader Thomas Catron are evil men—stoked by greed and arrogance.

Regrettably, Otero is not a sound source on Billy's life before the Kid arrived in Lincoln County—a weakness of most books published on Billy before the early 1950s. By following too closely the false facts in the Upson-Garrett biography, Otero jumbles the chronology of Billy's early life, mixes up his years in Silver City and Arizona, and incorrectly has Billy, after Arizona, in Mexico (following Garrett), where he did not go. These failings and mistakes in the Stinking Spring capture and the Lincoln County jail escape add to Otero's limitations. Keeping these shortcomings in mind, one cannot support Jon Tuska's greatly exaggerated claim that Otero's book "marked the first true breakthrough in scholarship on the Kid's life" (173, p. 135).

Even more upsetting to traditional historians are two other wrongheaded Otero techniques. Like many historical novelists, he feels free to create conversations for which no evidence exists. On several occasions he quotes Billy, his friends, and his opponents with words not known to exist. In addition, Otero fails to utilize important sources, especially New Mexico newspapers in Silver City, Santa Fe, and Las Vegas—and territorial documents as well—that would have enlarged his story with additional facts and helped him correct wrong assertions.

One wishes it were possible to salute the extensive "Introduction" that John-Michael Rivera wrote for this reprinted edition of Otero's book. That is not possible. Greatly smitten by emerging Chicano and other literary theories, Rivera focuses more on theory than on the historiographical place of this book. Nor does Rivera exhibit much understanding of what sources Otero was using, which ones he overlooked, and how much Otero was off track on Billy's early life and several of the crucial events of the Kid's post-1877 years: his capture at Stinking Spring, his trials at Mesilla, his escape from the Lincoln County jail, and his love for Paulita Maxwell. Generally,

Otero has not produced a novel, one-of-a-kind account of Billy the Kid; neither should his brief book, while to be praised for its extensive treatments of Hispanics and apt employment of interviews, be touted as a tipping point in the long, complex historiographical journey of Bill the Kid.

On balance, Otero deserves praise for his noted contributions and for his having produced a clearly written account of Señor Billy. On the other hand, his created conversations, slipshod research, and limited use of available sources must also be kept in mind.

159. Poe, John William. *The Death of Billy the Kid.* 1933. Santa Fe, N.Mex.: Sunstone Press, 2006.

First appearing in a British magazine in 1919 and then reprinted in 1922 and 1923 as "a brochure," this book was republished by Houghton Mifflin in 1933. That issue contained an "Introduction" (pp. vii–xli) and an "Epilogue" (pp. 52–60) by Maurice Garland Fulton, which together were almost as extensive as the text of John William Poe's story (pp. 3–50). Combined, the varied parts of this brief book provide authentic information from a diligent scholar (Fulton) and a partially eyewitness account of the Billy the Kid story (Poe).

Fulton, then about ten years into his decades-long research on Lincoln County during the 1878–1881 years of Billy's life, contributes a very abbreviated biography of John Poe. Turning to Billy, Fulton is less sympathetic to the Kid than some of his contemporaries. Billy was a "young hotblood," "a paragon of the bold, reckless life of the frontier," and generally a "nuisance, not to say an appreciable menace" (pp. 59–60). In his "Introduction," Fulton is the first to cite Billy's letter to Gov. Lew Wallace defending the Kid's position and expressing his willingness to testify against lawyer Huston Chapman's killers in exchange for clemency from his indictments. Fulton credits Billy with killing Jim Carlyle at the Greathouse Ranch and states that Billy's Lincoln County jail escape transformed him into the "darling" of the "popular imagination." Fulton follows Poe's account of Billy's death but does not speak of Billy carrying a pistol. The "Epilogue" contains Spanish and English versions of the coroner's jury report on 15 July 1881.

Poe's account is that of a semi-eyewitness. As Pat Garrett's deputy, he met Billy for the first time near midnight at the darkened Maxwell house in Fort Sumner. Although he was outside the bedroom and did not see Garrett shoot Billy, he heard the shots, witnessed the frenzied retreat of Garrett and Maxwell after the shooting, and heard Garrett's account of exactly what happened. Poe explains how he had joined Garrett in the hunt for Señor Billy, the details of what occurred in Fort Sumner on 14 July 1881, how he briefly encountered the Kid on the porch outside the Maxwell home, and the bedlam afterwards, including Poe's near shooting of Pete Maxwell as he scurried out of his bedroom. Poe claims Billy was armed with a pistol and knife when he met the deputies, including Kip McKinney, outside and then Pat Garrett inside. Finally, the author denies sensational rumors that he helped cut off Billy's fingers as trophies and that someone else and not Billy was killed by Garrett.

A brief but useful and fact-filled account, dependable beyond much of what was written about Billy the Kid in the 1920s and 1930s.

160. Poe, Sophie. *Buckboard Days.* Edited by Eugene Cunningham. 1936. Albuquerque: University of New Mexico Press, 1981.

The opening chapters of this biography-memoir deal with the life in Kentucky, the Midwest, and Texas of John William Poe, who was eventually Pat Garrett's deputy. These sections treat his labors as a farmer, railroad worker, buffalo hunter, and deputy sheriff and then his work as a Texas cattlemen's detective, an occupation that brought him to New Mexico in 1881 to hunt for stolen cattle—and also led him to Garrett and the hunt for Billy the Kid.

A long chapter—"Trailing 'Billy the Kid'"—details Poe's ride with Garrett to catch the Kid. The story here differs little from standard narratives in other reliable accounts, including John Poe's *The Death of Billy the Kid* (159), except that the author creates conversations between Garrett and Poe, for example, that cannot be verified. Sophie Poe says Billy stayed in Fort Sumner after breaking out of the Lincoln jail in late April 1881 to visit his girlfriend, whose name is not revealed. Poe identifies Billy as a "notorious . . . cow rustler and horse thief" (p. 99). But she mistakenly states that Catherine McCarty "operated eating houses in one 'camp' after another" (p. 99). She also identifies the Kid as a "born leader" (p. 100). He was a "grinning outlaw who . . . probably killed more men than any other gunman in New Mexico" (pp. 116–17).

The second half of the book treats the Poes' life in New Mexico after they married in 1883. We hear of John William's successes as a lawman, rancher, and banker. Of special interest are Sophie's descriptions of life as a rancher's wife in lonesome rural Lincoln County and of the physical and sociocultural surroundings before the Poes moved to Roswell.

Helpful for a woman's perspective, but her information on the Lincoln County War is secondhand because Sophie Poe was not in New Mexico until 1881 and was not involved in the events swirling around Billy the Kid.

161. Rasch, Philip J. *Gunsmoke in Lincoln County*. Edited by Robert K. DeArment. Laramie: University of Wyoming and National Association for Outlaw and Lawman History, 1997.

The second in the trilogy of Rasch essay collections, this volume gathers twenty-one contributions. The collection features essays on Lincoln County more than on Billy the Kid. We get discussions about the Pecos, Horrell, and Tularosa ditch wars and about a half dozen on the Lincoln County War.

Rasch hallmarks are evident in these contributions: diligent research, assertive conclusions, and arrays of little-known facts. These strengths are evident in essays here on L. G. Murphy, Lt. Col. Nathan Dudley (two essays), Huston I. Chapman, Ira Leonard, and Frank Warner Angel. In addition to these biographical treatments, the collection also gathers essays on the shootout at Blazer's Mill, the murders of John Tunstall and Juan Patrón, and the Five-Day Battle in Lincoln.

These essays are not primarily about Billy the Kid but other figures and contextual events that are important for an understanding of Lincoln County and its wars. But, on occasion, Rasch speaks of Billy. He was not "a moronic little killer," as Rasch notes others have attested, but the Kid was "a psychopathic personality" (p. 221). Even in an essay titled "The Governor Meets the Kid" (pp. 208–27) we get a good deal on Gov. Lew Wallace but little comment on Billy. The Kid appears in other essays, but not as the lead character.

This collection is most valuable for the background information about and the varied characters involved in the Lincoln County War. The earlier collection, *Trailing Billy the Kid* (162) is the source for several of Rasch's most valuable contributions on Billy the Kid.

162. Rasch, Philip J. *Trailing Billy the Kid*. Edited by Robert K. DeArment. Laramie: University of Wyoming and National Association for Outlaw and Lawman History, 1995.

Rasch published these twenty-five essays, mostly dealing with Billy the Kid, during a period of more than thirty years (1954 to 1987). This collection is selected from his nearly 170 essays on southwestern subjects. The works appeared first, by and large, in little-known publications. Most are brief—fewer than ten pages; a few extend to fifteen to twenty pages. Nearly all include footnotes or a list of references.

Rasch was a tireless researcher, interested in every tidbit of information about Billy and the Lincoln County War. One cannot say, however, that Rasch was a mindless fan of Billy; indeed, he had more reservations about than attractions to the Kid. He did credit himself with redirecting stories about Billy as he corrected the inaccuracies of the pioneering biography of Ash Upson–Pat Garrett, the popularizer Walter Noble Burns, and memoirists misremembering their past. Most of the self-congratulation is deserved. Rasch turned up hundreds of fresh details about the Kid and the New Mexico Territory.

Rasch's research sources were multiple and varied. He read long runs of newspapers, examined manuscripts in several archives, wrote to hundreds of correspondents, and carried out interviews with persons who knew, for example, Billy's stepfather, William Antrim, and Billy's brother, Joe Antrim.

On the other hand, Rasch was little interested in the big picture behind and surrounding his narrower, focused stories. We do not learn about the Gilded Age and discover relatively little about New Mexico politics and the Santa Fe Ring or about U.S. Indian policy—all important contexts for the life of Billy the Kid and the Lincoln County War, but they are not dealt with here. Nor do cause-effect relationships interest Rasch much. Something happened, and he tells us about that event and the people involved, not the issues that might have led to or shaped those events.

Generally, then, Rasch is more annalist than analyst. We are much the better for his fact gathering than for his systemizing or overarching conclusions.

163. Rasch, Philip J. *Warriors of Lincoln County.* Edited by Robert K. DeArment. Laramie: University of Wyoming and National Association for Outlaw and Lawman History, 1998.

This collection of twenty-one essays by Rasch, a leading scholar of Billy and the Lincoln Country War from the 1950s to the 1980s, displays the valuable research of a grassroots scholar. He wrote prolifically. This is volume 3 of the tripart collection of Rasch's numerous essays, the other two volumes being *Tracking Billy the Kid* (1995) and *Gunsmoke in Lincoln County* (1997). The National Association for Outlaw and Lawman History was the sponsoring group for these three volumes.

Rasch was an energetic researcher. His projects on the lawmen, outlaws, and other notorious as well as lesser-known southwesterners was a hobby—and something of an addiction. Here he focuses on "the warriors," the men who fought in dozens of conflicts and "wars" that erupted between the 1870s and 1890s. The author has turned up thorough factual information on dozens of fighters, especially those warring on the side of Englishman

John Tunstall, lawyer Alex McSween, and rancher John Chisum or on the side of The House and its leaders, L. G. Murphy and James J. Dolan. Billy the Kid sided with the former group, although he is more a supporting than a major figure here. On many occasions, Rasch sides more with Dolan than with McSween and Chisum. He is particularly unkind to Susan McSween, suggesting that her morals were as loose as law and order in Lincoln County. By and large, Rasch is more critical of the McSweens, Tunstall, and Chisum than the best evidence indicates.

The essays exhibit both strengths and limitations. Rasch turned up useful material on the lives of numerous men and helpful facts on several strings of dramatic events. Conversely, some descriptions of incidents or persons are repeated up to a half dozen times because the essays were not edited to cut repetitions when in book form. On other occasions dates of events occasionally disagree. Rasch deserves awards for diligence and thoroughness of research but not for style, organization, revealing contexts, or overarching themes.

164. Simmons, Marc. *Stalking Billy the Kid: Brief Sketches of a Short Life.* Santa Fe, N.Mex.: Sunstone Press, 2006.

Marc Simmons, New Mexico's leading historian, furnishes a collection of his storytelling articles on Billy the Kid and contextual subjects. The collection is not so much a groundbreaking source as a smoothly and invitingly written series of stories aimed at general rather than specialist readers.

Simmons begins with stories about Billy's early years and then moves through vignettes illustrating major events in the Kid's life, people he met or who wrote about him, and stretchers that people told about their knowing Billy. Simmons follows, for the most part, middle-of-the-road positions, making Billy neither villain nor hero. The longest chapter, thoroughly documented, is "A Grave Question: Where Is Billy Buried?" (pp. 137–71, 184–87), which concludes that, despite differences of opinion, Billy's remains likely are still interred in the Fort Sumner cemetery.

Overall, a pleasant collection of compact, strong essays demonstrating the author's clear storytelling power.

165. Siringo, Charles A. *History of "Billy the Kid."* "Foreword" by Frederick Nolan. 1920. Albuquerque: University of New Mexico Press, 2000.

The handful of writers who have undertaken careful studies of the rise and flowering of Billy the Kid's legends often follow similar interpretive paths.

They speak of the images of Billy as a devilish character that appeared in newspapers and dime novels at the time of his death and soon thereafter. The satanic Billy, they continue, dominated the scene until Walter Noble Burns's *The Saga of Billy the Kid* (1926) appeared, which turned the notorious outlaw into a sometimes hero.

But these generalizations about Billy's interpreters from roughly 1880 to 1925 need more scrutiny. The Upson-Garrett biography, appearing in 1882, does not depict a wholly evil Kid. In fact, as many positive as negative comments fill that first biography. The Woods drama in 1903 and 1906 (307) also portrays Billy in a sympathetic light.

The writings of cowboy author Charlie Siringo are also exceptions to the negative first views of Billy. From his *A Texas Cowboy* (1885) to his final work, *Riata and Spurs* (rev. ed., 1927), Siringo portrays a likeable, courageous outlaw. In his nearly half dozen writings on the Kid, Siringo emphasizes the positives of Billy's character. "With all his faults," Siringo writes in summary, "'Billy the Kid' had many noble traits" (p. 140).

Siringo's *History of "Billy the Kid"* (1920) is the author's most extensive work on the subject. Although written thirty-five years after his first work on Billy, this concise biography follows the point of view sketched out in his earlier works on the Kid. The life story also betrays its large indebtedness to the Upson-Garrett biography.

From its opening pages, Siringo's Kid biography speaks well of Billy. He was "a bright scholar" (p. 7) as a boy. He loved his "dear" mother and tried to protect her from evildoers. He was loyal to his friends, "a good natured young man," "always cheerful and smiling" (p. 71). He avoided drunkenness and helped those in need.

But Siringo's Billy is no saint. Early on he was "associating with tough men and boys." Although usually of a "sunny disposition," Billy "when aroused had an ungovernable temper" (p. 7). For instance, after Tunstall's assassination, Billy was driven by "vengeance and hatred" (p. 39). And Siringo's positive reactions are tempered by the author's less positive hesitations. Near the end of his book he speaks of Billy as "once the bravest, and coolest young outlaw who ever trod the face of the earth" (p. 132).

Regrettably, especially for those wanting, above all, an accurate story of Billy, Siringo was not an energetic researcher, and he was careless with details. He misspells many names and gets his chronology mixed up; he is also wrong in some statements about Billy, who did not kill his first man at age twelve, was not present when Tunstall was shot down, and did not spend several weeks in Mexico after leaving Arizona in 1877. Siringo follows, too often, the wrongheaded paths of the Upson-Garrett account without undertaking his own search for verifiable facts. Even though the author promises to state exactly what he learned from Billy himself, Garrett, Manuela Bowdre, and many other participants, he plainly gets wrong too many crucial events.

Surprisingly, too, this book was privately printed rather than published by an established publisher. If *A Texas Cowboy* had sold a million copies (though Siringo probably exaggerated with that figure), one would have expected that an ambitious, energetic, well-known publisher would have taken on this biography. Had Billy—and Siringo too—fallen that far in popularity? Second, Siringo moves little beyond the research contained in his earlier books. Third, he fails to deal with several important persons in the Lincoln County story, including Alex and Susan McSween, Jimmy Dolan, and Lew Wallace.

Most of all, however, Siringo must be remembered as an obvious exception to the negative portraits of Billy the Kid that dominated newspaper stories, dime novels, and books and essays published from 1880 to 1925. If Siringo's Billy was no saint, he was certainly no devilish desperado either.

166. Siringo, Charles A. *A Lone Star Cowboy.* Santa Fe, N.Mex.: self-published, 1919.

Billy the Kid is not a major figure in this volume. Siringo mentions that he has written this book because his best-selling *A Texas Cowboy* (1885) has gone out of copyright, so he has rewritten the book to keep his story before a larger reading audience. That is something of a dodge because this book contains little not already appearing in Siringo's first book.

The sections here on Billy the Kid repeat most of what he said in *A Texas Cowboy*, which was expanded on one year later in *History of "Billy the Kid."* Siringo adds that this account also draws on his conversations with Charlie Wall, one of the Lincoln County prisoners when Billy broke out of jail in April 1881.

Siringo does not avoid mentioning Billy's violent crimes, but the Kid is not pictured as a murderous desperado bent on killing at will. Indeed, the Texas cowboy and detective author states that on the LX Ranch, about thirty miles south of Tascosa, Texas, he and the Kid "became quite chummy" (p. 110) and even exchanged gifts as a sign of their quick friendship. Siringo's discussions later in this book, taken from Wall's and other accounts, summarize Billy's breakout from the Lincoln jail and his death at the hands of Pat Garrett; they are straightforwardly told with but the slightest, rather neutral comment about Billy's personality.

167. Siringo, Charles A. *Riata and Spurs: The Story of a Lifetime Spent in the Saddle as Cowboy and Ranger.* Rev. ed. Boston: Houghton Mifflin, 1927.

The last of Siringo's books to include a good deal of information on Billy the Kid, this volume includes four chapters that treat the Kid and another that describes his connections with Dr. Henry Hoyt. As with all of Siringo's writings, this book must be used cautiously.

Primarily, Siringo relied too much on faulty information. He was too tied to the Upson-Garrett early, error-ridden biography (127), and he used too many stories uncritically. For instance, he includes information on several killings (pp. 84–85) that did not occur and accepts hearsay stories from Ash Upson without evaluating their reliability. Siringo gets wrong the Lincoln jail escape and Billy's demise at the hands of Garrett, but one must realize, again, that Siringo was not on the scene for either of these dramatic events and had to rely primarily on the unreliable Pat Garrett and Walter Noble Burns for his information.

The chapter on Dr. Hoyt, Siringo tells us, is quoting the doctor's own statements. He describes Billy as having a "pleasing expression of countenance, and a ready smile for all" (p. 245). Even though Hoyt encouraged the Kid to leave the area and to go farther east into Texas for a space of time, as did several others, Billy refused to follow that good advice.

Read critically, this book demonstrates again how off track early sources—e.g., Garrett and Siringo—were in their accounts written in the first years after the Kid's death, thus leaving readers searching for the truth with little to follow for several decades.

168. Siringo, Charles A. *A Texas Cowboy; or, Fifteen Years on the Hurricane Deck of a Spanish Pony.* . . . 1885. Reprinted, with an "Introduction" by Richard W. Etulain. New York: Penguin Books, 2000.

Siringo's *A Texas Cowboy* (1885) probably did more to spread the word about Billy than any other writings published before 1900. It is rumored that over its life, Siringo's wildly popular cowboy autobiography sold more than a million copies. Siringo based much of his account on the earlier Garrett-Upson biography (127), John Poe's book (159), hearsay, and his own brief encounter with Billy in Texas. Later, Siringo dealt glancingly with Billy in *Lone Star Cowboy* (1919) and *Riata and Spurs* (1927) and published a brief biography of the Kid, *History of "Billy the Kid"* (1920).

Nearly all the final ten chapters of *A Texas Cowboy* make mention of Billy the Kid, but chapter 27, "A True Sketch of 'Bill the Kid's' Life," provides a capsule biography of the famous outlaw. But more myths than facts inhabit Siringo's story. He has, wrongly, Billy killing a "Negro soldier" in Fort Union; a blacksmith in Silver City; a Mexican card dealer in Chihuahua, Mexico; and several others, including eventually *all* those involved in the Tunstall murder in February 1878. Siringo also shovels out incorrect information about the Five-Day Battle in July 1878, including Billy's playing the piano because Sue McSween was not at home. Siringo's description of Billy's escape from jail and his account of the Kid's death at the hand of Pat Garrett are equally untrustworthy factually. Most of the names of participants and many of the place-names are likewise misspelled.

Generally, Siringo is not as negative about Billy as early journalists and dime novelists. He depicts the Kid not as a "cruel hearted wretch" but as an outlaw who "would kill a man now and then, for what he supposed to be a just cause" (p. 149). Still, he could also on occasion help a sick or needy person.

Unfortunately, Siringo's widely touted account of Billy the Kid spread bundles of misinformation that dominated the next two generations, from the 1880s to the 1920s.

169. Sonnichsen, C. L., and William V. Morrison. *Alias Billy the Kid.* Albuquerque: University of New Mexico Press, 1955.

This abbreviated volume—about one hundred pages of text, forty pages of legal documents in appendices, and sixteen pages of photographs—launched in book form a new legend: Pat Garrett did not shoot Billy the Kid in July 1881, so Billy came back on scene as ninety-year-old O. L. ("Brushy Bill") Roberts. The old man, now from Texas, claimed to be the real Billy, and Professor C. L. Sonnichsen and legal researcher William V. Morrison accepted his story and retold it in this startling book. Although most authorities on Billy have disagreed with—or even denounced—the resurrected Billy story, it has not died. In the subsequent sixty years or more, nearly a dozen other writers have trotted down the same suspect path, turning up bits of new information and stirring up continuing criticism as a story unworthy of credibility.

Some wondered why Sonnichsen—a well-respected professor of English at the University of Texas at El Paso and the author of several books and essays on southwestern literary and historical subjects—joined the project. Early on, Morrison brought the Brushy Bill story to Sonnichsen and talked the professor into writing this book based on Morrison's tireless work in legal and personal documents. Although the two authors and their publisher, the University of New Mexico Press, claimed not to be advocating for Brushy Billy's story, instead merely relating the solid facts they had gathered, the two writers nonetheless seemed convinced that Brushy Bill was indeed Billy the Kid.

The book includes a "Prologue," "Brushy Bill's Story," four concise sections dealing with the origins of this story, and the concluding forty-page compendium of reprinted documents and testimonies. Clearly, the volume's contents prove Brushy Bill knew a good deal about Billy the Kid, although thorough knowledge of the Garrett-Upson and Burns biographies would have acquainted him with most of what he knew. Still, Brushy Bill also knew facts unknown to many Billy fans and was acquainted with a few a people who personally knew Billy the Kid and signed affidavits asserting that Brushy Billy was Billy the Kid.

Several other facts undermine the believability of Brushy Bill's story, however. More than a few close friends and acquaintances in Fort Sumner testified to seeing Billy's dead body on 15 July 1881 before he was buried that day. Among these were Pat Garrett, Pete Maxwell, Deluvina Maxwell, Saval Gutiérrez, and more than twenty others. Brushy also claimed that the Kid had escaped from the Lincoln County jail without killing anyone, and then he reversed himself to state that Billy had shot down Bell and Olinger. Even more troubling for Brushy Billy believers, if one accepts his controversial story, then what diligent biographers have uncovered about Billy's mother and stepfather and the Kid's life in Indiana, Kansas, Silver City, and Arizona must be almost entirely dismissed. The careful, ongoing research of recent historians and biographers presents huge, insurmountable barriers to accepting the Brushy Bill story. See the books by W. C. Jameson (135–38) for expansion of the beyond-the-grave story of Brushy Bill Roberts.

170. Steckmesser, Kent L. *The Western Hero in History and Legend.* Norman: University of Oklahoma Press, 1965.

A half century after its publication, this pathbreaking study of the lives and legends of four western demigods remains a go-to source for understanding mythmaking. A revision of Steckmesser's doctoral dissertation at the University of Chicago, the book demonstrates how the lives of Kit Carson, Billy the Kid, Wild Bill Hickok, and George Armstrong Custer transitioned from history to legend, with those two paths often later competing with one another.

The section on Billy the Kid (pp. 55–102) includes four brief chapters. The first provides a thumbnail biography; then follow two parts on the competing treatments of "satanic" and "saintly" Billy and a closing chapter on Billy as "The American Robin Hood." If those writers portraying Billy as a thief, outlaw, and murderer turned out most of the first accounts of his life and deeds, those depicting him as hero, courageously standing up for individuals on the "right side," later dominated the ever-mounting legends of Billy.

Steckmesser's research and conclusions are thorough, illuminating, and balanced. For instance, in his evaluation of Walter Noble Burns's difference-making biography *Saga of Billy the Kid* (103), Steckmesser notes Burns's dramatic, interest-whetting style as well as his inaccuracies and imagined conversations. In his closing pages on Billy, Steckmesser discusses biographies, novels, and films written and released in the 1940s and 1950s. Unfortunately, Steckmesser's book was published before the most thorough and best biographies appeared in the 1980s and thereafter.

An invaluable source for understanding how western men were transformed from humans into larger-than-life legends. The author's general comments about the origins of legends, the making of mythic heroes, and the shaping power of popular culture are particularly illuminating for understanding Billy the Kid and other such frontier heroes and heroines. Provocative and instructive.

171. Tatum, Stephen. *Inventing Billy the Kid: Visions of the Outlaw in America, 1881–1981*. Albuquerque: University of New Mexico Press, 1982.

Students of western history often try to separate what they consider to be the myth and reality of the American West. Conversely, this provocative book on Billy the Kid presents both topics without trying to praise one and condemn the other. The work also points to the failures of historians who are so centered on small, insignificant facts that they fail to see that the shifting interpretations of Billy often reflect transitioning sociocultural outlooks.

In fact, literary scholar Stephen Tatum is even more interested in the mythic Billy the Kid appearing in fiction, film, and other popular arts than in the factual William H. Bonney detailed in dozens of biographies and other works of history. What were the cultural-intellectual origins of the legends surrounding the Kid, how have these myths reflected emotional and societal needs of Americans through the years, and how have these views changed over time—these are the central questions of this provocative volume. Scrutinizing numerous novels, films, works of art, biographies and essays, and historical accounts, Tatum charts the peaks and valleys of the Kid's reputation from satanic, buck-toothed killer to saintly Robin Hood to disturbed young man—with several variations on these themes. He also shows how those interpretive shifts were parts of shifts in narrative modes: from romance to tragedy to irony.

The author's discussions are balanced and insightful—and interesting. One emerges from his book with a larger understanding of mythmaking processes, how popular culture reflects shifting national attitudes, and the manner in which popular writers and film directors structure their products to fulfill cultural needs. A much stronger book than the volumes by Ramon Adams, *A Fitting Death for Billy the Kid* (1960), and Jon Tuska (173) pursuing similar goals.

172. Tsompanas, Paul L. *Juan Patrón: A Fallen Star in the Days of Billy the Kid.* Richmond, Va.: Belle Isle Books, 2013.

We have needed books like this for a long time—and more are necessary. Tsompanas, a veteran journalist, provides a valuable, smoothly written biography of Juan Patrón (1852–1884), probably the most significant Hispanic figure in the Lincoln County uproar in the 1870s and 1880s.

The author is particularly fulsome on Patrón's noncombatant role in the Lincoln County War and also on his educational, religious, and political activities. Tragedy shaped the active but short life of Juan Patrón. His father was murdered in December 1873, when Juan was in his early twenties, and Juan himself was shot and severely injured in September 1875, causing him to limp for the rest of his life. Then Patrón was shot and killed in 1884, a mysterious murder still not fully explained.

Tsompanas fills his pages with revealing commentary about Patrón and Hispanic activities in Lincoln County and New Mexico conflicts. His research derives mainly from the writings of Frederick Nolan and Robert Utley, some from newspapers and other printed sources, and least from manuscript sources. The coverage of Billy the Kid is understandably limited because Patrón and Billy were not close and at times on opposite sides of conflicts. On a few occasions the author ventures into interesting new subjects but ones not closely linked to Juan Patrón.

No one has given us a more thorough examination of Hispanic reactions to the Lincoln County roilings. This book deserves more attention.

173. Tuska, Jon. *Billy the Kid: His Life and Legend.* Albuquerque: University of New Mexico Press, 1997. Revised and expanded version of *Billy the Kid: A Bio-Bibliography.* Westport, Conn.: Greenwood Press, 1983, 1994. Also printed as *Billy the Kid: A Handbook.* Lincoln: University of Nebraska Press, 1983, 1986.

An indefatigable researcher and prolific writer, Jon Tuska was known for his work on movies, moviemakers, and especially Western films; literary West commentaries and anthologies; and as a literary agent for reprinted books on the American West. He became widely recognized as an authority on Hollywood and later in the western literary field.

This book on the life and legends of Billy the Kid illustrates the author's clear strengths and equally evident limitations. The book's first hundred pages provide a capsule biography of Billy with ample comments on Lincoln County. The book closes with a ten-page (pp. 251–60) "Billy the Kid Chronology." These two sections, helpful and nearly always accurate, furnish dependable bedrock for Tuska's other chapters. The sections on Billy and historians, Billy and novelists, and Billy and films overflow with extensive plot summaries.

Unfortunately, Tuska became—and very much remained—a man of very strong personal opinions. His extensive and thorough criticism of the fantasies (errors and wrong conclusions) in the Garrett-Upson and Burns biographies seems defensible. But his denunciation of Robert Utley's three books on Billy the Kid as "riddled with inaccuracies on just about every page and in almost every paragraph" (p. 133), his calling Utley a "racist" for using "Hispanic" rather than "Mexican" or "Mexican-American" for Native New Mexicans, his assertion that Utley's books "have influenced only two articles" (p. 136)—these and other attacks on other writers diminish Tuska's credibility. He also dismisses Stephen Tatum's *Inventing Billy the Kid* (171) as "the only complete failure" (p. 231) in treating the legends surrounding Billy the Kid. Tuska adds that Tatum's book is "the silliest" (p. 236) volume in its attempt to use "the Henry Nash Smith thesis" (in his classic book *Virgin Land* [1950]) in linking popular works to their times—e.g., dime novels to the post–Civil War decades and Western film and fiction to the 1920s. Tuska likewise downplays the works of Kent Steckmesser and John Cawelti for their emphases on the cultural-intellectual milieus rather than stressing the specific "moral ideas" (p. 236) of authors.

Conversely, Tuska, in his final chapter on Kid legends, provocatively urges subsequent writers to consider a three-sided Billy: the outlaw, the hero, and the Januslike figure embodying both. Good parting advice for thoughtful consideration of the Kid.

174. Utley, Robert M. *Billy the Kid: A Short and Violent Life*. Lincoln: University of Nebraska Press, 1989.

Immediately after its publication in 1989, Utley's brief biography of Billy the Kid gained notoriety as the best life story of one of the West's demigods.

Now, thirty years later, Utley's smoothly written and rigorously researched book remains the leading account of the Kid's life.

Utley's narrative approach, spiced with provocative conclusions, grabs readers' attentions. Although the major emphases in the book are on the Kid's actions, Utley also provides strong and persuasive interpretations of those actions. For example, he shows that the Kid continuously put forth self-supportive statements after the fiery shootout in July 1878 in Lincoln, New Mexico, which all but ended the Lincoln County War; in the next three years, while claiming innocence and self-justification, the Kid turned to a life of crime. Billy the Kid, in Utley's convincing view, was a criminal, a murderer, a horse thief, and a liar.

But this biography is no diatribe against the Kid. It shows how the sociocultural and economic milieus of the 1870s and 1880s in the United States and New Mexico sometimes spawned the corruption and violence that erupted in Lincoln County in the 1870s. Billy the Kid was fetched up in such times; he fit into what was happening and would happen in Gilded Age America.

Utley also shows the complexities of the Kid's personality. Jovial, friendly, and often cheerful, he was also swift into violent actions, using his scampering and gun skills to keep opponents at bay. Contemporaries of Billy, as Utley clearly shows, might be taken with Billy's boyishness and drawn to him, but they also feared his quick, violent ways. A major contribution of Utley's biography is to illustrate clearly the tenor of his subtitle, "A Short and Violent Life."

Readers will be impressed with Utley's thorough research. He utilized—indeed combed—all the major research collections of Billy the Kid materials. In addition, he made wide use of pertinent newspaper accounts and federal records dealing with Billy, the Lincoln County War, and New Mexico in the 1870s–1880s. No major sources on Billy the Kid and the Lincoln County War were overlooked.

The major strengths of Utley's appealing biography can be succinctly summarized: this is a stirringly written biography of a major demigod of the Old West based on diligent, thorough research.

175. Utley, Robert M. *Four Fighters of Lincoln County.* Calvin Horn Lectures in Western History and Culture, University of New Mexico, 11–14 November 1955. Albuquerque: University of New Mexico Press, 1986.

The first of Robert Utley's four books dealing with the Lincoln County War and Billy the Kid, this volume utilizes a biographical approach. The author devotes separate, well-researched, and smoothly written chapters to Alex McSween, Billy the Kid, Col. Nathan A. M. Dudley, and Gov. Lew Wallace. The biographical organization allows Utley to cover most of the complexities of the war. The character portraits, the role of the military, and the clash and conflicts of Lincoln County in the 1870s and 1880s are particularly strong.

Utley's interpretations are clearly and persuasively presented. McSween, Billy, Colonel Dudley, and Governor Wallace were all flawed men. An idealist, McSween could also be dragged into disreputable deeds, and sometimes may have followed too closely the desires of his assertive wife, Susan. Billy, beginning as a petty young thief and general rascal, turned more criminal and violent from 1878 to 1881. The mythic Billy, argues Utley, has been given a larger role in the Lincoln County War than he actually played. Perhaps the most flawed of the characters was Colonel Dudley. Arrogant, naive, belligerent, self-deceptive, and addicted to whiskey, Dudley and his unwise actions on the final, turning-point day of the Five-Day War, 19 July 1878, led to the assassination of McSween. Had Dudley acted much more wisely—and decisively—he might have helped end the war at that time. Governor Wallace similarly exhibited such damaging limitations that he failed to govern well and end the war. True, the war simmered down after 1881, especially after Sheriff Pat Garrett killed Billy the Kid in July 1881, but that downward trend of the war was not a result of Wallace's strong, decisive actions.

Altogether a succinct and essential account of these four central characters in the Lincoln County War. A valuable brief overview.

176. Utley, Robert M. *High Noon in Lincoln: Violence on the Western Frontier.* Albuquerque: University of New Mexico Press, 1987.

An expansion of Utley's *Four Fighters of Lincoln County* (175), particularly the earlier book's biographical information on John H. Tunstall, Alex McSween, Billy the Kid, and Lew Wallace, this superb volume treats more extensively the ideas, events, and other people who were important in Lincoln County history of the 1870s. This second Utley volume is more than twice as long as the *Four Fighters* book. Utley focuses primarily on the period stretching from Tunstall's murder on 18 February 1878 through the Five-Day Battle, 15–19 July 1878, in Lincoln. The penultimate chapter sums up events through Billy's death on 14 July 1881, and the final section provides useful conclusions on the events, ideas, and participants of the Lincoln County War.

Utley's first-rate talents as a (perhaps *the*) narrative historian of the American West are on clear display here. His forceful language, apt descriptions, strong storytelling talent, and thorough research add much to this valuable volume. In large part, Utley illustrates his achievements, particularly through his appealing narrative of dramatic events and attention-catching participants; here are the talents of a creative nonfictionist—without the excessive imagined conversations, dramatic scenes, and overly wrought writing too often on display in sensational and controversial mixes of history and fiction.

Utley's portrait of Billy is of a piece with his general approach to the leading characters of this story; this is, according to Utley, "a war without heroes" (p. ix). Murphy, Dolan, and Riley of The House contingent and Tunstall and the McSweens among their opponents, as well as Governor Wallace, proved to be unheroic in their actions and statements. Like the remainder of the protagonists, Billy was unworthy of heroic status. In fact, Utley tells us, from the beginning he "did not expect Billy the Kid to be a hero" (p. ix).

Obviously, then, this volume and Frederick Nolan's book on Lincoln County (153) remain the best biographical sources on Kid and the county. Readers will be particularly drawn to Utley's vivid historical writing, his extensive research, and his clear articulation of the meanings of the "high noon" days of Lincoln County.

177. Utley, Robert M. *Wanted: The Outlaw Lives of Billy the Kid and Ned Kelly.* New Haven, Conn.: Yale University Press, 2015.

Utley achieves here exactly what he sets out to do: he provides side-by-side narrative life stories of Billy the Kid and Ned Kelly, the Australian bushranger. This is the inviting story of two outlaws conflicting with their host societies. And the achievement is one of a kind: no one previously had written a book comparing one of the western demigods (e.g., Custer, Geronimo, Wyatt Earp, Wild Bill, or Calamity Jane) with a comparable legendary character from another culture—e.g., Ned Kelly of Australia.

Utley's comparative biographies are primarily narrative in form—and augmented by the author's valuable analysis and evaluation. We learn much about the places, people, and events that illustrated and shaped the lives of these two larger-than-life protagonists. Most of the book's content consists of the two brief biographies, but the closing section includes about ten pages of revealing comparisons of Billy and Ned.

Although the biographical section on Ned Kelly will likely be new to most American readers, they will recognize Utley's clear achievements in handling the Kid. Utley knows his American West as well as any living historian, and he's done several books on major western figures—including Sitting Bull, Geronimo, George Custer, and the best midlength biography of Billy the Kid (173).

Utley's treatments of and conclusions about Billy and Ned provide balanced, middle-of-the-road interpretations. He notes the strengths and limitations of both characters—their courage and derring-do but also their shortsightedness and foolhardy actions. No one will accuse Utley of bending the evidence to buttress an off-the-road interpretation.

Utley has chosen the right length for his biographical stories. He utilizes about 150 pages to tell Billy's story and about 110 for Ned's.

178. Wallace, Lew. *An Autobiography.* 2 vols. New York: Harper and Brothers, 1906.

In his 1,028-page, two-volume autobiography, Wallace devotes but ten pages to his turbulent times in New Mexico. Neither New Mexico nor Billy the Kid appears in the index, and Wallace does not mention them in his text, suggesting he saw these as quite unimportant times from his perspective.

But his wife, Susan Wallace, dealt revealingly with the subjects in her letter to Henry L. Wallace (the governor's relative) from Fort Stanton, dated 11 May 1879. "The Lincoln County reign of terror is not over," Mrs. Wallace wrote, "and we hold our lives at the mercy of desperadoes and outlaws, chief among them 'Billy the Kid,' whose boast is that he has killed a man for every year of his life." Billy has broken out of jail "and now swears when he has killed the sheriff and the judge who passed sentence upon him, and Governor Wallace, he will surrender and be hanged." Mrs. Wallace then quotes a Billy threat: "I mean to ride into the plaza at Santa Fe, hitch my horse in front of the palace, and put a bullet through Lew Wallace" (p. 921).

Heeding this dire threat, Mrs. Wallace was closing the palace's shutters so that Billy would not see the governor's nighttime shadow. She wrote further, "'Billy' (whose name is Bonney) has a gang of admirers and followers, and they dash up to a ballroom, shoot out the candles, and gallop away and nobody hurt" (p. 921).

A revealing source—for what it does not say rather than for what it includes from Lew Wallace.

179. Wallis, Michael. *Billy the Kid: The Endless Ride.* New York: W. W. Norton, 2007.

The author of this volume, a journalist with several books to his credit, employs a life-and-times approach, giving as much sociocultural background as biography of Billy the Kid. That method both adds to our understanding of the young outlaw and detracts from the Kid's story as it gets lost in backdrops.

First the strengths: Wallis is a talented writer and tells an interesting story, even when lost in settings and other nonbiographical matters. He does a good job, too, of depicting Billy as a drifter, a young man who wandered more than planned his life. His depictions of some of Billy's settings—Wichita, Kansas, and Silver City and Lincoln, New Mexico—add measurably to understanding the shaping influences at work on Billy.

But Wallis easily loses Billy. When the author names a person, place, or thing, expect that he will then abandon Billy to talk about backgrounds. We learn more about guns, the lives of P. T. Barnum and Buffalo Bill Cody, and dime novels than we need for understanding Billy the Kid.

Wallis is incorrect, too, in suggesting that most writers about Billy have seen him as either a hero or villain. Instead, Robert Utley, Frederick Nolan, William Keleher, and Maurice Garland Fulton are not one-sided; they depict a Billy who could be both congenial and cheerful but also violent and revenge-driven.

Wallis's book is best read to see Billy in context rather than as a biography with sharp, clear focus on the Kid.

180. Weddle, Jerry. *Antrim is My Stepfather's Name: The Boyhood of Billy the Kid.* Historical Monograph No. 9. Tucson: Arizona Historical Society, 1993.

When a portion of this monograph of less than one hundred pages appeared first as "Apprenticeship of an Outlaw: Billy the Kid in Arizona," *Journal of Arizona History* (Autumn 1990): 233–52, and then in book form, it was hailed as a superb piece of research on Billy's early years. Rightly so. Along with the writings of W. E. Koop (215) and Robert N. Mullin (151), Weddle turned up more on Billy's Silver City and Arizona years than any previous researcher. He drew heavily on contemporary newspapers, later oral interviews with Billy's boyhood chums, and obscure manuscript sources for his revealing account. His footnotes (pp. 49–67) and bibliography (pp. 69–82) are particularly extensive—and valuable.

Weddle strongly pushes his points of view. Although very brief on Billy's life before 1873, Weddle concludes that Billy was born in Indiana, that Joseph was his younger brother, and that the McCarty-Antrim party stayed briefly in Denver before traveling south to Santa Fe, where William Antrim and Catherine McCarty married on 1 March 1873 and where they stayed with Antrim's sister and in a hotel before going south by stagecoach to Silver City. Weddle especially disagrees with the writings of Frederick Nolan and Donald R. Cline among several others.

Nearly all of Weddle's fact-filled account deals with Billy's time in Silver City, 1873–1875 (pp. 3–30), and in Arizona, 1875–1877 (pp. 30–43). More than a generation after its appearance, Weddle's monograph remains a key source on Billy's boyhood years. The work is thorough, well researched, and clearly written.

181. Westphall, Victor. *Thomas Benton Catron and His Era.* Tucson: University of Arizona Press, 1973.

New Mexican historian Victor Westphall follows a different path from most Billy the Kid biographers in evaluating the life and career of Thomas Catron. Rather than seeing him as a domineering, hard-nosed dictator and chief rascal of a thoroughly evil Santa Fe Ring, Westphall provides a straightforward, clearly written biography of Catron. The best life story we have of the Santa Fe lawyer and politician, the biography is not a whitewash. But neither is it a negative treatment of the subject. Generally, Westphall draws heavily on extant Catron papers, court records, and published books and essays to depict, as the author states, "Catron's life and his career objectively" (p. iv).

Westphall obviously achieves this major goal. He notes Catron's tendency to push for his Republican Party goals, his remunerations from business deals, and his willingness to take sides in controversies. At the same time the author points to all the financial help Catron gave to small or impecunious businessmen and agriculturists and his support for his family.

This biography is a useful and dependable source for gathering information on an opponent of Billy the Kid's but one who was not the devil incarnate that many Kid supporters depict him as being.

182. Wilson, John P. *Merchants Guns & Money: The Story of Lincoln County and Its Wars.* Santa Fe: Museum of New Mexico, 1987.

This valuable volume provides specific information on Lincoln County not available in other books written about the area. Anthropologist-historian Wilson views the Billy the Kid and Lincoln County War stories as part of a much larger narrative, stretching from about 1850 until the early twentieth century. His focus is on the county and town of Lincoln, not on Billy. Wilson devotes several chapters, however, to the Lincoln County War and events leading up to and through the violent conflict.

The author utilizes numerous statistics and other specific information to good effect. For example, he provides shifting demographic trends, revealing the population changes from the 1870s through 1900. In addition, Wilson shows how shifts in economic development, racial and ethnic conflicts, and a few national trends shaped life in Lincoln County over nearly a half century.

The treatments of Billy the Kid and the Lincoln County War follow accounts in the best secondary sources. But the author does not overlook key manuscript and published primary sources. He draws heavily on the writings of Philip J. Rasch, William A. Keleher, Maurice Garland Fulton, and other secondary works but not on the still-to-be-published major works of Frederick Nolan and Robert Utley. He also quotes extensively from government documents, newspapers, and unpublished sources.

For the most part, the author is fair and balanced in his assessments. He does not indulge in the anti-House or negative portraits of Murphy and Dolan, a tendency that often occurs in the Billy the Kid partisan accounts. Yet he is much more critical of Alex McSween than of John Chisum or John Tunstall, laying at the feet of the Lincoln lawyer much of the chaos in the 1876–1878 period. His Billy the Kid is also a violent, devil-may-care young man. A gunman without second thoughts concerning killing Sheriff Brady and others, Billy is portrayed, generally, as a negative character. Wilson does not deal with Billy's life before 1877 and not much with his personal life in the next four years.

Wilson adopts a chronological framework, although not all discussions within each chapter follow clearly the chapter title. Some chapters are more catchall sections rather than coherently organized. The author's style is clear but a bit pedestrian and cluttered with too many long block quotes.

On balance, Wilson's strong contributions on new information and breadth of coverage far outweigh stylistic and organizational limitations.

183. Wilson, John P., ed. *Pat Garrett and Billy the Kid as I Knew Them: Reminiscences of John P. Meadows.* Albuquerque: University of New Mexico Press, 2004.

A brief series of interviews and reminiscences of John Meadows, a close acquaintance of Billy the Kid's, this book provides one of the few extant eyewitness accounts of the closing months of the Kid's life. The slim volume includes both the connections Meadows had with Billy and the stories he got secondhand from others. The closing chapters of the book deal with Meadows's links to Pat Garrett.

Meadows is remarkably balanced in his statements. He can admit that Billy "was too awful rough at times," but his "generous treatment brought a warm spirit in . . . [Meadows's] heart for that boy, and it's there yet" (p. 28). Meadows thought Billy was "pretty well-bred. He must have had good stuff in him, for he was always an expert at whatever he tried to do" (p. 54).

"Among some other good traits the Kid had," Meadows adds, "he was quite generous with his friends" (p. 54). To the end, Meadows sees both sides of Billy's character: "I can't endorse . . . for example when he killed Charlie [*sic*, Jimmy] Carlyle," but Billy also "had a good streak in him" (p. 28).

Meadows contributes equally positive comments about Pat Garrett, for whom he worked for several years after the sheriff killed the Kid. He sums up his reactions to Garrett in one remarkable sentence: "I can say with honest conviction that I never met in my life a man who was any more truthful, any more honorable, or any better citizen than he" (p. 55).

About half of the book deals with Billy, half with Garrett, especially about the sheriff in the latter section dealing with events after 1881. Wilson's introduction is especially helpful for understanding the life and character of John Meadows. Well researched firsthand source.

Essays and Book Chapters

184. Adler, Alfred. "Billy the Kid: A Case Study in Epic Origins." *Western Folklore* 10, no. 2 (1951): 143–52. Reprinted in Frederic Nolan, *The Billy the Kid Reader* (156).

Beware. An early attempt to understand Billy the Kid as an epic hero, this theoretical piece is provocative, complex, and frequently based on sources now considered faulty. Adler uses the ideas of Lord Raglan in his book *The Hero: A Study in Tradition, Myth, and Drama* (1937) to compare the journey of Billy the Kid as a rising folk hero with other folk heroes from ancient times through the middle ages. Only readers versed in the theories of folklore will be at ease with this essay and find it less than very convoluted. The author's complex prose, in conjunction with his excessive use of the now-questionable conclusions of Otero (158), Hendron (129), and Brothers (102), leads to an ambivalent achievement. But, one should keep in mind that this piece was written before the rock-solid research work of Philip Rasch, Frederick Nolan, and Robert Utley appeared. Adler attempted to move beyond earlier writings limited to arguments over the accuracy of facts about Billy's life to aim at larger patterns of meaning surrounding the Kid's rather mysterious life. He did so with mixed results.

185. Ball, Durwood. "The Tale of the University of New Mexico Libraries' Three Millionth Volume." In *Three Million and Counting*, edited by Steven R. Harris. Phoenix, Ariz.: O'Neil Printing, 2013, pp. 54–80.

A revealing and valuable piece of research and writing, this essay discusses the backgrounds and contexts of the landmark first edition of the Pat

Garrett–Ash Upson volume *The Authentic Life of Billy, the Kid* (1882, #127). Author Durwood Ball, editor of the *New Mexico Historical Review*, opens his essay with capsule biographies of Billy the Kid, Garrett, and Upson, showing how these lives are germane to understanding the first biography of Billy. The closing pages of this well-written and thoroughly researched essay deal with the publication of the book and with the life of journalist-historian-lawyer William Keleher, whose family gifted the book to the University of New Mexico libraries. An especially helpful contribution about the Garrett-Upson biography.

186. Bell, Bob Boze. "Big Art, Big Billys." *True West* 56 (October 2008): 8.

Bell testifies that reading Walter Noble Burns's *The Saga of Billy the Kid* (103) was an electrifying experience for him. It drove him up the Billy trail, rekindled his interest in the Old West, helped him launch his own research on the Kid, and eventually led him to purchase *True West* in 1999. Plus, his fascination pushed him to publish his own book *The Illustrated Life and Times of Billy the Kid* (1992) and a revised version in 1996 (99). In the nearly twenty years since, Bell has gained a strong reputation for his publishing of *True West* and for his innovative artwork on the Old West. A brief biographical piece about an important figure in popular publishing about the Wild West, including Billy the Kid.

187. Bell, Bob Boze. "Caught with His Pants Down? Billy the Kid vs. Pat Garrett." *True West* 57 (August 2010): 60–63.

Based on the research of writer Frederick Nolan, National Park Service employee Gregory Smith, and former lawman Steve Sederwall, Bob Boze Bell presents a new scenario for the last moments of Billy the Kid's life. He posits that Billy was staying in the Maxwell home on 14 July 1881, as he had been off and on earlier in the summer. He might have even been in the bedroom of fifteen-year-old Paulita Maxwell, the younger sister of Pete Maxwell, when he heard voices outside. The Kid entered the enjoining bedroom of Pete from inside the house and was shot down by Pat Garrett, already in the bedroom. A floor plan of the Maxwell home, discovered in the National Archives, suggests there were no outside doors to Pete's bedroom; if that design is correct, Billy and Garrett could not have entered through an outside door to the bedroom, which thus changes the details of the story.

No major study of Billy the Kid has yet to incorporate this provocative information into a new biography of the outlaw. The details merit more consideration

188. Bell, Bob Boze. "Classic Gunfights: The Kid's First Kill; Henry Antrim vs. Windy Cahill." *True West* 58 (June 2011): 56–57.

Bell builds on the research of Frederick Nolan and Jerry (Richard) Weddle to provide a two-page sketch of the Kid's killing of Windy Cahill in Arizona on 17 August 1877. The account squares with the most authoritative recent accounts of Billy's first killing.

The author includes Cahill's dying words that appeared later in the 23 August 1877 issue of the *Arizona Weekly Star* (20). Other sidebar facts and Bell's innovative illustrations add much to this very brief piece.

A capsule, dependable account of Billy's initial murder.

189. "Billy the Kid—100 Years of Legend." *New Mexico Magazine* 59 (July 1981): 8–9, 16–19, 24–25, 42–46, 48–54.

This special issue on the centennial of Billy's death includes four items: a brief essay by managing editor Scottie King, "Billy the Kid—A Brief Reprise" (pp. 8–9, 24–25); Lynda A. Sánchez's "Recuerdos de Billy the Kid" (pp. 16–19, 68, 70–71); Nora Henn's "The Ranch on the Rio Feliz" (pp. 42–46); and a reprint of John W. Poe's previously published account of "The Killing of Billy the Kid" (pp. 48–50, 52–54).

Surprisingly, the essays do not say that much about Billy the Kid and do not add up to a great deal. King's piece, acceptable for general readers, contains too many errors: Billy did not come to Lincoln County in 1876; he did not work for John Tunstall for two years; Tunstall and McSween were not legal partners; and Garrett did not accompany the Kid from the Santa Fe jail to his trial in Mesilla. And, strangely, King does not push Billy's story through to his death. Sánchez's piece, a composite of *recuerdos* (memories) of a half dozen or so Hispanics whose people knew or knew about Billy, is helpful, but she does not deal with Hispanics like the Baca family, who did not like Billy and testified against him. Also, one wonders whether Hispanics were as convinced that Garrett did not kill the Kid as she suggests. The Henn piece is more about the Hendricks family then owning what had been Tunstall's ranch than about Tunstall—and even less about the Kid. The Poe story had been reprinted several times previous to this publication.

One would have hoped that stronger pieces, more focused on Billy, would have appeared in this centennial issue on Billy's death.

190. Boardman, Mark. "The Lunacy of Billy the Kid." *True West* 57 (August 2010): 42–47.

This brief, well-illustrated piece treats the frenzied stories, the "lunacy" as the writer calls it, dealing with the possible exhumation of Billy's bones to see whether Pat Garrett actually shot him—or someone else—near midnight on 14 July 1881. Boardman's purpose, he says, is not "to prove or disprove Garrett's claim that he killed the Kid" but to treat the controversial story of those wanting to dig up Billy. The essay covers the complicated story from 2003 to 2010. The roles of Tom Sullivan and Steve Sederwall, elected and unelected officials of southeastern New Mexico, and their attempt to use sophisticated DNA studies to confirm or refute Billy's death at the hands of Pat Garrett are the major emphases of this smoothly written piece.

The brief essay treats the political, economic, public relations, and popular cultural implications of the back-and-forth story. Boardman explains how a writer like Frederick Nolan, Billy researcher Gale Cooper, historian Paul Andrew Hutton, New Mexico governor Bill Richardson, and several others were involved in these verbal and legal tugs-of-war. The story here remains incomplete and is more thoroughly treated—from a very partisan viewpoint—in Gale Cooper's mammoth *MegaHoax* (2010) and much more briefly in Bob Boze Bell's "Diggin' Billy," *True West* 57 (August 2010): 8.

A helpful treatment of a rather insignificant part of the Billy story but a subject that has captured major attention throughout the country.

191. Bommersbach, Jana. "Digging Up Billy." *True West* 50 (August–September 2003): 42–45.

This concise story plays off a recent *New York Times* article (5 June 2003) about the plan to dig up the remains of Texan Brushy Bill Roberts and New Mexican John Miller as well as Billy's mother, Catherine Antrim, to examine their DNA and determine the real Billy the Kid. The author also discusses the use of the Brushy Bill story in the recent blockbuster movie *Young Guns II* (1990) even though the screenwriter John Fusco deplored the Roberts story. A sidebar includes editor Bob Boze Bell's "Five Good Reasons Brushy Bill Is Not Billy the Kid" and "Five Good Reasons Why People Will Continue to Believe in Bushy Bill" (p. 45).

191a. Bommersbach, Jana. "Digging Up Billy the Kid's Mother." *True West* 51 (July 2004): 72, 80.

A brief, informative essay summarizing those who favored exhuming the body of Billy the Kid's mother, Catherine McCarty Antrim, in Silver City and Billy's body in Fort Sumner. They wished to prove whether Pat Garrett killed the Kid or someone else in Fort Sumner and perhaps to grant a pardon to Billy or to Brushy Bill Roberts, who claimed to be Billy well into the twentieth century. The author provides balanced commentary on the goals of sheriffs Tom Sullivan, Steve Sederwall, and Gary Graves who favored exhumation and of those in Silver City and Fort Sumner who opposed the "digging up." Contrary to what writer Gale Cooper asserts in her book *Cracking the Billy the Kid Case Hoax* (112), this essay and *True West* magazine are not clearly slanted toward the exhumers.

192. Chamberlain, Kathleen P. "Patrick Floyd Garrett: 'The Man Who Shot Billy the Kid.'" In *With Badges and Bullets: Lawmen and Outlaws of the Old West*, edited by Richard W. Etulain and Glenda Riley. Golden, Colo.: Fulcrum Publishing, 1999, pp. 53–69, 203–5.

Chamberlain's solidly researched and smoothly written essay provides a helpful capsule introduction to Pat Garrett for scholars and general readers. Her interpretations of Garrett are balanced and thoroughly dependable.

Not surprisingly, the essay does not break new ground (clearly not its purpose) but furnishes a compact overview of Garrett's life (1850–1908). The author covers Garrett's life from Texas to New Mexico and then back and forth in Texas and New Mexico. Garrett's pursuit and capture of Billy the Kid in 1880–1881 is clearly covered, with the author suggesting that Garrett and the Kid were more than acquaintances; they were "friends." Diligently following the Kid, Garrett shot him down in Pete Maxwell's darkened bedroom near midnight on 14 July 1881.

In the next thirty years, Garrett lived an up-and-down, troubled life. Not very successful as a lawman, state and county official, and rancher, he was also a distant and unfaithful husband. He had difficulty establishing a positive reputation beyond his notoriety as "the man who shot Billy the Kid." His own life ended in a controversial murder on 29 February 1908. His killer has never been entirely and persuasively identified.

In one succinct sentence, Chamberlain summarizes Garrett's uneven life: "In essence, [Pat] Garrett shot Billy the Kid through the heart, then spent the rest of his life shooting himself in the foot" (p. 54).

193. Chapman, Arthur. "Billy the Kid: A Man All 'Bad.'" *Outing Magazine* 46 (April 1905): 73–77. Reprinted in Frederick Nolan, *The Billy the Kid Reader* (156).

Poet and journalist Arthur Chapman furnishes an overwhelmingly negative portrait of Billy the Kid in this brief early piece. Billy kills Mexicans "just to see them kick," mindlessly murders Chisum cowboys, and is, according to Chapman, "the only white man who slew out of pure wantonness" (p. 79). Chapman was also the writer who imagined the scene in the Mesilla courtroom where he has Judge Warren Bristol sentencing Billy to hang "by the neck until you are dead, dead, dead" and the Kid retorting, "And you can go to hell, hell, hell" (p. 82). No fact substantiates any of Chapman's treatment of this court scene.

Chapman depicts the Lincoln County War as a murderous conflict between legitimate cattle ranchers and violent cow and horse thieves. Billy, for Chapman, captains the thieves. There's no mention here of the Murphy-Dolan contingent or The House business nor of Thomas Catron, the Santa Fe Ring, or the anti-Billy men in the courts. Pat Garrett is lionized as a sturdy, courageous lawman who went after Billy.

Chapman's short essay fits comfortably into the nay-saying pictures of Billy that appeared in the period from the 1890s to the early 1920s. It, too, suffers from the multiple miscues that undermined most of these writings.

194. "Chisum: 'Cattle King of the Pecos.'" *Wild West* 27 (August 2014): 30–37.

Although no author is listed for this essay, Richard Weddle is credited with assisting "with this article" (p. 37), and *Wild West* editor Gregory Lalire provides a sidebar story alongside the essay. The story follows a fairly well-known trail from Chisum's earlier years in Texas to and through his becoming the Cattle King of the Pecos. The piece opens with the rumor of Billy the Kid's threat to kill Chisum unless the cattleman paid him $500 for his role in the Lincoln County War supporting Alex McSween and Chisum interests. Chisum adroitly parried Billy, saying he made no such promise, and did Billy want to kill a white-haired old man who had fed and quartered Billy and some of his riders during the war? Billy backed down and, according to one shaky rumor, replied lamely, "Aw, you ain't worth killing" (p. 31).

A handy essay providing a brief overview of John Chisum's life. For more extensive information on Chisum, see the essays by Harwood P. Hinton (209) and Clifford R. Caldwell's book-length account *John Simpson Chisum: The Cattle King of the Pecos Revisited* (2010).

195. Cline, Don. "The Mystery of Billy the Kid's Home." *Quarterly of the National Association and Center for Outlaw and Lawman History* 12 (Winter 1988): 17–19.

Cline, who wrote a good deal about Billy the Kid, challenges much of what has been stated about the Antrim home in Silver City. Using a series of Sanborn maps, he argues that the house may have been made of adobe rather than sawn lumber (or both), that previously published photographs of the home are incorrect, and that the cabin was not virtually destroyed by a disastrous flood in 1894. Cline's arguments are shaky and in need of more substantiation. The essay is better at challenging previous assumptions and interpretations than in delivering substantial, believable new conclusions.

196. Cline, Don. "Secret Life of Billy the Kid." *True West* (April 1984): 12–17, 62.

This assertive piece unsuccessfully challenges much of the still-accepted information about a half dozen or so incidents of Billy's life. The author says Billy, born in New York, returned from New Mexico to New York City as a teenager and killed a man, then he killed Frank P. Cahill in Arizona, who was not a blacksmith or ex-soldier, and went on to Lincoln County to father two illegitimate children. Cline argues that Billy and John B. "Squire" Wilson stole two horses in Albuquerque, were apprehended, and were jailed in the city. The author hints that Joseph McCarty, the Kid's brother, came to Albuquerque, perhaps arriving there to help the Kid and Squire Wilson to escape. A final section gives additional but convoluted information on brother Joseph and Billy's stepfather, William Antrim. Use with caution; nearly all the best studies of Billy disagree with most of Cline's findings.

197. Corle, Edwin. "Billy the Kid in Arizona." *Arizona Highways* 30 (February 1954): 2–5, 34–35.

Novelist Corle's essay, appearing in the mid-1950s, omits important facts about Billy in Arizona that later researchers uncovered, and it also suffers from mistakes others avoided at that time. The assertive author, however, stood by his story when its accuracy came under challenge.

Basing his story too much on the Garrett-Upson (127) and Burns (103) biographies, Corle incorrectly has Billy's family coming to Coffeyville, Kansas, before he was of school age. Corle is also off track in stating that Billy spent his "formative childhood years and learned to read and write both Spanish and English" in Santa Fe. At twelve or thirteen, Corle mistakenly writes, Billy killed a man in Silver City who had insulted his mother. Generally, Corle salutes the Garrett-Upson book as the "cornerstone on which a whole superstructure of Billy the Kid literature has been built" (p. 3).

The Arizona section of the essay has Billy arriving in the territory in 1872, but he did not until 1875—in fact, he may not have even come to Santa Fe by 1872. Moreover, Billy did not kill three Indians while in Arizona. Nor, as subsequent research tells us, he did not become a partner with a twenty-year-old "Alien" and beat the Apaches in several competitions. The story about the Kid's killing of a soldier, perhaps a "Negro," lacks details about the victim's name, cites the wrong date for the incident as 1873, and scrambles what other informants were stating about Windy Cahill's death in 1877. Then follows false information about Billy's traveling to and staying in Mexico for several months.

Corle closes his piece by castigating wrongheaded dime novels about the Kid, continuing to praise the Garrett-Upson biography, and mentioning J. C. Dykes's new book *Billy the Kid: The Bibliography of a Legend* (14) but overlooks the very recent, pathbreaking essays of Philip Rasch (234–50) and Robert Mullin (249–50) that would have challenged much of what Corle writes here.

198. Cozzens, Gary. "A Parting Shot: At Lincoln Historic Site, Theories Have a Way of Coming Out in the Woodwork." *El Palacio* 121 (Fall 2016): 82.

A former manager of the Lincoln Historic Site, Cozzens disagrees with one of the widely held beliefs about Billy's escape from the Lincoln jail on 28 April 1881. The author dismisses as a hoax the story of Billy's shot bouncing off the stairwell wall and into the back of Deputy James Bell. According to information that Cozzens recently gathered, no such bullet hole was in evidence before the 1950s. The story of the caroming bullet was a put-up job, Cozzens asserts, of two mythmakers. Now, if Cozzens is to be followed, we will need a new story of Billy, his unusual shot, and the current bullet hole in the wall.

199. Curtis, John B. "A Footnote to Frontier History." *New Mexico Magazine* 5 (May 1953): 25, 40–41.

This article by a journalist caused firestorms of surprise and conflict among Billy the Kid researchers in the early 1950s and helped lead to the eventual rupture between Robert N. Mullin and Philip J. Rasch, two sterling Kid specialists. Once Mullin's daughter, Frances Daseler, located the records of the marriage between Billy's mother, Catherine McCarty, and William H.

Antrim in the Presbyterian Church files in Santa Fe, author Curtis heard the news from historian Maurice Garland Fulton and put the story on the AP wire and then wrote this story.

Locating the records of the McCarty-Antrim marriage on 1 March 1873 upset the chronology and names involved in the early Billy stories inherited from the Garrett-Upson biography (127). Now a new timeline with newly corrected names had to be pieced together. The first steps in that complicated process were the very important jointly authored essays by Mullin and Rasch (249–50). Several years later, emotional arguments between Mullin and Rasch ended their friendship and carried bitter feelings into the future.

200. "Deluvina Maxwell." *Outlaw Gazette* 29 (2016): 4.

This brief interview with Deluvina Maxwell, the Native American slave-servant of the Maxwell family, was conducted by Texas historian J. Evetts Haley and appears here for the first time in print. Deluvina expresses her feelings for Billy: he "was my compadre, my friend, poor Billy." She also states that Billy became angry after rancher John Chisum refused to keep a promise and pay Billy "if he would up and fight Murphy at Lincoln." The Cattle King broke his promise and refused to "pay [Billy] a cent and that is what made him so mean."

Deluvina also counters what most storytellers say about the hectic minutes following Pat Garrett's killing of Billy in Pete Maxwell's bedroom. She did not go immediately into the bedroom to see whether Billy was dead, as many accounts have it. In fact, she did not "see Billy the night after he was killed, but saw him the following morning."

This brief but important interview conducted in the 1920s, shortly before Deluvina's death, carries new, important information.

201. Etulain, Richard W. "Billy the Kid: Thunder in the West." In *With Badges and Bullets: Lawmen and Outlaws n the Old West*, edited by Richard W. Etulain and Glenda Riley. Golden, Colo.: Fulcrum Publishing, 1999, pp. 123–38, 209–11.

This concise essay foreshadows Etulain's conclusions in his later writings about Billy the Kid. In this brief biographical and interpretive overview, the author contends that the Kid was a complex figure, a combination of good buddy and murderous villain. For Etulain, the oxymoronic definitions work best: Billy was a good-bad man, a companion-desperado, neither a white nor a black hat but a gray one.

Etulain follows most of the contentions of writers such as Robert Utley and Frederick Nolan. He notes the mysteries surrounding Billy's origins, probably in New York City in 1859, and posits that the Kid killed his first man, "Windy" Cahill, in Camp Grant, Arizona, in August 1877. In dealing with the Lincoln County War, the author sides more with the Kid, John Tunstall, and Alex and Sue McSween contingent than with The House team of L. G. Murphy and Jimmy Dolan. He also contends that when Col. Nathan Dudley unwisely brought his troops into the town of Lincoln on the fateful morning of 19 July 1878, known as the Big Kill, the military leader turned the tide away from Billy's side toward that of his opponents. The author also briefly traces the nefarious links between the Santa Fe Ring and legal officials in southern New Mexico, all to Billy's detriment. This account neither praises nor criticizes the dealings of Gov. Lew Wallace and Sheriff Pat Garrett with the Kid.

The final two pages of the essay (pp. 137–38) discuss the shifting interpretations of Billy in the writings and movies following his death until the end of the twentieth century. A brief bibliographical essay (pp. 209–11) summarizes and evaluates the major histories and biographies about Billy the Kid.

202. Etulain, Richard W. "The Legendary, Mysterious Kid." *Wild West* 31 (February 2019): 38–43.

The author briefly addresses seven enduring mysteries surrounding Billy the Kid. These include his birthplace and early years, his family's life up to 1873, brother Joe and stepfather William Antrim, Billy's escape from the Lincoln jail in 1881, his possible sweethearts, Garrett's shooting of Billy in 1881, and the Kid's persisting hold on so many readers and viewers. Etulain also adds sections on "10 Things You Need to Know about Outlaw Billy the Kid" (p. 10) and "Must See, Must Read" (pp. 82–83) on key Kid movies and books (biographies and novels). Editor Greg Lalire supplies interesting information surrounding the Kid in his "Editor's Letter" (p. 4), and the magazine staff has put together a collage of book covers and movie stills in "Pop Culture Kid" (pp. 44–45).

203. Etulain, Richard W. "Is There Anything Else to Say about Billy the Kid?" *Journal of the Wild West History Association* 11 (December 2018): 26–29.

In this very short piece, Etulain encourages writers to think about the several large and less extensive projects still available to authors wishing to write about Billy the Kid. Although more than one thousand books and essays have been published, there is room for more.

The author notes among the larger topics that books are needed on Billy's connections with women, including adult women like his mother, Catherine McCarty Antrim, and women in Silver City and Lincoln County, New Mexico. Then there are the possible sweethearts, including several in the Fort Sumner area, especially Paulita Maxwell. We also need a book on Billy's important connections with Hispanics, particularly those who rode with him in Lincoln but also those who were his opponents.

The influences of several persons who had close or nearby contact with Billy still need to have those influences traced. Chief among these are Alex McSween, L. G. Murphy, and Jimmy Dolan—but also more distant men like Thomas Catron and other legal officials in Santa Fe and Lincoln County. And we still do not have enough on the important links between political leaders in Washington, D.C., and their shaping power on Lincoln County and Billy.

Finally, we need to think about the shifting interpretations of Billy over time. We still lack careful studies of the changing views of Billy in biographies and histories, novels, and specific films. In this regard, Etulain reminds us that persons' views about facts are often as important as the facts themselves in understanding Billy.

So, yes, there is still a good deal to be written about Billy the Kid, and judging from the past, readers will continue flocking to books about him.

204. Fergusson, Harvey. "Billy the Kid." *American Mercury* 5 (June 1925): 224–31. Reprinted in Fredrick Nolan, *The Billy the Kid Reader* (156).

Harvey Fergusson, a New Mexican from a distinguished political family, grew up in Billy the Kid country and wrote several historical novels about the Southwest. His abbreviated essay on the Kid appeared in cultural critic H. L. Mencken's *American Mercury*, which, only a year old, had already gained a wide, enthusiastic readership.

Fergusson opens his essay with a major question—and his answer: "Who remembers Billy the Kid? He is no more than an echo of a name today . . ." (p. 89). But, the author argues, Billy should be seen as the epitome of the "primitive pastoral epoch" (p. 90) of the West's history stretching from the Civil War to the 1890s.

Fergusson piles up mistakes. He has Billy hating William Antrim, stabbing to death a man in Silver City, and befriending Jessie Evans there. Arizona is overlooked, and Billy spends considerable time in Mexico, killing as he thinks warranted. Fergusson also mistakenly names Billy as leader of the McSween faction before that happened and incorrectly states that the Kid did not accept Gov. Lew Wallace's offer of a pardon for testifying against the murders of lawyer Huston Chapman.

Conversely, Fergusson gets right the conflict between The House (Murphy-Dolan) and the McSween-Tunstall-Chisum cohorts—much more specifically and correctly than other contemporaries writing about Billy. Most of the author's accounts of Billy's capture, escape, and killing are also close to the known facts. Like Walter Noble Burns (103) the next year, Fergusson views Billy as the last gasp of a disappearing Wild West that soon transitioned toward a civilized state.

Prolific Kid specialist Frederick Nolan points out that Fergusson was wide of the mark in 1925 speaking of the Kid as unknown when in the next year Burns's *The Saga of Billy the Kid* ignited a firestorm of rekindled interest in Billy the Kid that continues today. One might add that the 1920s and early 1930s were aflame with interest in the Old West, as the Western novels of Zane Grey and Max Brand; the films of William S. Hart, Tom Mix, and several others; and the new biographies of Wild Bill Hickok, Calamity Jane, and Wyatt Earp abundantly attest.

205. Fishwick, Marshall. "Billy the Kid: Faust in America." *Saturday Review*, 11 October 1952, 11–12, 34–36.

Fishwick provides a provocative comparison between the German legendary figure Faust and Billy the Kid. As the author notes, "like the historical Faust . . . Billy the Kid was not so much invented as endowed with traits of the great folk heroes of earlier cultures" (p. 12). In most of his essay Fishwick credits Ash Upson, Charlie Siringo, Emerson Hough, and Walter Noble Burns with transitioning the Kid "from history into legend so rapidly that no one has figured out just what happened" (p. 12).

An early, singularly important study of four writers who were central to the birth of Billy as a legendary figure, this essay deserves wider recognition as a valuable pioneering essay. Upson, Fishwick says, was "the major architect of the Kid's legend," but his and Garrett's book sold poorly. Siringo's book *A Texas Cowboy* (1885), on the other hand, sold by the hundreds of thousands, making him "by far the most important disseminator of the [Billy] legend to the average American reader" (p. 35). Emerson Hough, in the early twentieth century, "put horns and tails on the juvenile killer," picturing Billy as "Faust gone Western" (p. 35). Burns "revised" rather than "invent[ed] . . . the Kid's saga." A superb wordsmith, Burns used turns of phrase and dramatic storytelling that made Billy into "more of a god than a man" (p. 36).

Fishwick shows in this brief essay how this quartet of authors launched Billy the Kid legends from the 1880s to the 1920s. His insights remain eminently valuable for readers decades later.

206. Fulton, Maurice G. "Apocrypha of Billy the Kid." *Folk Say* (1930): 12–26.

Fulton, a leading authority on the Lincoln County War and Billy the Kid (whom Fulton did not like), reprints in this piece four sections of a dime-novel-like fictional serial appearing in the Santa Fe newspaper the *New Mexican* "toward the close of 1882 [sic, 1881]" (p. 14). Fulton's introductory and concluding remarks are too brief and general to add a great deal. The four reprinted sections—chapters 7, 9, 10, and 11 of the serial—illustrate the Wild West fiction of the 1880s that appeared in a dozen or so dime novels about the Kid. For more commentary on the series, see entry 63.

207. Gardner, Mark Lee. "Pat Garrett: The Life and Death of a Great Sheriff." *Wild West* 24 (August 2011): 28–37.

Gardner follows the Pat Garrett–Billy the Kid connection that powered his very good book on those two men (126). He provides a positive image of Garrett: an excellent law man, dependable and courageous, although at times challenged by his gambling addiction and unwise decisions. The first half of the essay deals with Garrett's links to Billy and his twice-launched hunt for and eventual killing of the Kid. Later, beset by people incessantly calling him "the man who shot Billy the Kid," he sometimes wished that he had missed and Billy had gotten free. Gardner thinks we are mistaken in what we say about Garrett: "The real tragedy of Garrett's legacy is that he was so much more" than merely the killer of Billy, "and we *have* forgotten that" (p. 37).

The second half of the essay treats Garrett's difficulties as a rancher, investor, and law officer. Garrett's mistake in bringing a saloon man to a photographing session with President Theodore Roosevelt ended his well-paid position as a custom's collector in El Paso. Garrett's career tumbled downward, ending in his controversial death from shooting in 1908.

A sympathetic, smoothly written account of Pat Garrett.

Gregory Lalire, editor of *Wild West*, adds a readable, valuable one-page editorial on the Garrett-Kid relationship (p. 4).

208. Gomber, Drew. "The Death of Alexander McSween." *Outlaw Gazette* 29 (2016): 3–4.

Gomber, a longtime fixture in Lincoln who gave valuable tours of the town and its environs, provides another perspective on the killing of Alex McSween on 19 July 1878, the final day of the Five-Day Battle. Derived from information that Kid researcher Maurice Garland Fulton gathered many years before but had not published because he was threatened with death if he did, Gomber's story came to him via Bob Mullin and Lewis Ketring, both of whom were dedicated students of Billy's life.

This story line states that McSween died after John Jones, son of the notable Barbara "Ma'am" Jones (and both friends of Billy's, though on the opposition side), shot Bob Beckwith, a Murphy loyalist, and then a bullet blizzard immediately broke out. In the avalanche of shooting, McSween and others were killed. No one person is credited with killing McSween after the lawyer supposedly stopped his escape and yelled out, "Never surrender."

New information on, and a challenge to, a long-held story about a high point in the Lincoln County War.

209. Hinton, Harwood, Jr. "John Simpson Chisum, 1877–84." *New Mexico Historical Review* 31 (July 1956): 177–205; 31 (October 1956): 310–38; 32 (January 1957): 53–65.

This three-part biographical piece on the final years of John Chisum remains, after more than half a century, the best source on Chisum during the Lincoln County War and thereafter. Hinton's research is remarkably thorough, his writing clear and straightforward.

Briefly tracing Chisum's career before he came to New Mexico in 1872, Hinton emphasizes the Cattle King's courageous and ambitious character. By the early 1870s Chisum had gained a reputation for watchfulness and a go-ahead drive. One succinct sentence sums up Hinton's take on Chisum: he was "singular and shadowy in character, but in personality and manner an extrovert in the fullest sense" (p. 184).

Chisum's connections with Billy the Kid were not extensive. In the early fall of 1877, Billy came to the Chisum ranch looking for work. The Kid was "with" Chisum for a few days but was never offered a job. Chisum stood, somewhat, for the Tunstall-McSween coterie that Billy backed, but after the Big Kill in summer 1878, conflict between the cattleman and the outlaw heightened, with Billy accusing Chisum of never "paying up" the riders who had supported him and kept his herds safe. Hinton has Chisum and Billy meeting in Fort

Sumner and Billy challenging Chisum to pay up, but Hinton does not quote the words that others use in suggesting that Billy was ready to shoot Chisum.

Hinton provides no conclusion or summing-up and does not put Chisum in much context, but he is strong in showing the Washington, D.C., influences on Lincoln County. It would have been helpful, too, for Hinton to have suggested why Chisum took such a distant position on the Lincoln County events of 1878.

210. Hough, Emerson. "Billy the Kid: The True Story of a Western 'Bad Man.'" *Everybody's Magazine*, September 1901, 307–10. Reprinted in Frederick W. Nolan, *The Billy the Kid Reader* (156).

An in-between piece by Hough, Billy as rogue or not, appearing after his *The Story of the Cowboy* (1897) and before his novel *Heart's Desire* (290) and *The Story of the Outlaw* (1907), this essay also is less off track than Hough's earlier work but more mistake-ridden than the later work by other authors on Billy. Hough lived for parts of two years in White Oaks, New Mexico, and knew Pat Garrett and Lincoln County War participants, but he frequently accepted mythic events and imagined others.

Hough disliked Billy the Kid, whom he describes as "the most thoroughly bad of all the bad men in the really bad times of the West" (p. 62). He begins by stating that Billy, at age fourteen and in Arizona, drew a knife and stabbed a man who had been disrespectful to Billy's mother. All wrong. The mistakes add up: Billy is buried in Las Cruces, he killed twenty-one men in his twenty-one years, and he lusted continually to shoot someone. Unfortunately, Hough also gets the details of Billy's escape and his death at the hands of Pat Garrett mostly wrong.

For Hough, the West was a wild place, with thousands of unruly and uncivilized men (mostly mixed-bloods, including "Greasers") and "few [women] entitled to the name of womanhood," and "of civilization . . . there was nothing" (p. 63). Billy grew up in these surroundings, both influenced by the lawless surroundings and adding to the violence. The Kid "was an animal," Hough writes, "an animal born with a cat soul, blood-thirsty, loving to kill" (p. 65).

Building on this blackguard image of Billy, Hough says the Kid and his buddies killed seven Hispanics "just to see them kick" (p. 66). Stories of exaggerated violence pile up deeper and deeper in Hough's account. Four hundred people were killed in the Lincoln County War, with Billy, the "little wild beast" (p. 70), continuing to kill.

Here is another example of an early portrait of Billy as an entirely bad man. Regrettably, the piece is, for the most part, undependable on facts.

211. Hutton, Paul Andrew. "Billy the Kid's Final Escape." *Wild West* 28 (December 2015): 28–32.

Hutton's dramatic, appealing essay proves that familiar information can be retold in a fresh, inviting manner. This abbreviated piece, describing Billy the Kid's famous escape from the Lincoln County jail on 28 April 1881, concisely treats the personalities, actions, and varied interpretations of Billy's flight and dash into continuing immortality.

Hutton sides with Robert Utley in arguing that Billy began his escape by overcoming Deputy J. W. Bell, grabbing his pistol, and shooting Bell when he tried to dash down the jail's back steps. Hutton also follows most writers in castigating Robert Olinger as the bully villain of the story. Finally, he likewise believes that the breakout and tales about it led to something new. As Hutton puts it, "the dramatic final escape of Billy the Kid was a daring leap into the mists of legend" (p. 32). An example of first-rate, inviting narrative history.

The page following this essay, also by Hutton, titled "Hollywood's Take on Billy's Break" (p. 33), features four movie stills and brief commentary. The next two pages (pp. 34–35), titled "A Look around Lincoln," furnish more than half a dozen photos on recent Lincoln.

212. Hutton, Paul Andrew. "Dreamscape Desperado." *New Mexico Magazine* 68 (June 1990): 44–57.

See entry 340 for discussion of this essay.

213. King, David. "The Pecos War." *True West* 43 (December 1996): 18–22; 44 (January 1997): 12–15.

King chronicles the mounting tensions between large ranchers John Chisum and Bob Wylie on one side and smaller ranchers including Seven Rivers men such as Buck Powell, Dick Smith, Andy Boyle, the Beckwith family, and the Olingers on the other. Disappointed with the rough life and small dollars they made as cowboys, the Seven Rivers contingent—including some of those who had ridden for Chisum—decided to rustle cattle from Chisum, the Cattle King, and launch their own herds. Conflicts intensified, shooting broke out, and the Pecos War began in spring 1877.

A full-scale war seemed on the near horizon on 20 April, when a contingent of as many as thirty Chisum-Wylie riders surrounded the Beckwith home. But heavy fire from the home defenders and the we-won't-give-up attitude of the house gunmen defused the situation. The attackers realized that to go after those in the Beckwith house meant certain death for more than a few men. So, rather than launch an attack, they withdrew. Later, as a compromise, Chisum and Wylie agreed to pay back wages owed to several of the Seven Rivers riders. Tempers cooled.

But, meanwhile, Chisum had connected with Tunstall and McSween, and the Seven Rivers men had linked up with the Dolan side of the mounting Lincoln County turmoil. Those forged contacts would come into play the next spring. In short, the Pecos War helped usher in the conflicts that would come to fore in spring 1878 in Lincoln County and would whirl around Billy the Kid.

214. Klasner, Lily Casey. "The Kid." In Frederick Nolan, *The Billy the Kid Reader* (156).

Nolan reconstructs from Klasner's manuscript notes, which are on file in the Brigham Young University Library Special Collections, her negative reactions to the Kid. Some of this information appeared in different form in Eve Ball's edited *My Girlhood among Outlaws* by Lily Klasner (1972), but here Nolan pulls together an essay from the raw materials of Klasner's scribblings about the Kid. Lily Casey Klasner was (from girlhood) highly critical of Billy, dismissing him as "a little outlaw tramp" (p. 240) and states in stories that circulated "he was just a trifling no account street urchen [sic] and little bum around town" (p. 244). True, she concedes, he had difficult early teen years, losing his mother and being virtually abandoned by his stepfather, but fell in with bad company and early on tumbled into trouble—and stayed there.

Lily's animosity boils over in her treatment of "Thunston" and "McLain" (Tunstall and McSween), including calling the latter a "jackleg" lawyer. Her criticisms of the Murphy-Dolan contingent are muted, her comments on John Chisum less opinionated.

This compilation of Lily's comments ends with her ruminations fifty years after the Kid's life. She warns readers to avoid applauding the deeds of Billy the Kid. Americans should "hang their heads in shame" for honoring Billy and his ilk. "He was [not only] a ruthless outlaw . . . but caught without arms he was a rat" (p. 246).

Despite Nolan's admirable efforts to put Lily's jumbled thoughts and writing in understandable form, this section reveals, most of all, Klasner's shortcomings as a writer and thinker. Still, she clearly represents those who hated Billy the Kid.

215. Koop, W. E. "Billy the Kid: The Trail of a Kansas Legend." *The Trail Guide* (Kansas City Posse of the Westerners) 9 (September 1964): 4–19.

This essay, for the first time, uncovered much of what we still know—more than a half century later—about Billy and his family in the Wichita, Kansas, area in the years 1870–1871. Koop digs out records of land and property ownership by Catherine McCarty and William Antrim, sometimes near to one another. Bracketing this helpful information in Kansas is a brief mention of possible earlier happenings in New York and Indiana and bits about events later in New Mexico. The author also deals succinctly with the Antrim family in and out of Kansas in later years.

What matters most here is that Henry McCarty had moved again—for at least the third time in half a dozen years or a bit more—from New York City to Indiana and now on to Kansas. Changes in living styles and settings, especially considering he moved three times more in the next two years, were already part of Billy's DNA when he arrived in Silver City, New Mexico, in 1873.

This brief piece by Koop remains our major and best source on Billy's short stay in Kansas even more than fifty years after its publication.

216. McCright, Grady C., and James H. Powell, "Disorder in Lincoln County: Frank Warner Angel's Reports." *Rio Grande History* 12 (1981): 1–24.

A brief, helpful overview of the Frank Warner Angel reports on New Mexico, this essay provides needed information on that key investigation and Angel's findings. The authors summarize the backgrounds of the Tunstall killing; the New Mexico and Washington, D.C., pressures for an inquiry on the murder; the Angel interviews; the Big Kill in July 1878; and the Angel reports and their impact on New Mexico. Although Angel dismissed wrongful actions by New Mexico political leaders as the cause of the Tunstall's death, he did criticize Gov. Samuel B. Axtell's faulty leadership and hinted at Thomas B. Catron's misdirected actions. Angel attempted to be nonpartisan but found The House supporters to be the more guilty party in Lincoln County conflicts. The investigator interviewed more McSween men than Dolan supporters, but he turned up little information on Billy the Kid and did not speak to Jimmy Dolan.

A useful summary of an important document. The writers are correct in stating that the Angel report "is possibly the most detailed primary source available on the famous civilian conflict" (p. 3). The report should be edited and published; it is an immensely important document for understanding New Mexico in Billy the Kid's time.

217. McCubbin, Robert G. "The 100th Anniversary of Pat Garrett's Life." *True West* 55 (January–February 2008): 32–41.

The leading collector of Old West photographs, Robert McCubbin provides a succinct, sweeping overview of Pat Garrett's up-and-down life. Throughout, the essay features valuable photographs from McCubbin's huge collection and from other collections. The first pages are on target in noting the false depictions of Billy as hero and of Garrett as villain in so many Wild West stories. McCubbin, in balanced fashion, points to Garrett's strengths—his "efficient and conscientious" actions (p. 34)—and to his "faults"—"fondness for drinking and gambling" (p. 33). The closing pages treat Garrett's faltering life as a lawman and his failures as a politician and rancher.

A short but evenhanded piece on Pat Garrett a century after his death.

218. Metz, Leon C. "Billy the Kid and Pat Garrett." *True West* 4 (July 1997): 12–17.

The biographer of Pat Garrett is not at his best in this essay about Billy and Garrett. His opening section on Billy is rife with small errors, including giving wrong dates for the deaths of Catherine McCarty Antrim and Buckshot Roberts, citing George (not Frank) Coe's injury at Blazer's Mill, and misspelling Huston Chapman's name. Plus, the story is told in an off-putting jerky style.

The section on Garrett, on the other hand, is entirely correct and more smoothly told. Metz does not take sides on how Billy obtained a pistol to kill Deputy Bell in his escape from the Lincoln jail and avoids commentary on what weapons Billy carried into Pete Maxwell's bedroom, an event that Metz dates as 13 July 1881, not 14 July.

A bit disappointing from a major authority on Pat Garrett because of the too-numerous mistakes.

219. Metz, Leon. "The Death of Billy the Kid." *Wild West* 11 (August 1998): 30, 73.

Metz succinctly summarizes what most of the well-researched accounts say about Garrett's shooting of Billy the Kid. But he advances alternate views, too: he says the shooting occurred on 13 July 1881 (not 14 July), and he thinks Garrett heard Billy's voice outside Maxwell's bedroom when he asked the two deputies there, *"Quien es?"* and prepared himself for a violent encounter. This is a very useful distillation of Metz's biography of Garrett (149), still the best source we have on the subject. Metz is wrong, however, to speak of Paulita Maxwell as Pete Maxwell's daughter rather than his younger sister.

A sidebar essay by Metz, titled "Ten Billy the Kid Myths" (p. 32), lists ten misconceptions about Billy. Another sidebar essay by Sherry Robinson, "Another Version: How Garrett Found the Kid" (p. 33), recounts the Floersheim family traditions that Solomon Floersheim was the person who informed Garrett that Billy was hiding out in Fort Sumner.

220. Metz, Leon C. "The Pat Garrett Nobody Knows." *The West* 6 (October 1972): 32–35.

Metz adeptly summarizes Garrett's life after his killing of Billy in 1881. That dramatic happening, Metz writes, "brought Garrett more misery than fame" (p. 32). When Garrett and writer Emerson Hough retraced the sheriff's tracks into Lincoln County, Garrett stated at Billy's grave in Fort Sumner that he hoped, if there was another life, that the Kid and his buddies Tom Folliard and Charles Bowdre were making "better use of it than the one I put them out of" (p. 43). Probing and revealing about Garrett's personality.

221. Metz, Leon C. "The Truth and the Tall Tales of Pat Garrett." *New Mexico Magazine* 86 (February 2008): 52–55.

Written at the one hundredth anniversary of Garrett's death, this abbreviated essay summarizes the major events of Garrett's life, especially after the shooting of Billy the Kid in July 1881. Not surprisingly, Metz dismisses the story of Brushy Bill being the real Billy who survived and defends Garrett's quick decision to take Billy's life rather than forfeit his own. A good brief story for general readers.

222. Miller, Darlis A. "The Women of Lincoln County, 1860–1900." In *New Mexico Women: Intercultural Perspectives*, edited by Joan M. Jensen and Darlis A. Miller. Albuquerque: University of New Mexico Press, 1986, pp. 169–200. Reprinted in *Writing the Range: Race, Class, and Culture in the Women's West*, edited by Elizabeth Jameson and Susan Armitage. Norman: University of Oklahoma Press, 1997, pp. 147–71.

No one has written a more revealing account of Hispanic and Anglo women's experiences in Lincoln County during Billy the Kid's time than Darlis Miller, longtime professor of history at New Mexico State University. Miller asks us to rethink Lincoln County history by focusing also on the experiences of women and families rather than solely on the actions of male ranchers, businessmen, outlaws, and laboring men. Through diligent research in census records, agricultural schedules, deed books, probate records, and newspapers, Miller illustrates this region's sociocultural history in revealing terms different from those in previous county histories. Miller's census-by-census examination profiles the shifting imbalances and balances of Hispanic-Anglo populations, gender distributions among both groups, intermarriage rates and mixed-race numbers, and the changes in occupational and economic status.

We get additional new information and contexts for such women as Ma'am Jones, Ellen Casey, and the Fritz and Baca families—all of whom had contact with Billy the Kid. Most extensive is the coverage of the remarkable career of Susan McSween Barber, from lawyer's wife to widow to Cattle Queen. Miller also emphasizes the class and inheritance patterns of these women, and we learn about important acts of cooperation across class and racial lines.

Seen whole, this piece means we should see the Kid's life in Lincoln County in new contexts—the shifting significance of women and family in a changing Lincoln County.

223. Mills, William A. "Kid Brother." *Journal of the Wild West History Association* 12 (March 2019): 26–41.

Finally we get here a well-researched essay on Billy the Kid's brother, Joe (Joseph McCarty Antrim, 1863?–1930). Mills has combed census, city directory, retirement and pension, and other records to provide the fullest account yet published on Joe Antrim.

Mills's research reveals that Joe was Billy's *younger* brother, not his older brother as more than a few have argued. The author turns up several documents that indicate Joe was born in 1863, not before 1859. Most of this valuable essay, however, deals with Joe's life after Billy's death. We learn of Joe's residing in New Mexico and Texas but mainly in Denver, Colorado, between 1890 and 1930. His occupations included laborer, deputy sheriff, clerk, and—particularly—gambler. He married Jennie Stone on 19 December 1891 in Pueblo, Colorado, and may have even fathered a child with her in about 1888.

Mills extensively quotes several pertinent newspaper stories about Joe, including those dealing with events in New Mexico and Colorado. He also summarizes useful information about William Antrim, the stepfather of Joe and his brother, Billy the Kid.

An important piece filling in new details about Joe Antrim. The essay suggests how much a diligent researcher might still turn up on Billy the Kid and his family.

224. Nolan, Frederick W. "The Birth of an Outlaw." *True West*, 17 May 2015. https://truewestmagazine.com/article/the-birth-of-an-outlaw/.

Nolan advances a new view of Billy the Kid's origins. Rereading and reconsidering the names of the witnesses at the McCarty-Antrim marriage in Santa Fe in March 1873, the author traces their backgrounds to Utica, New York, where he finds a Catherine McCarty and Billy McCarty living in 1860–1861. He reads the marriage witness name "Josie" McCarty as short for Josephine McCarty, whom he speculates was the controversial sister of Catherine. Squeezing the new information he has turned up, Nolan is convinced that Billy was born in Utica, New York, not in New York City in 1859. A speculative piece that deserves second thoughts and more research.

225. Nolan, Frederick. "Dick Brewer: The Unlikely Gunfighter." *Quarterly of the National Association and Center for Outlaws and Lawman History* 15 (July–September 1991): 19–27.

Typical of Nolan's writings, this essay runs full of new information on Dick Brewer (1850–1878), who came to Lincoln County in about 1870. Although the piece contains little on Billy the Kid, it provides never-before-stated facts on the life and activities of Brewer, who came to mean much to the Kid in late 1877 and early 1878. In these months Brewer was foreman of Tunstall's ranch on the Rio Feliz and also operating his own ranch—a testimony to Brewer's diligent, hardworking character. Once the Kid signed on with Tunstall in late 1877, he and Brewer were often together—up through Tunstall's death the next February and Brewer's own demise two months later at the shootout at Blazer's Mill. In the days between these two murderous happenings, the Kid rode with Brewer, who served as leader of the Regulators. Brewer did not take part in Brady's assassination on 1 April 1878, and Nolan states that Brewer, not the Kid, swore vengeance at Tunstall's funeral, promising "to get" those who killed the Englishman.

The place for information on Dick Brewer; well researched and thoroughly documented.

226. Nolan, Frederick. "First Blood: Another Look at the Killing of 'Windy' Cahill." *Outlaw Gazette* 13 (November 2000): 2–4. Reprinted in Frederick Nolan, *The Billy the Kid Reader* (156).

Nolan sets the scene and introduces the actors in the actions that led to Billy's shooting of Francis "Windy" Cahill. The essay deals with Fort Grant in eastern Arizona; nearby buildings such as the Atkins cantina and Bonita

Store; and persons like Miles Wood, an Arizona rancher, and John Mackie, Billy's horse-thief partner. Following Wood's remembrances, Nolan traces the escalating stealing of Kid Antrim and Mackie.

Cahill, nicknamed Windy "because he was always blowin' about one thing and another" (p. 229), was a former army man and now a blacksmith. A short but stocky young man, he began bullying the Kid. On the evening of 17 August 1877 Billy showed up at the Atkins saloon, and Cahill began harassing him, roughing his hair, throwing him on the floor, and pummeling him. They exchanged insults, and Billy asked Windy to stop hurting him. When Cahill refused and said he wanted to hurt him, Billy slipped a pistol out of his pants, poked it into Windy's belly, and fired off a killing shot. Cahill died a painful death the next day. Not waiting for any reactions, Billy bolted out of the cantina, grabbed an available horse, and galloped eastward toward New Mexico.

This piece, except for the final two paragraphs on Cahill's burial, includes no new information that Nolan had not provided earlier, but it is a very helpful brief recapitulation of the Kid's first killing. Without saying so, Nolan counters those who argue that Billy killed only when he faced death. The Kid was being mauled but not threatened with murder. He did not face a gun in Atkins's saloon in eastern Arizona on the night of 17 August 1877.

227. Nolan, Frederick. "The Hunting of Billy the Kid." *Wild West* 16 (June 2003): 38–44.

Nolan provides a concise account of the hunt for Billy the Kid in the closing weeks of 1880. Although the main outline of Nolan's story is well known, he includes quotes from previously unpublished sources including persons such as Jim East, Frank Clifford ("Big Foot Wallace"), and Garrett H. "Kid" Dobbs. These new quotations add fresh material to familiar stories. No one has yet utilized these findings in a new overview of Billy the Kid.

Intriguingly, Nolan posits that it is "more than possible that Pat Garrett . . . and his close associate Barney Mason accompanied the Kid and his men on some of these raids" (p. 38) to steal horses in the Texas panhandle in 1880.

Nolan adds a brief sidebar biographical profile, "The Kid's Life" (p. 44), and Gregory Lalire, editor of *Wild West*, contributes further information in a nicely phrased one-page editorial titled "The Kid Never Grows Up" (p. 6).

228. Nolan, Frederick. "So, Who was Dan Detrick?" *True West* 58 (June 2011): 34–35. https://truewestmagazine.com/so-who-was-dan-dedrick/.

A two-page piece of text and photos, this pen portrait traces the Dan Detrick family from Indiana to New Mexico and up to the present. Nolan follows the route of the tintype that Billy gifted to Detrick up to the time it was to be sold, which occurred in June 2011.

Interesting bits of comparison between the similar dress of Billy in his tintype and of Detrick in a tintype of him add value to the piece.

229. Nolan, Frederick W. "The Search for Alexander McSween." *New Mexico Historical Review* 62 (July 1987): 287–301.

Frederick Nolan displays here his tenacious across-the-Atlantic research in this short essay on Alex McSween's pre–Lincoln County days. Now thirty years old, this piece nonetheless contains much of we know about the enigmatic lawyer.

Nolan pieces together the first thirty-plus years of McSween's life. Like other biographers and historians, Nolan has had to rely largely on wife Susan McSween's vague comments. We still do not know whether McSween was born in Scotland or Canada; where he studied for the ministry; what he did, exactly, before enrolling in the Washington University Law School in Saint Louis; and how he made a living in Eureka, Kansas, before coming west to New Mexico Territory in 1875. Nolan reveals that, for the most part, McSween gained a good reputation as an upstanding man and lawyer, but he did leave Kansas with unpaid debts, which were not paid until after his death in 1878.

Nolan's research here was worked into his full-scale history, *The Lincoln County War: A Documentary History* (153). Only Kathleen Chamberlain's first-rate biography of Susan McSween, *In the Shadow of Billy the Kid: Susan McSween and the Lincoln County War* (106), expands on Nolan's findings. We still need a full-length biography of Alex McSween, although the scarcity and vagueness of research materials may turn away all but the most ambitious of researchers.

230. Nolan, Frederick. "She Taught the Kid a Lesson: The Life of Mary Richards." *True West* 53 (May 2006): 51–53.

This brief piece corrects previous information on Billy's teacher Mary Phillipa Richards Casey (1847–1901) and adds new facts to the story. Mary arrived in Silver City in 1874 and began teaching that September. Billy and his brother, Joe, were her students for about a year before Billy got in serious trouble by stealing clothes and "skinned" out of town in September 1875. Billy and his teacher both spoke warmly of their friendship, and others saw her as an extraordinary teacher who "had . . . [her students'] interest excited and their advancement was certain." Billy also felt an affinity for Miss

Richards because she, like him, was ambidextrous. He was certain that this two-handedness proved that they were related.

Billy's warmth for Mary Richards illustrates how much women influenced and impacted his life, including his mother, Clara Truesdell (the mother of his friend Chauncey), and a clutch of Hispanic *señoras* and *señoritas* in Lincoln County. Nolan is convinced that Richards was one of the "two most influential persons" in Billy's life. The other was John Henry Tunstall. And as an Englishman himself, Nolan likes to note they "were both English." As usual in all his writing, Nolan's piece overflows with new information, corrected mistakes, and lively writing.

Nolan included some of this information in another, earlier essay: "The Life of Mary Richards," *Outlaw Gazette* 11 (November 1998): 6–8.

231. Page, Jake. "Was Billy the Kid a Superhero—or a Super Scoundrel?" *Smithsonian* 21 (February 1991): 137–48.

This brief piece compares the factual information on Billy with the legends that surround him, including his possible resurrection as Texan Brushy Bill Roberts or New Mexican John Miller. Page draws especially on the works of Robert Utley to comment on the life and character of Billy and to compare those facts with the distorted stories that have emerged over time about the young outlaws. A well-written abbreviated essay for general readers.

232. Pawley, Eugene. "Buckshot Roberts—Fighting Man!" *True West* 2 (August–September 1954): 16–17, 40–41.

Not a piece to be trusted. The author gets too many facts wrong. He is also so pro-Roberts that readers will not get balanced information on his opponents, the Regulators, including Dick Brewer, the Coe cousins George and Frank, Charlie Bowdre, and Billy the Kid. What Pawley says about Billy is incorrect, and so is his treatment of the sequence of events in the shootfest. Roberts deserves a strong essay; unfortunately, this is not it.

233. Peterson, Barbara Tucker, and Louis Hart. "Billy the Kid's Great Escape." *Wild West* 11 (August 1998): 28–29, 31–33.

A straightforward account of Billy's escape from the Lincoln County jail/courthouse on 28 April 1881, this short piece follows the standard story contained in most of the best recent accounts of the breaking out. The authors summarize the major interpretations of how Billy obtained a pistol and shot Deputy James Bell, but they do not point to one of these views as more persuasive than the others. For a more dramatic retelling of these events and personalities, see the more recent account by Paul Andrew Hutton (211).

Three sidebar stories accompany the Peterson-Hart story. Pat Garrett biographer Leon Metz provides a short version of "The Death of Billy the Kid" (pp. 30, 73) and a list of "Ten Billy the Kid Myths" (p. 32). Sherry Robinson, a New Mexico journalist, supplies a capsule story, "Another Version: How Garrett Found the Kid" (p. 33). Metz mistakenly identifies Paulita Maxwell as the daughter rather than the sister of Pete Maxwell, and all three writers state that Garrett killed Billy on the late night of 13 July 1881 rather than on 14 July, as most authorities argue.

Most of this information is familiar to Billy the Kid followers, but Metz's "myths" outline his views on several Billy actions, and Robinson summarizes the point of view of the Solomon Floersheim family on how Garrett found out about Billy's being in Fort Sumner.

234. Rasch, Philip J. "The Bonney Brothers." *Frontier Times* 39 (December 1964–January 1965): 43, 60–61. Reprinted in Rasch, *Trailing Billy the Kid*, 110–15 (162).

Rasch asserts in the opening sentence that Ash Upson and Walter Noble Burns deserve harpooning for the truckloads of inaccuracies they dumped on unsuspecting readers. When he wrote this essay, Rasch did not know that William Antrim and Catherine McCarty lived near one another in Indiana and Kansas before marrying in New Mexico in March 1873. Rasch then references the information he and others gathered about the McCarty/Antrim brothers in Silver City, but the writers did not yet have the later facts collected about Billy in Arizona. About Joe, Rasch devotes a half dozen paragraphs, tracing his life from Silver City to his later gambling years in Colorado. Joe Antrim's Colorado obituary indicates he was five years older than Billy, a disparity that Rasch thinks unlikely.

235. Rasch, Philip J. "Clues to the Puzzle of Billy the Kid." *English Westerners' Brand Book* 4 (December 1957–January 1958): 8–11. Reprinted in Rasch, *Trailing Billy the Kid*, 53–58 (162).

This piece begins with a mishmash of stories, accepted and rejected, about Billy. Next, Rasch provides a brief summary of what his research on Billy's life between 1873 and 1878 has turned up. Silver City, Arizona, and the early days in Lincoln County are emphasized. Oral evidence and anecdotal stories are sources for the new information.

236. Rasch, Philip J. "How the Lincoln County War Started." *True West* 9 (March–April 1962): 30–32, 48, 50.

About fifteen years into his rapid-fire, nonstop rising career as a hobbyist researcher on Billy, Philip Rasch stated what he thought to be the causes of the Lincoln County War. Later, after a good deal of additional research, he changed his opinions from several of those expressed here.

If one keeps in mind that this essay was written in the early 1960s and not forty years later, following the appearance of the masterful writings of Frederick Nolan and Robert Utley, one will realize that Rasch turned up a good deal in this essay intended primarily for general readers. He points to the ongoing conflicts between The House camp of Murphy and Dolan and the Tunstall-McSween-Chisum group, the controversies surrounding the Fritz insurance settlement, and the Chisum and Seven Rivers ranchers' contests as major reasons for the Lincoln County War. He concludes that McSween embezzled the Fritz monies, that Tunstall claimed he and McSween were legal partners, and that The House men, though sometimes rascals, were not the everyday evildoers writers asserted. Many recent writers disagree with Rasch, and with each other, on these latter points, but all agree that the shooting of Tunstall on 18 February 1878 did the most to ignite the tumultuous war that followed.

A helpful overview, although now dated. Almost nothing on Billy the Kid here.

237. Rasch, Philip J. "The Hunting of Billy the Kid." *English Westerners' Brand Book* 2 (January 1969): 1–10; 2 (April 1969): 11–12. Reprinted in Rasch, *Trailing Billy the Kid*, 119–42 (162).

This rather extensive essay, at least for Rasch, is one of his most thoroughly researched pieces. He cites the Billy–Lew Wallace correspondence, the Ritch Papers at the Huntington Library, National Archives records, and New Mexico territorial records—along with the usual newspapers and secondary and primary published sources. The "hunting" period focuses on Billy's life from summer 1878 to his death three years later. The essay deals largely with persons pursuing Billy, especially Pat Garrett, and the events from the Kid's apprehension in December 1880, his trial and sentencing in Mesilla, his escape in Lincoln, and on to Garrett's shooting him in July 1881. Reasonably researched and well organized compared to Rasch's other brief discursive pieces. Rasch quotes several words he says are Billy's and cites several Kid actions after killing Bell and Olinger that other later sources have questioned.

238. Rasch, Philip J. "A Man Named Antrim." *Los Angeles Westerners' Brand Book* 6 (Summer 1956): 48–54. Reprinted in Rasch, *Trailing Billy the Kid*, 38–45 (162).

    As he often does, Rasch opens this essay by discussing the inaccuracies of the Garrett-Upson biography, *The Authentic Life of Billy, the Kid* (127). Then he moves step by step through the evidence that disproves Garrett's account and supports his own conclusions. The author rehearses the Santa Fe evidence (the McCarty-Antrim marriage in 1873) and the Silver City years (1873–1875) but asserts wrongly that nothing is known of Billy's life after he left Silver City until he appeared in Lincoln County in 1877. Relying on oral interviews, his own correspondence, and newspaper articles, Rasch's work is most valuable here in his information on stepfather William Antrim's life from 1877 forward. Antrim stayed in the Silver City and El Paso areas for several years, working as a miner and laborer, gaining a good reputation as an affable Uncle Billy. Rasch traces Antrim's life up to his death in California in 1922. The fullest account of Antrim's life to this point.

239. Rasch, Philip J. "And One Word More." *Chicago Westerners' Brand Book* 18 (August 1961): 1–2. Reprinted in Rasch, *Trailing Billy the Kid*, 85–88 (162).

    Rasch was certain his six essays on Billy the Kid published between 1952 and 1958 had covered all the known information on the Kid. But, he says here, bits and pieces continued to roll in, and he lists that new information in chronological order in this jumbled piece. Rasch has not yet latched on to the census of 1880 and its questionable entry that Billy was born in Missouri in 1855; instead, Rasch speaks here of two women who contended they were relatives of the Kid's. He discredits most of their claims. He also denigrates statements from several old-timers who claimed to know or know about Billy, including the wrong facts about Billy as Billy LeRoy, the Colorado bandit.

    Interestingly, Rasch furnishes bits of information about Billy's possibly fathering children. He mentions the rumored daughter with Nasaria Yerbe and perhaps the son with Juanita "Tullida" Montoya. Rasch, unable to find further facts, does not come to any conclusions on these stories.

Rasch suggests that Joe Antrim was the younger brother of Billy. He adds more information about Joe's meeting with Pat Garrett in Albuquerque's Armijo House in summer 1882 and argues that it was a friendly encounter. Two or three other stories add other information about brotherJoe.

Rasch wonders whether the "lode of information on the Bonneys has just about pinched out" but nonetheless encourages others to read more local newspapers and dig even deeper.

240. Rasch, Philip J. "More on the McCartys." *English Westerners' Brand Book* 3 (April 1957): 3–9. Reprinted in Rasch, *Trailing Billy the Kid*, 46–52 (162).

Rasch provides here an updated summary of what his half dozen years of research on the McCarty family has turned up. He follows his unusual methods of discussing "leads," accepting or dismissing them. Admitting that little if anything is known of the McCartys' lives before 1873, Rasch then adds information on Billy in Arizona, photographs of Billy, and Joe Antrim's meeting with Pat Garrett in Albuquerque in 1882. Rasch, undoubtedly referring to his own labors, asserts that more has been discovered in the past five years about the McCartys than in the previous half century. Surprisingly, almost nothing here on Catherine McCarty.

241. Rasch, Philip J. "Old Problem, New Answers." *New Mexico Historical Review* 40 (January 1965): 65–67. Reprinted in Rasch, *Trailing Billy the Kid*, 116–18 (162).

Rasch shares here his discovery of Billy in the census of 1880 in listings from San Miguel County. He states that the Kid was living with Charlie and Manuela Bowdre at Fort Sumner and that his birth took place in 1855 in Missouri, where both of his parents were also born. Rasch does not mention the doubts of other researchers who believe that the census taker may have talked to someone else rather than Billy in taking the census. It is difficult "to venture an intelligent guess at this point," Rasch states, but he sticks closer to this information than to the story of Billy's New York City birth that Garrett-Upson and most other biographers have accepted, without substantiating proof, since the death of Billy in 1881. Rasch introduces, too, the two alternative views of Lois Tefler, a New Yorker who claimed to be a relative of the Kid's, and William H. Carson, who stated he had found records of Billy's parents in New York City and that his name at birth was Patrick Henry McCarthy. Even at this point, Rasch is less inclined to follow either of the

Tefler or Carson claims; rather, he is more inclined to accept the listing in the census of 1880.

242. Rasch, Philip J. "The Quest for Joseph Antrim." *Quarterly of the National Association and Center for Outlaw and Lawman History* 6 (July 1981): 13–17. Reprinted in Rasch, *Trailing Billy the Kid*, 151–64 (162).

This piece was one of Rasch's last and most extensive essays, his most thorough work on Billy's brother, Joseph Antrim. The author reviews the known information about Joe, suggesting he was older than Billy and perhaps a half brother, but does not comment on the validity of these assertions. By carefully checking city directories, particularly those in Denver, and scattered newspaper sources, Rash pulls together a fairly thorough portrait of Joe Antrim. Unfortunately, as is often the case, Rasch fails to draw conclusions about his findings, not telling us the significance or the veracity of information he gathered.

243. Rasch, Philip J. "Sidelights on Billy the Kid." *Quarterly of the National Association and Center for Outlaw and Lawman History* 8 (Autumn 1983): 2–7. Reprinted in Rasch, *Trailing Billy the Kid*, 167–81 (162).

Curious in its organization and content, this essay is both self-congratulatory regarding Rasch's work on Billy and an admission that he is dealing here with "sidelights" that other writers have overlooked or dismissed. Rasch, in adjoining paragraphs, discusses Billy's missing a trigger finger, the location of his skeleton, and his favorite horse. It is not the information so much as the author's disorganization that mars this disjointed essay. And, unfortunately, most of the tidbits discussed seem irrelevant; however, the comments on photographs of Billy and those reputed to be of his mother, his sweethearts, and his guns have more substance.

244. Rasch, Philip J. "Some More Grist for the Mill: Has the Last Word Been Said on Billy the Kid?" *Los Angeles Westerners' Branding Iron*, December 1960. Reprinted in Rasch, *Trailing Billy the Kid*, 74–76 (162).

A very brief piece with three stories that one Numa A. Strain told a reporter for the *Las Angeles County Employee* in its September 1930 issue. Strain claimed to have heard about the killing of Billy from Pat Garrett, participated at a distance in the shooting of Buckshot Roberts at Blazer's Mill, and listened to an account from an eyewitness of how Billy escaped from the Lincoln jail. Curiously, Rasch tells the stories, which are not far from what later stories advanced, but makes no comments about their authority, merely asking readers "to winnow these additional grains" and no more.

245. Rasch, Philip J. "The Trials of Billy the Kid." *Real West* (November 1987): 32ff. Reprinted in Rasch, *Trailing Billy the Kid*, 194–201 (162).

Rasch is at his best in delivering this brief, focused survey of Billy's two court trials in La Mesilla in March–April 1881. The first trial, U.S. Criminal Case No. 441, dealt with Billy's indictment for killing Andrew "Buckshot" Roberts. That charge was thrown out, largely because the crime occurred off government land. The second charge, for the murder of Sheriff Brady in Lincoln, Territorial Case No. 532, quickly led to a guilty verdict from an all-Hispanic jury. Rasch adeptly summarizes the issues and persons involved in the two trials and describes Billy's reactions to the court sessions and his continuing attempts to gain his freedom. A strong, helpful essay.

246. Rasch, Philip J. "The Twenty-One Men He Put Bullets Through." *New Mexico Folklore Record* 9 (1954–55): 8–14. Reprinted in Rasch, *Trailing Billy the Kid*, 23–35 (162).

Rasch deals with the twenty-one men Billy allegedly killed in his twenty-one years. The author concludes what others later, with more evidence, have concluded: Billy killed, we know, F. P. "Windy" Cahill, Joe Grant, J. W. Bell, and Robert Olinger. He was also involved in the killings of William Morton, Frank Baker, William Brady, George Hindman, and James Carlyle. But he was not the killer of Andrew "Buckshot" Roberts, Bob Beckwith, and Morris Bernstein. The distorted early account of the Garrett-Upson biography started this "folklore" and these "fantasies" of twenty-one deaths in twenty-one years. Strong research in a variety of sources but published here in scattered form. Notice, too, the author places no blame on Walter Noble Burns for exaggerations.

247. Rasch, Philip J. "Why So Much on Billy the Kid?" *Quarterly of the National Association and Center for Outlaw and Lawman History* (Autumn 1983). Reprinted in Rasch, *Trailing Billy the Kid*, 165–66 (162).

This two-page piece zeroes in on a central question: Why is there so much interest in and writing about Billy the Kid? Rasch fingers the Ash Upson–Pat Garrett (127) and Walter Noble Burns (103) books as launching the fascination and keeping it going. They presented a dramatic, romantic figure who protected the reputation of his mother; became a Robin Hood, attacking the bad guys and helping the less powerful good ones; and embodied heroic qualities. These are the major reasons, Rasch suggests, that have kept writers and readers enthralled with Billy the Kid. But, Rasch insists, nearly all the writings about Billy before the 1950s, were inaccurate and off track. Still, the romantic legend expanded decade by decade. Rasch implies, wrongly, that no real facts surfaced until his own work began appearing in the 1950s. He is overstating the point, giving himself too much credit. Others such as Maurice Garland Fulton (as early as the 1920s) and Robert Mullin (in the 1950s) had also begun their important work on Billy and the Lincoln County War.

248. Rasch, Philip J., with Allan Radbourne. "The Story of 'Windy' Cahill." *Real West* 28 (August 1985): 22–27. Reprinted in Rasch, *Trailing Billy the Kid*, 182–93 (162).

This essay furnishes backgrounds and actions involved in Henry Antrim's (Billy's name at the time) first killing, his shooting of blacksmith Francis P. "Windy" Cahill on Sunday, 17 August 1877, at Atkins's saloon in Bonita (near Fort Grant), Arizona. Rasch provides context about Cahill, scattered information on Henry's activities in Arizona, and varied stories about the Kid's killing of Cahill. He depicts Henry as an escape artist before and after the shooting and lists parallels among Henry/Billy's escapes in Silver City, Arizona, and Lincoln County. Reminiscences, newspaper articles, National Archives records, and Rasch's earlier essays are the sources for this valuable but rambling essay.

249. Rasch, Philip, and R. N. Mullin. "Dim Trails: The Pursuit of the McCarty Family." *New Mexico Folklore Record* 8 (1953–54): 6–11. Reprinted in Rasch, *Trailing Billy the Kid*, 12–22 (162).

The authors review and dismiss most of the information given in previous essays on Catherine McCarty and her two boys. They throw out nearly all the stories that authors John B. Curtis, F. Stanley, and Edwin Corle wrote, showing that these accounts cannot withstand the factual information Rasch and Mullin have uncovered about Mrs. McCarty-Antrim, Henry (Billy), and brother Joe. The two writers admit, however, that their research on the mother and her two sons raises more questions than answers. Still, they turned up much of the information about Joe's life in New Mexico and Colorado that we now have. A final paragraph provides a capsule summary of the outcome of their diligent research by the mid-1950s.

250. Rasch, Philip, and R. N. Mullin. "New Light on the Legend of Billy the Kid." *New Mexico Folklore Record* 7 (1952–53): 1–5. Reprinted in Rasch, *Trailing Billy the Kid*, 3–11 (162).

> The authors open their important essay by showing the numerous inaccuracies in the Pat Garrett–Ash Upson biography, *The Authentic Life of Billy, the Kid* (1882, #127). They then branch out into a rather disjointed list of information they have uncovered about the Kid's stepfather, William Antrim—his birth date, military service, and marriage to Catherine McCarty in March 1873 in Santa Fe. What they have turned up, they admit, creates more puzzles than solutions. Still, they have dug up information about Antrim in Indiana, Kansas, and New Mexico—and alongside those Antrim stories are helpful facts on Billy, his mother, and brother Joe. The authors close with a call for more research in New York newspapers and interviews with persons who could have known Joe Antrim.

251. Sanchez, Lynda A. "They Loved Billy the Kid: To Them He Was 'Billito.'" *True West* 31 (January 1984): 12–16.

> The author aims at telling why Hispanics were so attracted to Billy the Kid. She points to his kindnesses to Hispanic men and women (both older and younger), his interests in their daily doings, and his willingness to help needy people, including Hispanics. His fluency in Spanish and his warmth toward *señoritas* were also draws for Mexican-heritage people.
>
> Unfortunately, Sanchez's rambling approach that jumps from one topic to another, her factual mistakes, and her tendency to accept unreliable stories without corroboration undermine the value of her essay. For example, she accepts the story told by Billy's good pal Yginio Salazaar (*sic*) that Billy was not shot by Pat Garrett but someone else without placing that very doubtful story in context or asking questions about it.
>
> A worthy subject but a flawed treatment.

252. Sanderson, Wayne. "The Kid and the McCarty Name." *Wild West Magazine*, 23 November 2016. www.historynet.com/kid-mccarty-name.htm.

> Sanderson, drawing on a letter from one Catherine McCarty, written and published in a New York newspaper, speculates that the McCarty family—and perhaps Billy—were from New Jersey rather than New York City. He also concludes that Catherine, pregnant and unmarried, left Billy in 1860 with her sister, Margaret, and did not come back for him for nearly a decade before going west to Indiana and Kansas. A new, provocative guess about

Billy's origins that deserves consideration and more research. If this is our Catherine McCarty, we now know that she was in Nevadaville, Colorado, in 1872, a mining town about thirty miles west of Denver.

253. Smith, Mike. "Great Escape." *New Mexico Magazine* 86 (January 2008): 44–47.

The author describes Billy's holing up for a very brief time at Black Hill, a part of the Robledo Mountains, about twenty miles northeast of Las Cruces. Here in an arroyo are scratched the words/names/initials of "Bonney," "Bowdre," "OF" (O. Folliard), and "DR" (Dave Rudabaugh). The author surmises that sometime in 1880 the quartet of outlaws inscribed their names, graffiti-like, on the rocky sides of the arroyo. Interesting history tidbit.

254. Smith, Robert Barr. "The Short, Nasty Life of Dave Rudabaugh." *Wild West* 9 (June 1996): 40–44, 81.

Smith comes to his major point in his opening sentence: "It was hard to say anything good about Dave Rudabaugh" (p. 40). The rascal "was a hulking, nasty, treacherous bully, seen in his best light" (p. 40), the author adds. And he stunk, avoiding bathing like a plague of smallpox.

Smith writes with flair and wit, sketching out Rudabaugh's background and subsequent years in addition to his contacts with Billy the Kid in southeastern New Mexico.

The author believes Billy greatly feared the ruthless, arrogant, and murderous Rudabaugh. Perhaps he did, although Rudabaugh traveled with the small Billy-led group without fighting the Kid. When Billy's gang was captured on 23 December 1880 and taken to Las Vegas, a bloodthirsty mob wanted Rudabaugh's head because he had earlier killed a popular Hispanic lawman there. Rudabaugh was jailed but broke out and went to Mexico. Rumor says he was captured there after killing others and decapitated, and his severed head was marched around a small northern Mexico town.

255. Snell, Dave. "Of Buckets, Bullets, and Buckshot: A New Look at Billy the Kid's Escape." *Journal of the Wild West History Association* 8 (December 2015): 13–27.

Snell advances a new, never-previously-argued theory about Billy's escape from the Lincoln jail on 28 April 1881. Like a good debater, Snell attempts to discredit earlier theories before pushing forward his own view. First, there is the "Harry Houdini Thesis" that has Billy getting free from his handcuffs, grabbing J. W. Bell's pistol, and killing the deputy when he tries to flee. Next is the "Half-Moon Hideaway Hypothesis" in which a pistol was hidden in the backyard privy, which Billy used to kill Bell on the jail's back stairway. And third is that a handcuff key was hidden away in the privy that the Kid used to break free.

In contrast, Snell asserts that other facts in plain sight offer a better explanation of the jailbreak. He argues that Billy, having emptied a chamber pot out back, bashed Bell over the head with the pot on their way up the back stairs and raced upstairs to get Olinger's shotgun to shoot the other deputy. Snell is convinced that this new interpretation "dovetails with all the known facts of the escape" (p. 230): the tussle heard on the back stairs, the gash on Bell's head, and the alleged ricochet damage to the stairway wall.

This is an intriguing theory. Like the other interpretations, it has strengths and limitations. Snell's argument merits more consideration as a provocative *theory* but is not a proven conclusion. We still lack additional needed information, and some questions remain unanswered—for example, how Bell's pistol was obtained and proof that it was not used to kill Bell. The treatment of the chamber pot and Billy's carrying and using it is all supposition—interesting but not conclusive and, to some, not convincing.

Snell calls out the partisanship of more than a few writers dealing with Billy. True enough. But when Snell states that Sheriff Brady "sent a posse of fifteen . . . to hunt down and murder John Henry Tunstall" (p. 13), calls Jimmy Dolan "Lincoln's head gangster" (p. 15), and argues that Governor Wallace "double-crossed the Kid" (p. 15), some will think he, too, has become partisan.

In short, a provocative piece that merits more consideration—and more evidence for it to be accepted as *the* theory of Billy's jail escape.

256. Special Billy the Kid issue. *Visions of New Mexico* 2 (1988): 6–38, 46–55.

Seven essays and a short poem by poet Keith Wilson comprise this Billy the Kid issue of a short-lived New Mexico arts and culture magazine in Las Vegas. Robert Utley contributes the brief opening essay, "Billy the Kid Rides Again" (pp. 6–7), discussing the conflicting, changing images of Billy as hero and antihero. Mary Carroll Nelson's "Pat Garrett's Son" (pp. 8–12) is as much about Sheriff Garrett as about his son Jarvis. Lynn Koenig deals with Billy's connections with New Mexico settler Robert M. Gilbert in "A Tale of Two Men" (pp. 13–17). Jerry Weddle's "Billy Bonney in Arizona" (pp. 18–20) includes a two-page excerpt from the revealing but unpublished journal of Miles L. Wood, an Arizona rancher and lawman who unsuccessfully tried to keep Billy under lock and key.

Two of the most extensive essays are Donald R. Lavash's "Conspiracy and Murder in Lincoln County" (pp. 26–31) and Ray John de Aragon's "Billy the Kid: A Victim of Circumstances" (pp. 32–38). Neither works well, with Lavash far too pro–Sheriff William Brady and de Aragon's sympathetic piece on the Kid rife with errors.

The strongest essay—by far—is Frederick Nolan's "Dirty Dave" (pp. 46–55). It is the best compact biography we have of Dave Rudabaugh, part of the Kid's small gang in 1880–1881.

Unfortunately, this collection is disappointing, with too many typos and the use of too many questionable photographs.

257. Stahl, Robert J. "Billy's Bastard Child." *True West* 64 (March 2017): 40–43.

Many Billy biographers think he had an electric love affair with Paulita Maxwell in Fort Sumner. Some have even asserted that since Paulita was pregnant with Billy's child in midsummer 1881, she hurried into a cover-up marriage to José Jaramillo, the son of a well-to-do Hispanic rancher. Author Robert Stahl argues against such stories in his brief essay and provides strong evidence that the couple did not marry until January 1883 (not 1882) and that no child was born to Paulita until January 1884. The author also adds much to what was previously unknown about Paulita and José's unhappy marriage and later separation.

A valuable piece, this essay should cause historians and biographers to be more hesitant about speaking of a torrid romance between Billy and Paulita. Yet Stahl does not address and answer all questions, including the emotional and passionate embrace between Billy and Paulita in the Maxwell house just after he was captured at Stinking Spring in December 1880 and the letter Paulita wrote to Billy when he was awaiting trial in Mesilla in March–April 1881. A brief piece alongside this essay argues that "historians generally agree the Kid's main interest in Fort Sumner was Celsa Gutiérrez." Not entirely true. Some do, some do not. Celsa was a love interest, certainly, but there were others besides her. Now, even if the story that Paulita was expecting Billy's child when Pat Garrett shot him down in her brother Pete's bedroom is clearly scotched, a less intimate romance between Billy and Paulita nonetheless still seems possible—and maybe probable.

258. Stahl, Robert J. "The January 1883 Marriage of Paula Maxwell to Jose Jaramillo." *Outlaw Gazette* (2008–9): 8–10.

A very brief essay that Stahl, a retired professor, expanded on in entry 257. He shows that Paulita and Jaramillo did not marry until January 1883. Hence, Paulita did not hasten into a marriage to cover up her pregnancy from Billy since her marriage did not occur until eighteen months after Billy's death. The author cites newspapers, marriage records, and death records to make his strong case. Stahl wonders whether the Telesfor Jaramillo that previous scholars cited as the "love child" of Billy and Paulita was not the older brother of José, although another Telesfor Jaramillo was born to Paulita and José in 1895. The author here does not dismiss a Billy-Paulita romance, as he does later in his 2017 essay (257).

259. Strykowski, Jason. "An Unholy Bargain in a Cursed Place: Lew Wallace, William Bonney, and New Mexico Territory, 1878–1881." *New Mexico Historical Review* 82 (Spring 2007): 237–58.

Written while Strykowski was a graduate student at the University of New Mexico, the essay provides a helpful overview of the connections and disconnects between Gov. Lew Wallace and Billy the Kid in New Mexico Territory, 1878–1881. The author draws primarily on the published books of Frederick Nolan and Robert Utley and the manuscript correspondence in the Lew Wallace Papers in the Indiana Historical Society and the National Archives.

Strykowski is pleasingly fair to both men, noting the up and down sides of Wallace and the Kid. The governor, although a bit reluctant and alienated from New Mexico as an isolated and tumultuous place, nonetheless tried to solve what were probably unsolvable problems in Lincoln County. Billy courageously fulfilled his side of the promised pardon of Wallace but also easily backslid into outlaw actions after Wallace reneged on his promise.

The author concludes that Billy, considering the huge legends his name and life have engendered, probably won in the contest since Wallace never was able to satisfactorily deal with his failures in New Mexico. A balanced introduction to an important part of Billy's life.

260. Thorp, N. Howard (Jack), as told to Neil McCullough Clark. In *Pardner of the Wind*, 168–93. Caldwell, Idaho: Caxton Printers, 1945. Reprinted in Frederic Nolan, *The Billy the Kid Reader*, 110–34 (156).

Thorp moved into new terrain in Billy the Kid historiographical country: he was one of the first writers to evaluate the legends that grew up surrounding the Kid in the first two or three generations after his death. In preparation for the writing of his book *Pardner of the Wind*, Thorp read the previously published books by Ash Upson and Pat Garrett (127), John Poe (159), Charlie Siringo (165–68), George W. Coe (109), Miguel A. Otero (158), and Walter Noble Burns (103); he also chatted with eyewitness participants in the Kid story: Pat Garrett, George Coe, and Charlie Siringo.

It is not the life of Billy that Thorp addresses, however. His purpose, he writes, is "to separate the truth about him from falsehood, the facts from the fiction" (p. 111). Thorp does not begin with a high regard for the Kid: he "was just a little, small-sized cow- and horse-thief who lived grubbily and missed legal hanging by only a few days" (p. 111).

Thorp's approach is to cast doubt on or deny the validity of stories that could make Billy a "hero." He especially points to the Upson-Garrett biography as a beginning place of the false facts that launched misguided legends about a heroic Billy. Thorp cites the Morton-Baker, Buckshot Roberts, Sheriff Brady, Bob Beckwith, Morris Bernstein, Joe Grant, Jimmy Carlyle, J. W. Bell, and Bob Olinger killings as examples of either false facts or actual facts that illustrate Billy's entirely unheroic actions. As Thorp puts it, his analysis "certainly removes a good deal of the glitter from the 'hero' halo" of the legendary Billy (p. 129).

Thorp likewise credits Garrett, in the sheriff's biography of the Kid (127) and in his later statements, with making Billy a hero to overcome his own doubts about killing the outlaw. Thorp also points out that stories need heroes and many readers have accorded Billy hero status for the Lincoln County War story because they want a hero for that interest-catching story.

Finally, Thorp thinks that Billy's actions in the O. Folliard killing, the mistreatment of Mexican haymakers, and his cowardly giving up at Stinking Spring (though he had vowed he would never be taken alive) are examples of Billy's "short weight for a hero" (p. 134).

A pioneering but not entirely satisfactory discussion of the falseness of the Billy-as-hero legend.

261. Traylor, Leslie. "Facts Regarding the Escape of Billy the Kid." *Frontier Times* 13 (July 1936): 506–13. Reprinted in Frederick Nolan, *The Billy the Kid Reader*, 316–29 (156).

Traylor, a lay historian, traveled to southeastern New Mexico and interviewed several participants and/or later residents of Lincoln County and nearby to piece together this influential essay on Billy's escape from the Lincoln jail on 28 April 1878. Later findings contradict several of Traylor's conclusions, but other of his assertions have become long-accepted parts of subsequent legends about the Kid.

Traylor discusses several unsolved questions concerning Billy's escape: (1) Was the escape at noon or in the evening? (2) How did Billy obtain the gun with which he killed the jail guard J. W. Bell? (3) What were the exact details of Billy's death in Pete Maxwell's bedroom? (4) And was Billy the person killed on the evening of 14 July 1881? In his closing paragraph, Traylor sorts out his oral evidence from interviewees and provides his conclusions: (1) Billy's escape was at noon; (2) the Kid's gun was one hidden for him in the privy out back of the jail; (3) Garrett, seeing Billy, moved swiftly into Maxwell's bedroom and shot the Kid when he entered; (4) and "there are reasons to doubt," Traylor states, "that W. H. Bonney was the person killed in Pete Maxwell's room on the night of July 14th, 1881" (p. 329). Most of Traylor's conclusions, and other small points as well, have been overturned by subsequent researchers.

262. Trujillo, Francisco. "The Mackyswins and the Marfes." In Frederick Nolan, *The Billy the Kid Reader*, 257–67 (156).

Despite its several errors in dating and naming, this interview has become a major source for some leading authorities on Billy the Kid. Interviewed in 1937, when he was eighty-five, by the WPA worker Edith Crawford, Trujillo spoke about several important events in the Lincoln County War and then, curiously, overlooked or forgot about several others. Even more problematic are Trujillo's mistakes in chronology and on details involved in the Lincoln County and Billy stories. For example, the best-known accounts of the Morton and Baker deaths, the Big Killing, the Lincoln jail break, and the killing of Billy are all jumbled here. Nor is the timing of the events in the correct order.

All these mistakes make it difficult to embrace other parts of the Trujillo conversation. He tells his interviewer, for instance, that McSween offered to pay any of his followers $500 if they shot down a Murphy partisan. No other contemporary of Billy's has so stated. Many historians, including this writer, want to hold on to all Hispanic accounts of Lincoln County and Billy, but the erroneous information and the snafus in chronology make this interview problematic—at best.

263. Turk, David S., with Sallie Lynn Chisum Robert. "Much Misunderstood Miss Chisum." *Wild West* 30 (February 2018): 52–57.

Drawing in part on information from Sallie Chisum Robert's great-granddaughter Sallie Lynn Chisum Robert, Turk very briefly traces out the life of John Chisum's niece. Following the information from Chisum Robert, Turk concludes that Sallie's brief contact with Billy the Kid "suggests a possible flirtation between the pair . . . at minimum a friendship between them, but not necessarily a romance." Their "interaction . . . was situational rather than romantic" (p. 54), Turk adds, meaning they happened to come into contact rather than planning such meetings.

The author has not turned up much more on the Billy-Sallie connection than the widely cited snatches of information recorded in Sallie's journals. In these happenings, Sallie indicates that Billy gave her an "Indian tobacco sack" on 13 August 1878 and "two candi hearts" (p. 54) on the next 22 August. A descendant of Sallie's also recounted a family story in which Billy warned Sallie away from a shootout that may have saved her life.

Bits of information; one wishes there were more.

264. Utley, Robert M. "Billy the Kid Country." *American Heritage* 42 (April 1991): 65–66, 68, 72–73, 76, 78.

Utley helpfully distinguishes between the Billy the Kid of history and his "towering significance" (p. 65) as a world-renowned legend in folklore. The Kid, Utley asserts, is neither hero nor villain "but a little of both" (p. 65). And we have made him what we have wanted, sometimes a courageous, violent individualist and on other occasions a villain and evil brat. Drawing on his extensive research for several books on Billy and the Lincoln County War, Utley summarizes the events of the war and Billy's actions, all the while evaluating Billy's personality and character. In addition, the author provides a capsule description of the places, especially Lincoln and Fort Sumner and the countryside of the Rio Bonito and Rio Pecos, as valuable backdrops for his Kid story. A skillfully and smoothly written condensation of the longer, larger story.

265. Walker, Dale. "Few Know the Kid like the Englishman behind the Annotated Edition of Pat Garrett's 1882 Book." *Wild West* 13 (April 2000): 66, 68.

Part interview, part book review, this valuable piece from the late, well-known, and popular western writer Dale Walker with Kid authority Frederick

Nolan provides valuable information about Nolan's first steps into Billy the Kid and Lincoln County history as well as about the Garrett-Upson biography of Billy. Nolan sent hundreds of letters across the Atlantic to gather information about territorial New Mexico well before his book on John Tunstall (152) was published and before he visited the United States. Most valuable here are Nolan's contentions not only that Ash Upson filled the first half of the 1882 book with "a farrago of nonsense" but that Garrett "was lying about insignificant matters" and distorted more important matters in the later chapters of the book. Nolan was convinced that Garrett thought "quite a number of sleeping dogs [were] better left undisturbed" in his chapters in the biography. Perhaps Garrett, worried about keeping his sheriff position and not alienating participants in the Lincoln County War who were still alive, chose to be "reticent" (p. 68) about what he said. A brief exchange with important information from Frederick Nolan.

266. "What If Everything We Know about Billy the Kid Is Wrong?" *True West* 62 (June 2015): 22–30.

This provocative potpourri of bit pieces includes seven bylined essays and several other tidbits of information—along with helpful photographs and artworks. Frederick Nolan contributes "Believe Billy" (p. 24) and "How Did the Kid Get His Gun?" (p. 30). Chuck Usmar deals with Billy's backgrounds in "Billy the Irish" (p. 27), and Mark Lee Gardner asks, "How Did Henry Get His Alias?" (p. 27). Dr. Robert Stahl authors "Seeking the Creation of the Kid's Death Record" (p. 29), and Steve Sederwall writes "Billy Bonney's Bad Bucks" (p. 29) on the counterfeiting controversy. Alongside these essays are sketches on Billy's interviews, the controversial croquet photograph, and Paul Hutton's everywhere quote on the "dreamscape" desperado. All of these brief essays have something of value for Kid followers.

267. Wilson, John P. "Building His Own Legend: Billy the Kid and the Media." *New Mexico Historical Review* 82 (Spring 2007): 221–35.

Wilson, a thorough researcher and innovative thinker, utilizes known sources to take them in a new direction. He advances a very useful thesis: Billy the Kid "played a substantial role in creating his own legend" (p. 221).

Wilson deals with newspaper stories, interviews with Billy, Pat Garrett's important book about Billy in 1882, several other Kid stories, essays in the *National Police Gazette*, and several dime novels to show, more often than previously realized, that Billy did a great deal to launch and shape the early legends about him that continue to the present. Wilson provides an eye-opening, if brief, discussion of the formation of Billy the Kid legends just before and after his death.

The author demonstrates, alongside his signal thesis, that researchers looking at familiar research materials may, through probing reflection, arrive at fresh readings of and important conclusions about those sources. No one previously advanced this interpretation as forcefully and persuasively as does Wilson.

A strong and valuable contribution.

268. Wilson, John P. "With His Boots Off: First Newspaper Reports on the Death of Billy the Kid." *Rio Grande History* 14 (1983): 11–13, 23.

Independent scholar John Wilson provides a brief account of which New Mexico newspapers—there were five daily and twenty-one weekly New Mexico territorial newspapers in 1881—printed stories about Billy's death. Original stories (over and above wire service and reprinted accounts) appeared in three extant newspapers. The stories, according Wilson, were "widely and wildly different" (p. 13). Those accounts are reprinted here.

Wilson's essay is not an evaluation of the contents of these stories and their role in forming early legends about Billy but an account of how and where the newspaper stories about Billy's death were printed. The reprinted stories remain useful for Billy biographers and students of the legends surrounding the Kid.

Novels, Other Literary Works, and Criticism

269. Aragon, John A. *Billy the Kid's Last Ride.* Santa Fe, N.Mex.: Sunstone Press, 2011.

A longtime Billy collector, researcher, and Santa Fe lawyer, Aragon has produced a novel with balancing strengths and limitations. Aragon is a skilled writer, especially in his scenes of action and violence. In the first half of his novel, he also follows quite closely what is known historically about Billy's life. In second half, however, the author's imagination is on the loose. He sends Billy south into Mexico after his escape from the Lincoln jail in April 1881 and allows him to be involved in a horrendous shooting war among cowboys, Indians, and Mexican *ricos*. Part 2 falls apart as a work of verifiable historical fiction because almost nothing in this section is factual history.

Aragon's Billy is a character with a complex personality. He can be compassionate, passionate, and very sexy and identifies with down-and-out Hispanics. They love him as El Chivato. But the Kid can also be dangerously assertive and murderous in his actions, particularly, for example, in his wanting to kill Morton and Baker soon after they are involved in the murder of Tunstall. When Aragon allows Billy to reflect on his life and his future, we get some interesting suggestions about his personality. Unfortunately, Billy is off scene too frequently, especially in the imagined second part.

Aragon adopts the narrative frame of a stuffy eastern journalist who comes to the Lincoln County area in the early 1920s to find out about Pat Garrett. Instead, he falls in love with the Billy the Kid story, New Mexican ways, and a vivacious *señorita* who proves to be the descendent of a Billy-

Hispana union. Percy, the narrator, goes home a wiser man and, following Billy's passionate ways with women, decides to move on to a single woman at his own newspaper office.

Aragon tries to be innovative in his plot, in his use of Spanish-English narration, and his imagined historical events for the second half of the book. Unfortunately, his reach exceeds his grasp in most of these attempts.

270. Bean, Amelia. *Time for Outrage.* Garden City, N.Y.: Doubleday, 1967.

Bean's novel of nearly 450 pages is one of the most extensive works of historical fiction about the Lincoln County War. Focusing almost entirely on the events of 1877–1878, the author provides numerous pen portraits of the major participants in the war. She deals negatively with the Lawrence Murphy gang, including Jimmy Dolan and John Riley, as well as Sheriff Brady. Nor does she overlook their web of connections with Thomas Catron and the Santa Fe Ring and territorial officials such as Warren Bristol and William Rynerson, both sympathetic to the Murphy House contingent. Col. Nathan Dudley is pictured as a belligerent, drunken, misguided supporter of the Dolan faction in Lincoln.

But Bean does not overlook Murphy's competitors. She deals with Alex McSween, John H. Tunstall, and, glancingly, John Chisum. The author's sympathies are with this group, even though she's not positive on Chisum, surprisingly critical of McSween, and sympathetic to Tunstall, although viewing him as something of an English naïf adrift on a wild frontier.

Alongside these historical characters are two imagined figures, Luke Pender and Magdalena Perez. Luke, an irrepressible red-haired cowboy, and Maggie, an orphaned Mexican, Indian, or mixed-race young woman, get entangled in a quick, torrid romance. Luke is the novel's main character, whose actions and thoughts provide the central continuity in the novel's thick plot.

Notably, Bean does not deal extensively with Billy the Kid. Following the nonfiction writings of William A. Keleher, Taylor Ealy, and Frederick W. Nolan, the author asserts that Billy was "never . . . during the war a leader of any group or contingent." Or, again, "Bonney could not have been a leader of men fighting for McSween" (p. 443). Prone to strong opinions and quick violence, as seen in his part in the Brady killing, Bean's Billy is pushed aside by Luke Pender as the main presence in the novel.

In two ways, Bean enlarges the fictional recounting of the Lincoln County War. She deals extensively with the ethnic-racial mix in the region, showing how Mexican-heritage and African American people were intimately involved in the events of 1877–1878. Bean also integrates women's roles more thoroughly into the Lincoln County story. Sue McSween is a lively, assertive, and sometimes foolish participant in several events, and Mrs. Brady, the Mexican wife of Sheriff Brady, is known in Lincoln for her opinionated, outspoken ways. More intriguing is Tia Lupe, a local *Hispana médica* (*curandera*) who plies her skills as a healer and source of folk wisdom in the village of Lincoln.

271. Boggs, Johnny D. *Law of the Land: The Trial of Billy the Kid*. New York: Signet, 2004.

The opening pages—and much of the entire novel—display the author's dedication to historical accuracy. Most of what Boggs writes is sound history, following a good deal of the information biographers and historians have provided about Billy the Kid. Whether dealing with the Kid, Lincoln County or La Mesilla, or the reactions of Gov. Lew Wallace, the author stays close to the known facts. True, he adds imagined conversations and enlarges on characters' temperaments, but even these additions, for the most part, will strike his readers as true to history.

Most of the story's action is seen through the consciousness of Billy the Kid, with bits from the perspectives of other characters, and large sections via the thoughts of Ira Leonard, Billy's lawyer in the last months of his life. Part 1, about 120 pages, traces Billy's life from his entrance into Lincoln County in fall 1877 until his travels to La Mesilla in early 1881 as a prisoner. Part 2, of 140 pages, the longest section, is an almost entirely imagined set of chapters, but they, too, are based on sound historical generations; these chapters deal with Billy's trial for murder in La Mesilla in April 1881. Part 3, the briefest section of about fifty pages, treats the last three months of the Kid's life.

Boggs also adds a good deal of historical information through flashbacks. For instance, we learn through those returns to the past about the details of Tunstall's killing, the murders of Morton and Baker, the assassination of Sheriff Brady, the shootout at Blazer's Mill, and the Big Kill on 19 July 1878. Even in these turns back the author follows the main tracks of the Kid's known history.

The conversations and the trial testimonies at La Mesilla depict a two-sided Billy. He can be loving, friendly, and gregarious with his mother, John Tunstall, and his pals. Conversely, Lew Wallace comes to see Billy as an evil rascal who became a turncoat. The talks between Leonard and Lew Wallace picture the complex Billy, mainly positive in the lawyer's conclusions and negative in the governor's comments.

Given this extraordinary emphasis on historical accuracy, it is surprising how much Boggs deviates from the conclusions that the best essays and books follow in dealing with Billy's last weeks. Boggs, for instance, has Pete Maxwell meeting with Pat Garrett in Roswell and telling him that Billy is in Fort Sumner; he depicts Billy and Paulita making love in her Maxwell bedroom before he goes for meat to cook, a journey that leads to his death at the hands of Pat Garrett; and he moves away markedly from what dependable sources say about events immediately after Billy's violent death.

Still, one comes away from this novel pleased with how much solid history it is based on. Moreover, Boggs is a skilled writer, keeping his story open to general readers, remaining true to the facts, and providing a provocative and persuasive interpretation of a dualistic Billy the Kid. For all these strengths, the work should be considered one of the best handful of novels about Señor Billy.

272. Braun, Matt. *Jury of Six*. New York: Pocket Books, 1980.

Combining history and sheer imagination, veteran Western novelist Matt Braun produces a mixed-bag novel. The author clearly is acquainted with the general outlines of the Kid's last months in 1880–1881, but he also chooses to present a one-sided, negative view of Billy and reorganizes several of the well-known events of the Kid's final days to fit his dark purposes.

Braun grafts the imagined life story of Texas stock detective Luke Starbuck's career onto the journey of Pat Garrett with confusions, irregularities, and unbelievable resultant events. All historical novelists must face the dilemma of how much history and how much fiction will characterize their works; this author errs on the side of excessive invention.

For Braun, Billy the Kid is "nothing more than a common murderer." He killed eight men (not true) and "had given none of his victims an even break." Even worse, the Kid was like a "mad dog terrorizing the countryside," with his terrible actions a "passing similarity to a rabid animal" (p. 60). The author's fictional character, Starbuck, is, in contrast, a courageous, driven, and dependable man.

The author's reorganizations, often without clear reasons, are also often off track. He wrongly lists Sallie Chisum as the daughter of Cattle King John Chisum, renames Jimmy Dolan Jack Dobson, shifts Billy's loyalties, and turns Pat Garrett into a cautious, entirely self-aggrandizing monster.

A disappointing fictional effort from a well-respected writer of Westerns.

273. Burnett, W. R. *Mi Amigo: A Novel of the Southwest.* New York: Knopf, 1959.

Skilled and veteran author W. R. Burnett adopts a popular approach among historical novelists (inventing characters to accompany well-known historical figures) and then carries it further than most other writers dealing with Billy the Kid. The young villain in his novel—Bud/Smith/Jamie Wiggan, also known as "the Kid"—is indeed Kid-like. A superb shootist, a friend of Mexicans, drawn to young *señoritas*, and by turns a pleasant companion and a heartless killer, Bud-Jamie ramrods one side of a vicious civil war in La Paz, something of a Lincoln, New Mexico.

But Burnett is most interested in his hero, army man John Desportes, known as "Sergeant" or "Soldier." A seasoned and devoted veteran, a bachelor, and a never-give-up soldier, Sergeant nonetheless works well with numerous men and gains a widespread, positive reputation for courage and fairness. His first "amigo" (a friendship theme that persists throughout, as indicated by the novel's title) is Natty Bugworth, a longtime but profligate frontier nomad. Natty is later gunned down by the Bud-Jamie sharpshooter. Earlier Sergeant found the Kid injured, brought him into a fort reminding one of Fort Stanton and established a father-son relationship with the twenty-year-old. Months later, the Kid reveals his evil nature, lying, cheating, and murdering; he is rumored to have killed a man for every year of his life.

The author is most interested in the character of Sergeant and his cycling through three "amigo" relationships: first Natty, then Bud-Jamie, and finally Blackpony, a young Apache desperado who comes in from the wild to become Sergeant's third amigo. Subsequent amigos wipe out earlier friends, with Kid killing Natty and Blackpony shooting down the Kid.

Although more a plot borrowing from Billy the Kid's life and surroundings than a fuller story of the Kid himself, *Mi Amigo* is nonetheless an engrossing example of strong historical fiction from a veteran novelist in which a character resembling the Kid plays a major part.

274. Coolidge, Dane. *War Paint.* New York: E. P. Dutton, 1929.

Dane Coolidge draws on the tradition of the Western that under the leadership of Zane Grey, Max Brand, and several others had zoomed to the top of best-seller fiction lists by the late 1920s. The triplex at the center of the newly defined "Western"—heroes, villains, and heroines—is at the hub of this novel.

Coolidge also makes extensive use of several elements of the Billy the Kid story. Like most fiction written about Billy before the 1920s, Billy is obviously a devilish villain here. Although he is primarily off-scene in the novel, his reputation as a killer—having murdered nearly twenty people—hangs over and threatens to bedevil the good guys and their attempts at communal acts. Named Tuffy Malone, the Billy-like character is described as "bad medicine," "the best pistol shot in the country" (p. 35). "You'll hear from [Tuffy/Billy]," for "there is one of the worst characters on the whole frontier—a city tough, gone wild in the West" (p. 36).

True events in Billy's life appear in this story, but usually in garbled form. Like Billy, Tuffy is involved in the killing of the Lincoln sheriff, takes part in the Lincoln shootouts, is captured in a stone house like Pat Garrett's capture of Billy at Stinking Spring, and is shot down by the hero (who in some respects resembles Pat Garrett) in a darkened room.

Coolidge's novel reminds one of the strengths and limitations of several Zane Grey Westerns. The author provides a speedy plot overflowing with action; a stalwart hero; deplorable villains; a lively, vivacious heroine; and numerous settings lovingly described. But Coolidge is unsuccessful in handling human emotion, overblowing the characters' passions, fears, and stubbornness. Surprising, too, is the blatant racism throughout the novel, with more than a few references to "greasers" and "niggers."

275. Cooper, Gale. *Joy of the Birds*. Bloomington, Ind.: Author House, 2008. Reprinted under the title *Billy and Paulita: A Novel*. 3d ed. Albuquerque, N.Mex.: Gelcour Books, 2012.

The first of several recent books by Gale Cooper, this hefty novel of nearly six hundred pages is what the author terms "docufiction," which, one supposes, is meant to be history or documents presented in a fictional format. The 2012 edition is about twenty pages longer than the initial version but differs very little in content or format.

The huge novel exhibits several strengths. Gale Cooper knows the history of Billy the Kid and Lincoln County. She begins the story with the Kid's mysterious origins in New York City and ends the book with Pat Garrett's gunning down of Billy on 14 July 1881. The story is told in context, with a good deal of Washington, D.C.; Santa Fe; and southeastern New Mexico contexts. And Billy is surrounded by those who did so much to shape and influence his life: his mother, John Tunstall and Alex McSween, Pat Garrett, and Paulita Maxwell.

Cooper is a better historian than literary stylist. She has difficulty not falling into stereotypes and overblown scenes. Billy's putative father, Michael McCarty; his stepfather, William Antrim; Jimmy Dolan; Tomas Catron; and Pat Garrett among several others are either blackhearted rascals, mentally unbalanced, or sexual predators. Cooper is also hard on Alex and Susan McSween, depicting the lawyer as a naive Bible-pounder and his wife as sexually hungry. The same with Celsa Gutiérrez, who lusts for Billy's electric lovemaking each time she sees him in Fort Sumner.

Cooper's Billy is an attempt at a complex characterization. Loving his mother, John Tunstall, and Paulita Maxwell, he likewise exhibits murderous hatred toward Sheriff Brady, Jimmy Dolan, and Governor Wallace. Billy desires, above all else, freedom ("the joy of birds"), a theme that Cooper frequently repeats, and wants to represent the Hispanics in their attempt to break from under the lion's paw of the Santa Fe Ring. Although a bit clumsy in its presentation, Cooper's many-hued Billy is one of the strengths of her otherwise too-lengthy and sometimes awkwardly presented novel.

Overall, this is not a successful novel on literary grounds. Excessively overwritten, too often blustery in style, and containing too many stereotypical characterizations, the work needed strong developmental and copy editors to straighten out the author's writing. Cooper's talents obviously lie more in her historical research than in her literary contributions.

276. Corle, Edwin. *Billy the Kid: A Novel.* 1953. Albuquerque: University of New Mexico Press, 1979.

Corle's novel fits smoothly into the historical fiction category. In fact, some sections of the novel read more like history and biography than fiction. Rarely does the author invent, whole cloth, scenes that did not happen. All major characters seem to be historical—and quite true to form historically.

Like many other novelists, then, Edwin Corle draws heavily on the known history of Billy the Kid but then plays with that history, often adding imagined scenes that expand on Billy's fictional character and frequently distorting facts. For instance, in the early pages of his novel Corle speaks of Billy's birthplace as New York City, and then he moves Billy to Silver City in the second scene. Well and good, but he distorts what we know by having frontier badman Jessie Evans as Billy's chum in Silver City and having Billy stab a Chinse laundryman while on a robbery jaunt with Jessie. Billy also kills a "nigger" while he is next in Arizona and two Mexicans while in Mexico before coming to Lincoln County. This marriage of fact, imagination, and sometimes distortion runs throughout Corle's novel.

Corle's Billy is an irrational killer. On several occasions he kills because he is angry or uncomfortable but not because he is threatened or in a violent confrontation. He even tells Abrana Garcia, his *novia*, that he does not think about killing; he just does it because he wants to. Corle has him killing twenty-one men in his twenty-one years. Billy kills often, placing him in the early devilish Billy line even though Corle's novel was not published until the 1950s. It was, however, drafted in the 1930s.

Corle drives his plot with two engines. The first is Billy the killer. The second comes later, when he meets Abrana Garcia and falls hard for her. Although she is Hispanic in a world that sees Hispanics as lesser mortals (they are followers, servants, and yes-sir men and women in Corle's novel), Billy says nothing about her ethnicity. Nor, at first, is he bothered much that she is the teenage wife of a nearly sixty-year-old man. He bullies his way into her heart—and then into her bed. The romance and lust theme comes increasingly on scene in the second half of the novel. It's difficult to accept that Manuel Garcia allows his wife to bed down with Billy without reacting in any way negatively.

Corle treats Abrana as Billy's sole *novia*. Billy has not known girls before, has not visited the local prostitutes as have some of his gang members, and he does not pay attention to Paulita Maxwell or Celsa Gutiérrez as does the historical Billy. Nothing is suggested about his returning to Fort Sumner for Paulita; it is for Abrana. On the last night of his life, he arises from Abrana's bed to cut a steak from Pete Maxwell's recently killed beef before he carries out his plan of going to Mexico. Nothing is hinted about Billy's fathering children with Abrana, as several biographers have suggested.

It is intriguing to think that Corle drafted this novel soon after Walter Noble Burns had published his very sympathetic portrait of Billy in the mid-1920s, a work that seemed to swing other accounts away from the earlier, more negative pictures of Billy. But this novel is a negative portrayal.

Corle's position on the major actors in the Lincoln County drama merits comment. He dislikes Chisum, who is pictured as a self-serving fraud and two-timer bent on turning things to his own benefit. Conversely, Pat Garrett receives very positive attention. A very good early friend of Billy's, the thoughtful, dependable Garrett takes the sheriff position that Wallace had earlier offered to Billy, who rejected that position out of hand, saying he still had to kill those involved in the Tunstall murder and would never give up his gun in an armistice deal. Garrett says he must bring in Billy, but he works at it in a balanced, must-do-it manner, not in an irrational method or out of hatred of Billy. When Garrett becomes sheriff, Billy immediately says he will kill his former friend—without any thought to the contrary.

Corle is generally more friendly to the Murphy-Dolan contingent than to the McSween and Chisum faction. Of the latter, Tunstall is portrayed more positively. None of these characters is on scene as much as Garrett and Olinger. Olinger becomes the devil incarnate figure, limned as a trigger-happy killer who wants Billy's scalp in any way—and soon. Billy's killing of him seems almost OK since Olinger has been such a violent, vile opponent.

Bartender Beaver Smith and Pete Maxwell are on the edge of things quite often as Billy's friends—almost as supporters. Jessie Evans is the sole Tunstall killer whom Billy is unable to wipe out because he has run away. Like Garrett, Evans is another former friend who becomes a deadly enemy.

An important early novel in the development of the literary Billy, it is disappointing in its treatment of history, however.

277. Cotton, Ralph W. *Cost of a Killing.* New York: Pocket Books, 1996.

Historical novelists are expected to stick close to the actual history in their fiction. They are to avoid distorting the lives of historical figures or events for their novelistic purposes. True, they may add incidents and characters and plumb the thoughts of historical characters, but readers expect their handling of actual figures of the past to be realistic and accurate.

Unfortunately, author Ralph W. Cotton is guilty of several inaccuracies and distortions in this paperback-original novel. Employing the familiar technique of creating an imaginary character to ride alongside a historical personage, Cotton spins his yarn around Jeston Nash, who, as a first-person narrator, tells a sensational story of intrigue, hidden gold, and lusty romance. It is Nash, a hero in Cotton's series of novels about him, who is the lead character; Billy rides alongside Nash and is tailored to fit authorial needs. Billy is pictured as a previous acquaintance of Nash's, but here rides with him in a plot of unbelievable, unrelieved dramatic actions.

Cotton fails to provide a credible portrait of Billy the Kid. In the more than one hundred pages where Billy is on scene or just offstage, we encounter but a page or two of his actual life. Only the Kid's contact with John Tunstall and Pat Garrett are more than mentioned, and Cotton (wrongly) says of Billy's relationship with Garrett, "The man was my best friend"

(p. 70). Scene after scene in this overly sensationalized work of fiction portrays Billy in actions in which he did not participate. And when Billy says he wants only three things in life—a "fast horse," a "pretty woman," and to "let no sumbitch tell me what to do" (p. 148)—we also see nothing of that credo played out here.

But Cotton does raise several questions about Billy's character that are realistic and believable. He describes Billy, in actions and words, as a young man who does not plan ahead but acts instead on the spur of the moment. The author also has Billy saying of his reluctance to leave Fort Sumner, "It's been home . . . after a long time without one" (p. 77). One wishes that Cotton had not appropriated Billy so clearly for his novelistic purposes and chosen to deal so sparingly with his actual life. Instead, the novel seems primarily a steady series of dramatic events, including truckloads of action and steady threats of scene after scene of violence. In the overemphasis on mayhem, the author fails to develop his characters, including Billy the Kid. Disappointing.

278. Cowdrick, J. C. *Billy the Kid from Frisco*. Beadle's Pocket Library 321. New York: Beadle and Adams, 1890.

Most Billy the Kid dime novels attempt to get his biography and his historical context into their pages. This one does not. In several ways Cowdrick's work breaks from the usual mold of Kid dime novels. It is decidedly an imagined mystery story overflowing with action, adventure, and entertainment, with little emphasis on place, historical events, or known characters. The author spins a tale of drama and frenetic action, not unlike the well-known Deadwood Dick series—which Cowdrick assumed as author of the Deadwood Dick Jr. series when the original author, Edward L. Wheeler, died.

Billy the Kid makes a few brief appearances here. In none of these is he on scene for very long. He appears first in capturing the story's heroine before she is quickly set free. In that episode and those that follow about him, Billy is described as a "mighty chief," but as one character says, he is really "only a common cut-throat." Another adds that Billy is "a man of great nerve and daring," and a third describes Billy as being dressed like something of a Mexican dandy (p. 11).

On two different occasions, Billy escapes jailing even though closely guarded in a cabin. One of the desperado's opponents explains that the Kid is too strong and supported by too many followers to remain locked up. He "has got more friends right here in this very town than ye'd ever dream of"

(p. 16). As predicted, Billy busts out in a few hours. Later, he will again break out of a lockup.

Cowdrick braids several strands into a mystery story about a Spanish ship that sinks and about a buried treasure in a lost city of an isolated New Mexican town of Indians. These events, part and parcel of the mystery of this Cross of the Golden Keys, are overflowing with adventure, clashes, and strange events. The episodic narrative jumps back and forth from the town of Golden-Egg and its characters to the lively adventures surrounding the mystery of the Cross of the Golden Keys. The author marshals incredible coincidences, complex disguises, mistaken identities, and fantasies of all sorts to drive his narrative.

In the final sequence of events, Billy the Kid and his riders are caught up in the search for the lost city and its hidden treasure. A mysterious figure, Silver-Mask, helps capture the Kid. Again, Billy escapes. The final line, after the loose events of other strands of the narrative have been tied together, states, "How Billy, the Kid from 'Frisco ended his days, is known to all." Perhaps some readers understood this cryptic closing line. Most might be puzzled, however, because the novel never explains Billy's origins, the development of his character, his personal life—or what happened to him. Indeed, the novel's ending is but one more of the differences between this Billy the Kid dime novel and others about him. Cowdrick produced a skilled dime novel that brought Billy the Kid on scene, but only as a minor background figure—perhaps for interest's sake. In the end, he contributed an enigmatic story of mystery.

279. Daggett, Thomas F. *Billy LeRoy, the Colorado Bandit; or, The King of American Highwaymen.* New York Police Gazette. 1881. New York: Richard K. Fox, 1883.

The first and the most curious of the dozen or more dime novels about Billy the Kid, this work appeared originally in 1881, then with a slightly altered title in 1882, and was reprinted again in 1883. Published about two weeks before Pat Garrett shot down Billy, the sixty-six-page dime novel was the first in publisher Richard K. Fox's Police Gazette Series on Famous Criminals.

The curious part is the divergent content in the work. Said to be a "biography" of Billy LeRoy (Arthur Pond), an actual Colorado highwayman, it is also, in lesser part, a fictionalized portrait of portions of the life of New Mexico's Billy the Kid. After tracing the violent and mindless exploits of LeRoy's dramatic life in Indiana and Colorado, author Thomas Daggett conflates LeRoy's career with that of the New Mexican Billy the Kid. Even more confusing, the Colorado outlaw is also known as Billy or the Kid. A few months earlier, publisher Fox had published essays in his magazine, the *National Police Gazette*, on both the Billys, sometimes mixing up the details of their two lives.

Although LeRoy is never identified as Billy Bonney, he meets and travels with the New Mexico Kid's friends and participates in events in which Bonney took part. While in southern Colorado, LeRoy encounters Tom O'Phallier (Tom O. Folliard), "one of the most notorious desperadoes in the West" (p. 27), and his fellow outlaw Dave Rudabaugh. In a cave ritual, LeRoy is initiated into the O'Phallier gang and soon proves himself as highwayman in holding up a stagecoach and robbing a man of his considerable cash. LeRoy does so well that the outlaws call for his elevation to captain of the gang.

When things get too hot in Colorado, LeRoy rides south to New Mexico. He is pictured taking part in activities there in which Billy Bonney participated. LeRoy rustles cattle and is involved in a red-hot shootout in Lincoln, and his extralegal activities bring groups from Texas, White Oaks, and other parts of Lincoln County in pursuit. He and his gang try to work out something with Gov. Lew Wallace, but the New Mexico leader does not keep his promises. The outlaws think of assassinating the governor, but then, realizing Wallace is a courageous, valiant fellow, decide they will only capture and spank him!

The New Mexico event treated most extensively is the shootout between Billy's gang and the White Oaks posse at the Greathouse Ranch. Some of the details are accurate, others are not, and Billy is singled out as the killer of Jim Carlyle. Soon thereafter Billy rides into a Chisum cow camp, quickly shoots three of the four cowboys, and sends the fourth off to John Chisum himself, warning that Billy will murder other cowboys because the Cattle King has not paid Billy for "riding shotgun" in earlier conflicts.

LeRoy returns to Colorado again after pursuers are close on his heels in New Mexico. Going back and attempting to reignite his romance with girlfriend, May Vivian, the author tells us, was the "resolution [that] cost [LeRoy] his life" (p. 60). He is captured, with his less energetic brother Sam (sometimes also Arthur), and a mob breaks into the jail and lynches the two Pond brothers in May 1881.

Billy LeRoy, in Colorado and New Mexico, is depicted throughout as a vicious, driven killer. Without much cause, Billy whips out his pistol and shoots down many opponents; he seems immune to the bullets of others and always on target in his own shots. Assertive, desperate, his soul "dead to remorse" (p. 16), and never haunted by "the consequences of his deeds" (p. 43), Billy "stole, murdered, [and] ravished women" (p. 56) after arriving in New Mexico. Defiant to the end, Billy tells his gang of lynchers, "I am ready to meet the cashier. Go on with your cart" (p. 62), as he faces the rope.

This initial Billy the Kid dime novel features familiar facets of the genre. The West is a wild place, ruled by the strongest and most desperate characters and without much law and order. Close families, farmers, and mushrooming cities are nearly nonexistent, with individualistic miners, outlaws, and cowboys dominating the scene. Women's virtue is protected even among bands of murderous outlaws. Indeed, sexual subjects in the main are taboo. Plot tricks including fantastic disguises, false identities, and strings of dramatic action rule the scene. Dime novels were meant to entertain, titillate, and perhaps inform (often with false facts), and this work is no exception. Excessively sensational, unbelievable, and contrived, the story of Billy LeRoy (and some of Billy Bonney's) nonetheless evidently proved sufficiently entertaining and sold well enough to be reprinted twice. It also helped launch the legendary life of New Mexico's Billy the Kid, albeit in an imagined, altered form.

280. "Dead Desperado, Adventures of Billy, the Kid, as Narrated by Himself." *Las Vegas Daily Optic*, 12–23 December 1881.

See No. 63.

281. Doughty, Francis W. *Old King Brady and "Billy the Kid"; or, The Great Detective's Chase.* New York Detective Library 411. New York: Frank Tousey, 11 October 1890.

One of the last of the Billy the Kid dime novels, published nearly a decade after the Kid's death, Doughty's *Old King Brady and "Billy the Kid"* features a well-known New York detective, Old King Brady, pursuing Billy the Kid in a distant, lawless New Mexico. The novel includes both familiar and innovative fictional ingredients.

Like so many other dime novels, this one intersperses episodes of dramatic, violent conflict with scenes of adventure and travel. Dime novel authors could keep readers engaged with gunfights and other horrendous clashes and then follow up with depictions of major characters traversing awe-inspiring and almost placid landscapes of a mysterious and scenic West.

Most memorable in this novel is the skewed depiction of Billy the Kid. He is the worst of human beings, a brutal murderer. He leads violent attacks, viciously assaults opponents, and kills on a whim. Early on, Billy shoots down a pious minister who does no more than to try to protect his virtuous daughter from the Kid's rapacious actions. Later Billy kills several others—again without cause.

In the opening and closing scenes of the novel, Billy is described in the darkest of hues. As one acquaintance puts it, Billy "is the blood thirstiest little cowpuncher whatever straddled a horse"; he "thinks he owns the earth." In the final sentences, the narrator, taking to his preachy pulpit, asserts that no one in New Mexico was "so vile a specimen as this bloodthirsty boy, whose chief delight was murder" (pp. 4, 29).

Regrettably, the East Coast author understood little about Billy and New Mexico. The author of more than a thousand fictional works, including a series on Old King Brady, Doughty makes distorted comments that undermine the authenticity of his fiction. Billy did not hang out in Ojo Caliente in northern New Mexico, and he did not live in a cabin surrounded by a lake and rushing river; once the Kid passed through the Silver City area in his flight to Lincoln County in 1877, he did not return to stay there; and he and old John Chisum were not hand in glove in mutually dominating a murderous civil war in eastern New Mexico. In fact, the biographical details, scanty and false as they are, present an off-track Billy the Kid.

What this dime novel illustrates is that by the early 1890s, a satanic Billy dominated portraits of him in fiction and newspaper stories. Nearly all the dime novels about the Kid—at least a dozen and perhaps as many as seventeen—portrayed a villainous Billy. When the dime novel depictions were combined with the dark views of Billy in contemporary national and New Mexican newspapers, this meant that Billy the Kid rode violently across fictional and biographical landscapes in the United States at the end of the nineteenth century—and for the next quarter of century as well.

Old King Brady and "Billy the Kid" also moved to its excessively negative view of Billy somewhat by default. Similar to other dime novels built around a heroic protagonist, such as Old King Brady here or Deadwood Dick or Buffalo Bill elsewhere, those who oppose the central heroes quickly descend into the villain category. When Billy confronts the New York detective in the first scenes of this work, he is immediately cast into the outer darkness of villainy, where he remains as a blackhearted killer. From James Fenimore Cooper through the dime novels and on to the fictional and cinematic Westerns of the twentieth century, a man who challenges Leatherstocking, Buffalo Bill, or John Wayne quickly and thoroughly descends into hell. No spaces of compromise between upright and evil-minded scoundrels are in existence.

282. Fable, Edmund, Jr. *The True Life of Billy the Kid.* Published as *Billy the Kid, the New Mexican Outlaw; or, The Bold Bandit of the West!* Denver, Colo.: Denver Publishing, 1881.

Reprinted; College Station, Tex.: Creative Publishing, 1980.

Two of the dozen or so dime novels about Billy the Kid were reprinted about a century after his death and enjoyed a modicum of circulation and renewed interest. One of the duo was this work. Commentaries on this book have been as extensive as on any of the Kid dime novels.

The publication date of the novel was 15 July 1881, the day after Billy's death, with the copyright not applied for, however, until the following September. The title page and preface of the novel reveal the author's and publisher's intentions. The cover page carries the statement that this work will be "A True and Important History of the Greatest of American Outlaws." It will deal with "His Adventures and Crimes Committed in the West. The History of an Outlaw Who Killed a Man for Every Year in His Life."

The preface likewise makes large promises. The author argues that eastern readers have been led astray about Billy the Kid's life. These writers have portrayed Billy as being rich, living in a castle, and possessing elegant, gentlemanly manners. These wrongheaded accounts, Fable tells us, were "made up of whole cloth"; if eastern readers believed these stories about Billy, they had as much understanding about him "as a burro has of the beauties of Milton" (p. 5).

The author promises that his dime novel will be accurate in all "incidents narrated" and will feature "correctness of . . . details." He has not had to "draw upon a vivid imagination to enhance" the story's draw because Billy's "true history . . . eclipses any border romance, and dims by comparison the tales woven from the realms of fiction" (p. 5). These comments are all the more noteworthy because the author diverges repeatedly from known details and again and again resorts to embellished scenes. Here is another building block for constructing the negative legendary edifice of Billy at the time of and soon after his death.

Fable states that William Bonny (*sic*) was born in New York in a "tenement house in the Fourth Ward of that city." His father, William Bonny, "was an honest, hard-working man" who labored diligently to support his family and unfortunately died when Billy was just six (p. 9). After Billy's widowed mother failed in trying to make it on her own, she married Thomas (*sic*) Antrim and moved west. Nearly all of this is false or unconfirmed regarding names, place of marriage, and the role of William Antrim.

After being reared in Colorado, Billy sets off on his own and arrives in Silver City, New Mexico. On his first night there, he goes to a dance, gets drunk, is robbed, and ends up in jail on false charges that he has been involved in a violent robbery. A turning point occurs, the author tells us, when Billy, suffering in jail under this trumped-up penalty, decides that thereafter "I'll hold my own with the best of them" (p. 14).

Escaping up the chimney, the young Billy then happens into a freighter's wagon and ends up in Lincoln County, New Mexico. Almost overnight, he kills a bullying blacksmith who was threatening him and becomes embroiled in the Tontsill (*sic*) and Chisom (*sic*) side of the county civil war. When Chisom tries to cheat him, Billy kills Chisom's riders—murders, the author says, that show Billy as a "heartless Kid" guilty of "cold-blooded murder" (p. 31). The killings continue, one almost every other month. Sometimes Billy thinks about his vicious actions but mostly gathers followers like Tom Phaller (*sic*) to help with rustling and killing, although most of the time he acts on his own.

None of the incidents Fable describes follow closely the actual events of the last years of Billy's life. The killing of Sheriff Brady, the Lincoln shootout at the McSwain (*sic*) house, the gunfight at the Muscalero (*sic*) reservation, and finally Billy's death at the hands of Pat Garrett are wide of the mark. So is the author's faulty treatment of geography: riders in southeastern New Mexico go "down" to Las Vegas, and nearly fifty miles separate Lincoln and Fort Stanton. Fable's large promises of authenticity fail in nearly every aspect of the novel.

One is surprised, too, about some of the rearranged details. Billy's mother, brother, and stepfather never make it to Silver City; Billy stays out of Arizona; and Susan McSween and Paulita Maxwell are nonexistent. In addition, the roles of Bell and Olinger are exchanged in the Lincoln jail escape, with Olinger shot first. Moreover, almost nothing appears about any of the major characters of the story save for Chisum and Folliard, whose lives are greatly revised.

If readers expected to "get the facts" about Billy and the Lincoln Country War—and evidently some believed Fable's claim that he was telling the truth—they would have eventually been disappointed about how distant this dime novel was from facts. Like nearly all the dime novels about the Kid, this one depicts Billy as a shoot-and-think-later murderer. Fable's Billy lacks depth, warmth, and substance as a character; he enters numerous scenes in which he took no part; and he is kept from other scenes where he was a central figure. Those hungering and thirsting for a veracious literary portrait of Billy the Kid would have to look elsewhere. Unfortunately, such truthful and polished accounts would not come until decades later.

283. Fackler, Elizabeth. *Billy the Kid: The Legend of El Chivato.* New York: Forge Books, Tom Doherty, 1995.

This lengthy historical novel provides an extensive fictional life of Billy the Kid from his midteen years until his death in 1881. Running to more than five hundred densely packed and small-printed pages, the novel furnishes almost as much biographical and historical material as most nonfiction works on Billy. Indeed, it can be said that Fackler generally follows known facts and along the way adds conversations and thoughts based on thorough historical research.

Fackler clearly backs the Tunstall, McSween, Chisum, and Billy side of the Lincoln County conflicts. Although all of these characters display human limitations, they are not the devil figures of the opposing side: The House, the Santa Fe Ring, military leaders, and biased judicial-legal figures. Yet both John Tunstall and Alex McSween are naive, failing to understand the hard-nosed, violent ways of their opponents. Chisum, fighting for his own interests, is unwilling to go to the mat to support Tunstall and McSween. Generally, the Hispanics, especially *los pobres*, are heroic, too, in their gentle, loyal, and rural ways. And they love Billy the Kid.

Fackler's Billy the Kid is an appealingly complex figure. At times fun-loving, genial, and loyal, he can also be violent, vicious, uncaring, and murderous. In fact, the author achieves depth and breadth of character in demonstrating that in one scene Billy can win the hearts of *señoritas* and *señoras* but in the next he can mow down those who stand in his way or challenge his actions. Many recent books on Billy are sympathetic to him; a few others, conversely, see him as a desperado whose selfish, arrogant actions bring on his own demise. To Fackler's large credit, she portrays Billy positively as well as negatively, showing that his complex character embodied humanity and even love but also violence and evil. Not many historians, biographers, or novelists have been as successful as Fackler in portraying Billy the Kid as a complex historical character.

Along the way Fackler sticks close to the major historical events of Billy's life, but where she diverges from those known actions is of note. For example, she has Billy's mother, Catherine McCarty, and his stepfather, William Antrim, meeting for the first time in the far West rather than beforehand in Indiana and Kansas. In her account, Billy says he did not know his father and then later tells a story of his parents, unmarried, in New York City, with the father running a fruit stand when they met. Surprisingly, Fackler also asserts that Billy stabbed a man, which is not true. Also she is much more negative on William Antrim than most biographers, picturing him as a negative, hateful, and uncaring man.

Other additions in Fackler's novel increase rather than diminish its value. Her treatment of Hispanics and women is expanded much beyond most accounts of Billy. The depictions of Susan McSween and Billy's *señoritas* and his relationship with Paulita Maxwell are much more thorough than in other fiction. Generally, Fackler adds a great deal on the roles of women in what is usually a man's story. Sexual relationships likewise play a large role in this story, with Billy sometimes employing his penis more than his pistol.

Overall, this novel is a probing and interest-whetting account of Billy and the Lincoln County War. Although a bit too negative about Billy's opponents and a tad too sympathetic to his supporters, Fackler's account is a superb work of historical fiction, one of the most comprehensive novels we have on this complicated, complex subject.

284. Grey, Zane. *Nevada*. New York: Harper, 1928. New York: Bantam Books, 1986.

Although Billy the Kid never appears on scene in this novel, Zane Grey mentions him and the Lincoln County War about ten times. These references link the novel's hero—known variously as Nevada, Texas Jack, and Jim Lacy—with the Kid and his gunman role in the Lincoln County War. A year earlier Grey had introduced the character Nevada in a prequel novel, *Forlorn River*.

Nevada illustrates both the attractiveness and the large limitations of Grey's Westerns. The author's descriptions of several scenes, his handling of action sequences, and his nonstop tempo—all appealed to and still draw beef-and-potato readers. Conversely, Grey's overreliance on contrived secrets, hyped emotions, and fainting females—some of the author's hallmark limitations—undermine this novel.

In the final pages, Grey dramatically changes directions regarding Billy the Kid. He has a major, well-respected character argue that characters like the novel's hero, Wild Bill Hickok, Wess (*sic*) Hardin, and Billy the Kid are not "bloody murderers." Instead, they are necessary for the settling and civilizing of the West. "There are bad men and bad men." Billy and the others are, at the worst, good bad men. "They are a product of the times. The West could never have been populated without them" (p. 279). Waiting until the closing paragraphs to launch this provocative idea that differs so markedly from the other references to Billy and the Lincoln County War greatly lessens the persuasiveness of the contention.

285. Grey, Zane. *Shadow on the Trail*. 1946. New York: Pocket Books, 1970.

Grey opens this later novel, published after his death, by expressing his fascination with the fact that so many western "desperate characters and hunted outlaws disappeared without leaving a trace." He adds this was true of Henderson, who was "one of the Billy the Kid gang." Not so. Grey is also misleading in asserting that Billy "helped to instigate the Lincoln County War" (n.p.). Later in the novel the author has Pat Garritt (*sic*) killing Billy in the town of Lincoln (*sic*). Not a promising start for a historical novel.

Most of Grey's ten or so references to Billy the Kid and the Lincoln County War picture him as a violent desperado and the war as ruinous for cattle raising and livestock selling across the West. On one occasion, a character describes Billy as "the chain lightnin' an' poison of the frontier" (p. 68). Another asserts that Billy "is all thet's bad on the frontier rolled into one boy of eighteen years" (p. 68).

But, of special note, Grey brings the novel's hero—variously known as Wade Holden, Blanco, and Tex Brandon—and Billy on scene together as Holden is escaping Texas and riding through New Mexico on his way to Arizona. In this meeting, Billy proves friendly to Holden, inviting him to join the Kid's outlaw gang and go after rancher Jesse (*sic*) Chisum and the killers of Tunston (*sic*).

Why Grey refers to Billy and brings him front and center in one brief incident is not clear. The Kid plays no active role in the novel.

286. Hall, Oakley. *Apaches*. 1986. New York: Bantam Books, 1988.

A multitalented and prolific writer, Oakley Hall illustrates in this five-hundred-page novel what a first-rate author can do with the Billy the Kid and Lincoln County stories. Hall utilizes many familiar ingredients, adds new ones, and transforms many of the best-known participants and events in these much-written-about facets of New Mexico history.

Most of the leading characters in the Lincoln County story appear in Hall's novel, all renamed and frequently recharacterized. Alex and Sue McSween become Frank and Lily Maginnis, with Frank/Alex retaining his rather alienating high-mindedness and Lily/Sue transfigured into a beautiful, sex-hungry woman pushing for her rights and justice. John Tunstall becomes Martin Turnbull, who, with Frank Maginnis, naively thinks they can compete with "the store" leaders Ran Bolond (L. G. Murphy) and Henry Enders (Jimmy Dolan), the latter being the worst villain in Madison (Lincoln). John Chisum (Penn McCall), Sheriff William Brady (Pogie Smith), and Pat Garrett (Jack Grant) play familiar roles, but many of the details of their personalities and actions are changed.

Johnny Angell is the Billy the Kid character, who comes on scene well into the novel. He is depicted by an opponent as a young "gun-toter" whose life is dramatically transformed after the shooting of Turnbull and the dramatic Big Killing in July 1878. Johnny murders his stepfather, kills several in Madison (Lincoln) County, and seemingly is unable to leave despite several encouragements to decamp for Mexico. Hall's Johnny/Billy gradually emerges as a bifurcated character: he murders but is much loved, appeals to Hispanics, makes love to Lily Maginnis, and saves the life of the other hero of the novel, Patrick Cutler.

As the other lead character, Cutler is a lieutenant in the army working with Apache scouts to keep the peace. Hall places the two plots of Cutler and Angell side by side and then increasingly combines them as the novel progresses. The military happenings, the changing roles of Cutler, and the extensive coverage of the Apaches, especially their social and cultural customs as they reside on reservations and try to keep the peace with the "white eyes," enlarge and enrich the complex story Hall narrates.

History purists will wish Hall had not changed so many facts or been guilty of mistakes. He has Billy killing William Antrim and Henry Enders, attending Turnbull's funeral, traveling from Madison County toward Mexico, hanging out frequently with Grant (Garrett), not killed but badly wounded by the sheriff, and after death buried in the ruins of the Old Ones near Madison. All wrong.

But even more intriguing and valuable are the novel's multiple strengths. It is an engrossing story well told with an expansive narrative encompassing the Apaches and the military as well as Johnny (Billy) and the Lincoln County story; careful, probing discussions of the characters of the two heroes, Cutler and Johnny; provocative comments on history as science and art; and the emerging legendary Johnny/Billy in newspapers and nickel and dime novels even before his death.

A top-drawer novel with some questionable uses of history but even more major achievements in plot, character, intellectual content, and human history.

287. Hansen, Ron. *The Kid.* New York: Scribner, 2016.

The largest challenge for Ron Hansen and other historical novelists writing about Billy, as it is for biographers and historians, is how one is to tell a believable story about the Kid when so little is known of his first fourteen years and so often there is not much more than controversial bits and pieces about his last seven years.

The best of the historical novels about the Kid are Edwin Corle, *Billy the Kid* (1953); Charles Neider, *The Authentic Death of Hendry Jones* (1956); Amelia Bean, *Time for Outrage* (1967); and Elizabeth Fackler, *Billy the Kid: El Chivato* (1995). Also of note are Larry McMurtry's *Anything for Billy* (1988), N. Scott Momaday's *The Ancient Child* (1989), and Johnny D. Boggs's *Law of the Land* (2004).

Hansen's *The Kid* surpasses all these in its careful, inviting combination of historical accuracy, skillful scene setting, and plausible interpretations of Billy. Hansen's work might be the most historically accurate of any novel written about the Kid. Drawing thoroughly on important Billy books by Robert M. Utley, Frederick Nolan, and several others, the novelist sticks closely to the known facts of Billy's life. We see the conflicting theories about the outlaw's journey from his natal New York through brief stays in Indiana, Kansas, and Colorado and on to New Mexico in 1873. Most of the book deals with Billy's life in Silver City, New Mexico (1873–1875); Arizona (1875–1877); and Lincoln County, New Mexico (1877–1881).

Along the way Hansen nearly always gives us accurate scenes of Billy's actions in these three locations. We are shown his love for his mother, his alienation from his stepfather, and his tendency to fall in with older, off-track men leading him to thievery—and even murder in Arizona. More attention-getting are Hansen's treatments of the major events in Lincoln County: the killings of John Tunstall and Alexander McSween, Billy's big-brother/father-figure friends; the Kid's part in the murder of Sheriff Brady, Bad Billy's worst offense; and his participation in thievery and other inexcusable killings.

Hansen gets a few things wrong or distorts events beyond known facts. William Antrim, Billy's stepfather, was not a mean man, although distant and sometimes disinterested. Hansen overemphasizes Billy's amorous adventures and conquests. He is also too negative about Sue McSween and indicates that Celsa Gutiérrez is both sister and cousin of Pat Garrett's wife. No major biographer has identified Yginio Salazar as Billy's cousin, but Hansen does. Finally, Billy did not tell Judge Bristol to go to "hell, hell, hell" at the end of his murder trial in Mesilla.

Billy the Kid interpreters often fall into opposing categories: Billy as villain or Billy as hero. But Hansen provides a more provocative, appealing portrait: Billy the complex protagonist who can be a murderer, thief, and liar but also a carefree, joyous, and upbeat companion. In avoiding either-or and embracing both-and interpretations, Hansen furnishes a full-bodied picture of the controversial Billy.

Finally, the author's noteworthy story is presented in an appealing, straightforward manner. No reader will have trouble following Hansen's plot, characterizations, or ideas. All are lucidly and understandingly presented.

In short, a first-rate, on-top historical novel on one of the West's most written-about characters. A delightful read.

288. Henry, O. "The Caballero's Way." In *Heart of the West*, 187–204. New York: Doubleday, Page, 1904.

O. Henry (William Sydney Porter) obviously drew on the Billy the Kid story in this short fictional work but changed the details while telling some of the general story. The young, "quick-tempered" hero, named the Cisco Kid—but called "the Kid" for short—has killed a large number of men, "mostly Mexicans." When O. Henry writes that the Kid killed Mexicans just "to see them kick," he was clearly referencing Emerson Hough's wrongheaded and racist conclusions in his book *The Story of the Cowboy* (1897). O. Henry's Cisco Kid can shoot faster "than any sheriff or ranger," and the *señorita* Tonia Perez loves him (p. 187).

Then things change for Tonia and the Kid when Lieutenant Sandridge, a blond sun god, is sent to capture the desperado. Tonia, the half-Mexican girl of Spanish Basque heritage, and the soldier immediately fall in love, imperiling the Kid's love. He learns of Tonia's infidelity, overhearing her comments about him as El Chivato but also about her newfound love for the blond giant. But later, after the lieutenant leaves, the Kid rides to hug Tonia and acts as if nothing is amiss.

In a quick O. Henry ending, the Kid writes a letter to the lieutenant (but disguises it as having been written by Tonia), saying the Kid will be dressed as the Mexican girl and to kill her/him immediately. Sandridge, thinking he has been told the truth, smiles and shoots several times only to find that the Cisco Kid has gotten his revenge; the lieutenant has killed his *novia* rather than the outlaw.

The popularity of the Cisco Kid in subsequent writings and movies indicates that Kid-like figures in disguise could attract large crowds of readers and viewers. As time went on, however, the Cisco Kid became increasingly modeled on Billy the Kid.

289. Henry, Will. "A Bullet for Billy the Kid." In *Sons of the Western Frontier.* Philadelphia: Chilton Books, 1966, pp. 165–209.

If historical fiction is to include a verifiable factual foundation on which to erect a fictional edifice, Will Henry's long short story fails in nearly every respect. Henry relies heavily on the false conclusions of Pat Garrett's and Walter Noble Burns's earlier books, which the strong research and writings of Philip Rasch, Maurice Garland Fulton, and Will Keleher had replaced before "A Bullet for Billy the Kid" appeared. Henry has Billy killing twenty-one men, including a man in Silver City said to have insulted his mother and several Mexicans and Indians. Billy, a "wolfish outlaw boy" (p. 188), as the author describes him, is a heartless killer.

Henry's Billy is entirely negative. He never keeps his word, kills only for his own benefit, and never thinks about befriending anyone else. He is a wanton murderer with a "wily mind, if limited" (p. 183). Or, even worse, "Billy was a boy, no more, and rotten to the sapwood of his spine" (p. 199).

The author creates a shadowy character named Asaph, who accompanies Billy, both off and on the scene but is never fully human from birth to death. Perhaps based on the biblical gatherer of King David's time, Asaph flits in and out of the plot, sometimes helping Billy, other times pushing him into drastic deeds. In the closing scene, just after Garrett shoots down the Kid, Asaph gathers up the resurrected Billy, and together they ride off into eternity.

A strange and rather disappointing work by a noted historical novelist who produced several superb works of historical fiction about other western figures and events.

290. Hough, Emerson. *Heart's Desire: The Story of a Contented Town, Certain Peculiar Citizens and Two Fortunate Lovers.* New York: Macmillan, 1905.

Billy the Kid plays a distant, minor role in this romantic, sentimental novel set in Edenic Heart's Desire (White Oaks), New Mexico. Billy never appears on scene, although Hough includes a mainly imagined chapter on Billy's capture at Stinking Spring. After Billy has broken out of jail, Sheriff Ben Stillson (Pat Garrett) and a handful of posse members (some from Heart's Desire) capture him and some of his gang and haul them off to Las Vegas. Hough evidently cared little about following history in this minor novel even though he would deal extensively and much more importantly with the same history in books and an essay about Billy (see entries 131 and 210).

Rather, Hough deals with a woman-starved passel of men in Heart's Desire who see their place as a Valhalla until a married woman with daughters, another woman, and two young twin girls invade their sanctuary. The women represent civilization (the East, the "States") and disrupt the gaggle of cowboys, errant former husbands, and men at odds with the demands of family, occupation, and responsibility. Hough evidently had tongue in cheek in most of his comments dealing with women as barriers to masculine independence. When given the opportunity, the freedom-loving men welcome the females who come on scene.

Not a major fictional work on Billy the Kid.

291. Jenardo, Don (John Woodruff Lewis). *The True Life of Billy the Kid.* Five Cent Wide Awake Library 451. New York: F[rank] Tousey, 1881. Reprinted in Frederick Nolan, *The Billy the Kid Reader*, 3–49 (156).

Even though Jenardo (Lewis) called this work a "biography," it is a dime novel with shaky historical content. The false facts, sensational plot, and one-sided story betray its dime novel content.

The author combines fact and fiction throughout his plot. Billy comes from New York to New Mexico, lives for a space in Silver City and Arizona, and then spends most of his days in Lincoln County, New Mexico. Billy sides with John Chisum and Alex McSwain (McSween) and viciously opposes the Murphy-Dolan combine. He's involved in the killing of Sheriff Brady and Morton and Baker and heads up a gang of thieves and shooters after the firing of Lincoln. Pat Garret (*sic*) apprehends Billy, but the gunman breaks out by shooting deputies Bell and Ohlinger (*sic*). Garret catches up with Billy in Pete Maxwell's bedroom and shoots Billy—with Maxwell absent from the scene.

Most of these segments of Billy's story are mistakenly told or narrated from a different slant. Billy is a bloodthirsty killer, and John Chisum is an equally barbaric cow thief. Murphy-Dolan, Sheriff Brady, and Pat Garret are all good guys entirely. Santa Fe and Washington, D.C., governments play almost no roles, although Gov. Lew Wallace is portrayed as a weak-kneed, changeable, deeply flawed leader.

The number of imagined strains and scenes of the Jenardo/Lewis story rival those intended to be factual. Billy kills his first man as a rival for the hand of a pretty *señorita*. He deeply admires and loves Susan McSwain and will do anything for her. Later he captures warmhearted Nettie Jones (who had helped him to escape jail in Silver City) and forces her into a marriage, and his ill treatment leads to her death.

The largest divergence from fact is the author's off-key treatment of Billy's character. The novel's leading man is a total villain with no heroic qualities. A diminutive, pale-faced killer, Billy murders dozens of people, even dipping his finger into the blood of some he has gunned down. There's not a sympathetic or empathetic bone in his little body.

Occasionally the author enters the narrative to preach a bit—to comment on Billy's action, for example. He damns the characters of Chisum and McSwain and praises those of their opponents. The final paragraph carries a preachment that if Billy had been given proper upbringing and education, he might have accomplished much because of his verve and energy.

Published just weeks after Billy's death in July 1881, this dime novel helped to establish a negative image of Billy as a frontier barbarian and murderer. That black image continued well into the twentieth century. A work much more important historically and historiographically than as a work of literature.

292. Lehman, Paul Evan. *Pistols on the Pecos*. 1953. London: Chivers Press, 1992.

Author Lehman weaves a few historical details of Billy the Kid's life and the events of Lincoln County around the actions of his hero, Cole Claiborne. A Texan, twenty-two, and previously diminished because of excessive drinking and gambling, Cole rides away from his father and five older brothers to find a new path. He travels to Arizona, gathers a herd of about fifty horses, and drives them back to sell at Fort Stanton. One day before the sale, a band of rustlers, who turn out to be Billy and his riders, steal the horses. Over the next three to four years, Cole and Billy frequently tangle and come close to killing one another on several occasions.

Cole and Billy also compete for the affections of pretty red-haired Susan Roberts. Cole has known Susan in Texas, and she, with her Uncle Bill Roberts (who proves to be a re-created Buckshot Roberts), moves to New Mexico and reacquaints with Cole. Billy tries to win Susan too, and the tensions among the threesome power much of the plot.

Lehman's Billy is decidedly a rascal—if not a murderer. The author piles up the negative evidence on the Kid, including his involvement in the killings of Morton and Baker, Sheriff Brady, and Buckshot Roberts as well as other shootings. But the author does not bring Billy's opposite side—his generosity, kindness, and congeniality—into the story. Nor are the Kid's strong ties to Hispanics and adult women mentioned.

The historical elements of the novel are inaccurate and off the beam in separate sequences. Billy's relationships with John Chisum, John Tunstall, and Alex McSween are skipped over, and Dick Brewer is depicted primarily as an outlaw. The specifics of the Big Killing in July 1878 are wrong, but the treatments of the Stinking Spring capture and the killing of Billy in Maxwell's bedroom stick close to authentic history.

The largest shortcoming in Lehman's novel is his unfortunate adherence to the formula of the popular Western: the hero, the villain, and the heroine. The author rearranges actual history and characterizations to fit his plot needs in sticking to this confining formula. As a result, Billy the Kid is here depicted as a flat, stereotypical, and villainous character without much complexity or reader interest.

293. Lewis, Preston. *The Demise of Billy the Kid.* New York: Bantam Books, 1994.

Veteran historical novelist Preston Lewis adopts an oft-employed technique of his guild. He invents a character, H. H. Lomax, to move alongside a well-known historical figure, allowing the imagined participant to fill in the gaps and silences in a historical protagonist's life and mind. Here, the just-discovered diary of Lomax is the source of information on both Billy the Kid and himself; his indefatigable travels throughout the Old West introduced him to several of the demigods of the region. The author dovetails Lomax's plot into Billy's actions in Lincoln County, including his reactions to the Tunstall killing, his participation in Sheriff Brady's murder, his sentencing in the Mesilla courtroom, and his death in Pete Maxwell's bedroom. In most of these dramatic scenes, Lomax is an eyewitness, not only viewing the unfolding actions but also commenting on them.

In the early pages Billy rides alongside Lomax as a cheerful, joyous companion. But the killing of Tunstall changes everything, with the Kid desperately vowing to kill all of Tunstall's murderers. Billy may be the grinning, warm buddy at first, but his negative side emerges and enlarges; his personality shift is chronological, with not much positive remaining after February 1878. Only after he vows vengeance on Tunstall's killers does he surface as a heartless murderer himself. Thenceforth, Billy is driven up a dark, violent path.

Lewis depicts nearly all major characters in the Lincoln County story as flawed individuals. Lawrence Murphy is a drunken despot, Warren Bristol and William Rynerson manipulators of law and order, Alex McSween a hopeless moralist and conniver, Tunstall a naive and rather senseless young man, and Sue McSween a voraciously lustful redhead. Even John Chisum is portrayed as a selfishly driven egoist, and his niece Sallie as an immature, thoughtless young woman. So, the Kid is surrounded by warped individuals, with some of their flaws almost as bad as his. Only Pat Garrett seems an upright, honest lawmen.

The author's otherwise-above-average novel suffers from two limitations. Lewis is addicted to similes and metaphors, dotting nearly every page with too many examples: someone is "hungrier than a tick on a skeleton," another person thinks he is "smarter than a perfesser in a nuthouse," and still another man is described as being "as useless as a Democrat with integrity." A few chuckling or risqué examples sneak in, too: a sharpshooter "could hear a flea break wind in a thunderstorm," and something is straighter "than a preacher's pecker in a whorehouse."

More off-putting is Lewis's attempt to graft on a romance story late in his novel. It is a hopeless, ill-conceived romance between Lomax and a *señorita*, Rosalita, who plays musical beds with Lomax and the Kid. Authentic history—which much of the novel is—suffers from an imagined romance that seems contrived, unbelievable, and out of place.

A more-than-adequate historical novel with interesting comments on Billy, other major figures of Lincoln County, and events of the 1870s.

294. McGeeney, P. S. *Down at Stein's Pass*. Boston: Angel Guardian Press, 1909.

McGeeney's novel of about 115 pages tells the story of narrator Alden Raymond, a Boston native who travels to New Mexico to work as an engineer with a government agency. The story overflows with violent action, surprising clashes, and, unfortunately, authorial manipulations.

Like Emerson Hough's *Heart's Desire* (290), published four years previously, McGeeney's novel depicts "Billie" the Kid as a minor, negative character. He is introduced as the leader of a pack of gunmen, which the narrator describes as "overbold in committing crimes against God and man." Pat Garrett, clearly a heroic character, vows to take on the "lawless band" (p. 21). After Raymond and Billie meet and briefly chat on the streets of Stein's Pass, a small town near the Arizona border, they exchange threats and warnings. Raymond concludes that Billie is "without a doubt the coolest customer I have ever met . . . the most daring of outlaws" (p. 23). Billie rides as the chief gunman for the novel's villain, Francis Livingston, the half brother of another heroic character, Patrick Livingston.

McGeeney's novel has little to do with the actual history of Billy the Kid and Lincoln County. True, Pat Garrett is on the scene as a sheriff of Grant County, is something of a hero, and kills Billie in the second half of the novel at the Maxwell "ranch." Otherwise, the novel fails as a work of *historical* fiction.

Unfortunately, McGeeney is guilty of other artistic miscues. He manipulates the plot with a series of contrived happenstances, having characters meet and overhear conversations in miraculous circumstances. The novel's narrator, Raymond, loses his mind after near-deadly gunshots, and even his own father, sister, and stepmother fail to recognize him or his voice. Raymond saves Beatrice Livingston, Patrick's five-year-old daughter, and much later falls in love with her, now renamed Marcia Lewis and also bereft of her memory.

In short, *Down at Stein's Pass* never engaged readers after its publication, undoubtedly because of its major literary flaws. But it also fails, regrettably, as a work of historical fiction.

295. McMurtry, Larry. *Anything for Billy*. New York: Simon & Schuster, 1988.

McMurtry limns an unusual portrait of Billy, here named Billy Bone, in perhaps one of the best-known novels about the Kid. Uncertain, irrational, and weepy, Billy exhibits few—if any—of the characteristics of the historical Billy. Giving his youthful, diminutive protagonist a less-than-brave demeanor allows McMurtry to depict a far different lead man than most other novelists or biographers portray.

Billy Bone demands to have his way. Ben Sippy, the imagined narrator, and Joe Lovelady, Billy's cowboy buddy, try—not very successfully—to bend to Billy's will and actions. He brooks no disagreements with his opinions or deeds, bullies his acquaintances into following his irrational ideas and activities, and falls into a depression when he dreams of the mysterious Death Dog and his own demise.

McMurtry tells his skewed story through the consciousness of a fifty-something Ben Sippy, a dime novelist from Pennsylvania who has fled west to avoid his termagant wife and nine daughters and embrace his dreamed-up wild frontier. Ben is trying to understand the West and Billy Bone, but both are at odds with his preconceptions of the region and its uncivilized ways and valiant heroes. The huge differences between Ben's before and after conceptions are major ingredients of the novel.

The novel eventually evolves into something of a spoof, even though McMurtry's intentions are probably more serious. *Anything for Billy* reminds one of McMurtry's novel about Calamity Jane, *Buffalo Girls* (1990). Both works satirize western demigods, Billy and Calamity, but move little beyond the satire. When compared with McMurtry's strengths and major achievements in his Pulitzer Prize–winning novel, *Lonesome Dove* (1985), these two novels falter. They are so tied to satire that the depictions of the major characters suffer as a result.

Along the way, Ben Sippy provides intriguing bits and pieces of commentary about Billy's character. First of all, he tells us he would have "done anything for Billy" (p. 12). Yet he also describes Billy as "violent all right . . . [but] in his case the reputation [as a gunslinger] just arrived before the violence" (p. 15). Billy's nonchalance about shooting and killing dumbfounds Ben, but he is careful not to criticize Billy. He sees Billy as a sassy, contrary, and sulky killer, but he also considers Billy "a wandering boy one step ahead of his doom" (p. 91). Billy moves, too, without thinking: "Billy Bone was just a puppet to his instincts, jerked this way and that by strings whose pull he couldn't predict" (p. 168). Although Billy is a cocky killer, Ben cannot avoid his mysterious attraction to and attempted protection of Billy.

How much of what Ben tells us in first person represents McMurtry's thoughts about Billy the Kid is an unanswerable question. One might speculate, judging from McMurtry's numerous other comments about the mythic West, that he attempted here to question the huge, dominating legends about the region, particularly in the person of Billy the Kid, while writing a strong novel. That's as far as the speculation ought to go—perhaps.

296. Mann, E. B. *Gamblin' Man.* New York: William Morrow, 1934.

Mann warns readers from the outset that his book is a novel, not a work of history. His "story makes no claim to accuracy," for he "added some [and] changed here and there to fit the needs of this specific tale" (p. v). He also admits his "tak[ing] sides" and his "partisanship," which he considers "permissible" (p. v). If readers wish "the historical facts more accurately portrayed," he urges them to read Walter Noble Burns's *The Saga of Billy the Kid* (103), William McLeod (sic) Raine's *Sheriffs and Famous Outlaws*

(1920, 1929), or Pat Garrett's *The Authentic Life of Billy, the Kid* (127). These books were notable sources that Mann drew "upon in the preparation" of his novel (p. vi).

But too many changes, distortions, mistakes, and wrong conclusions—all these and more—greatly undermine the value of this novel. Historical novelists, including E. B. Mann here, promise to follow Billy's story, but Mann's *Gamblin' Man* illustrates what happens when writers fail to keep their promises.

Most significantly, Mann's changes and his major perversions of facts distort the Billy the Kid story. The author grafts a romance story—Billy's abundant love for pretty, vivacious Kathie Haskel—onto his action plot, but in so doing undermines the authenticity of Billy's life, especially in his days in Lincoln County. Revealingly, no Paulita Maxwell or Hispanic *señoritas* walk through these pages; instead it is the author's imagined and not very believable heroine.

Consider the ways Mann's other changes misinterpret Billy's life. The author removes Billy from the Buckshot Roberts incident and the killing of Bernstein at Blazer's Mill, and he makes Billy the very close friend of Pat Garrett and, for the most part, close to John Chisum. He overemphasizes John Tunstall's love for Billy (although Billy is not even mentioned in Tunstall's long, voluminous letters to his family), makes Sue McSween a close friend, and changes the details of the killing Morton and Baker and the Five-Day Battle in Lincoln. No Huston Chapman incident appears here to explain Governor Wallace's meeting with Billy, and Alex McSween is a stick figure reduced to a Bible-caressing caricature.

Most important, Mann has Garrett killing a Billy look-alike in Peter Maxwell's bedroom and allowing Billy and sweetheart Kathie to ride off to begin a new life in Mexico or elsewhere. Earlier, Kathie had been the one to deliver a gun to Billy in a Lincoln jail visit, which allowed him to shoot his way out.

If the historical novelist is to follow known history, Mann fails miserably in his changes and mistakes that lead to distortions. His alterations and miscues, large and small, shift the Billy the Kid story away from history and allow the author's transformed and imagined Kid rather than the historical Billy to ride through these troubling pages.

297. Momaday, N. Scott. *The Ancient Child.* New York: Doubleday, 1989.

One of the most unusual of the novels written about the Kid, or with a considerable focus on Billy, is Momaday's innovative work *The Ancient Child.*

It was the first work of fiction by Momaday after his Pulitzer Prize–winning novel, *House Made of Dawn* (1968). This experimental novel combines several ingredients: Native American myth and lore, Old West legends, and modern Indian life. The work is a magical marriage of past and present, memory, dreams, and history.

Two characters are at the center of the novel. Set, an adopted Indian artist, is on a traumatic identity search, trying to find his real father and his own true self. His journey turns him toward Grey, a young part-Kiowa, part-Navajo medicine woman. It is through Grey's dreams or visions that we see Billy the Kid and his times.

Momaday portrays Grey not only dreaming of Billy but becoming his lover and a companion to or onlooker of several of the most written-about events of his life. It is she who delivers the note about a hidden pistol in the privy, which he uses to shoot down one of the deputies in the Lincoln jail and escape. Grey also observes Billy's capture at Stinking Spring and his involvement in the killing of Sheriff Brady, and she dreams about the other women in his life. On one occasion they are also involved a scene of enthusiastic lovemaking.

The images of the Kid in Grey's memories and dreams—and in the novel generally—are those of the bifurcated Billy. He can be involved in killings (although never labeled a murderer), but he is also a jolly, clever, and loving companion. From her dreams, Grey constructs a brief account titled "The Strange and True Story of My Life with Billy the Kid."

It is not easy to follow all of Momaday's novel because it is, essentially, a work of fiction without a plot. Dreams and memories, descriptive passages, bits of poetry, strands of legends, and other experimental literary forms are jammed together without clear or explicit connection. Once Set sets out to find himself after the death of his adoptive father, the search leads him to Grey, and, once that contact is made, leading to love and marriage, Grey's dreams of Billy disappear.

298. Neider, Charles. *The Authentic Death of Hendry Jones.* 1956. Reno: University of Nevada Press, 1993.

Neider's imaginative work of fiction illustrates how much a gifted writer might follow and yet diverge from the known facts of Billy the Kid's life. Neider's novel both mimics the stories that biographers and historians tell based on solid, defensible research but also reimagines those stories, moving along new paths in the characters, actions, and ideas that inhabit his novel.

Even though the setting, characterizations, and plot of Neider's work employ recognizable facts about the Kid, the author's changes, at first, gather more attention. Most unusual is the author's dramatic shift of scene—from the activities of Hendry Jones (the name Neider gives Billy the Kid in his novel) in Lincoln County, New Mexico, to Jones's actions on the Monterey coastal area of California. In making this major shift, Neider abandons the cattle country culture and isolation of remote territorial New Mexico and places the action in the more settled seacoast of California. In the new setting, mists, gloom, abalone fishing, and a trip to Old Mexico replace sun, heat, open-ranch ranching, hunting, and Texas connections. The shift mitigates any possibility of a regionalist's demonstrating the shaping power of place on events and character. As much as Neider tries, he cannot transform coastal California in the early 1880s into the life and times of Lincoln County, New Mexico, more than a thousand miles to the east and an obviously variant sociocultural world.

In his characterizations, Neider duplicates some of the known acquaintances of Billy—and creates new ones. There are equivalents to Pat Garrett (Dad Longworth), Pete Maxwell (Hijinio Gonzales), deputy James Bell (Pablo Patron), Bob Olinger (Lon Dedrick), and Deluvina Maxwell (Francesca Zamora). There may even be parallels for Abrana García (Nika Machado Gomez) and Tom O. Folliard (Harvey French). But no equivalents of The House people—Murphy, Dolan, and Riley—or John Chisum and John Tunstall appear in Neider's novel.

The most obvious change in the cast of major characters is Doc Baker, the narrator. A close friend of the Kid's, Doc tells the central story in Neider's book. Much of the reaction to the Kid, comments about other characters and central events, and descriptions of terrain, climate, and place come from Doc. How much Doc's ideas and viewpoints reflect those of the author is not clear, but the vernacular tone, the straightforward narrative, and the informal style all give Doc's story a veracious tone.

Doc tells us little about Hendry Jones's—the Kid's—background. We learn almost nothing about his life before he arrives at Punto del Diablo (Devil's Point). But Doc imparts a good deal about the Kid's character in the months immediately preceding his violent death. Doc's Kid is courageous, often cheerful, and gregarious, but he's also a callous, nonchalant killer. He is secular, even antireligious; sexual; and will wipe out, without apparent reason, a close acquaintance. Still, Doc loves the Kid, wants him to quit his wayward journey, and urges him not to overreact to untoward events.

Generally Doc abhors some of the Kid's negative actions, but not sufficiently to break their friendship.

A few of Neider's other additions and changes deserve attention. In several scenes, he makes explicit mention of the second-class status Mexican-heritage people faced in 1880s California. That racial-ethnic tension is spotlighted when Neider transforms deputy James Bell, an Anglo, into Pablo Patron, a much-loved Mexican whose admiration for his wife and family is emphasized. The Kid feels clear remorse in killing Patron in his dramatic escape. Neider also portrays Nika as sexually promiscuous—she is the Kid's lover who marries another man when she thinks the Kid will be hanged but is soon back in the Kid's bed before his ultimate demise. Perhaps her actions follow some of those of Abrana García, but Nika's assertive, opinionated personality moves well beyond what is known about Abrana.

Several literary scholars praise Neider's novel as a breakthrough in fiction about Billy the Kid. Obviously an innovative, appealingly written work of fiction, it nonetheless fails as a believable account of Billy the Kid sans the Lincoln County setting. The author's new setting—physical, occupational, and sociocultural—does not work as an entirely veracious account of the historical Billy the Kid and the weeks leading up to his death.

299. Nye, Nelson C. *Pistols for Hire: A Tale of the Lincoln County War and the West's Most Desperate Outlaw, William (Billy the Kid) Bonney.* New York: Macmillan, 1941.

Although Nelson Nye was a practiced craftsman with more than one hundred books to his credit, his novel about Billy the Kid and the Lincoln County War is one of the least impressive of the historical novels written about these topics. Nye's weak narrative strategy, his faulty uses of history, and his slanted viewpoint greatly undermine the value of his brief novel.

Nye's novel covers most of the period historians label as the Lincoln County War. Taking up the story just after John Tunstall's murder in February 1878, Nye treats the next weeks and months of increasing conflict, ending with the Five-Day Battle in July 1878. The yarn is told through the consciousness of Flick Farsom, a twentysomething cowboy who begins as a Chisum rider but transfers his loyalties to the Murphy-Dolan House side. Farsom is an inadequate vehicle for the narrative, unable to think clearly, act coherently, and deal with his emotions.

As the first-person narrator, Farsom clearly places his loyalties with the Murphy-Dolan side. But so does the third-person narrator. The almost heroic Murphy and Dolan are pitted against the sanctimonious and devious McSween, the conniving Brit John Tunstall, and the erratic and crooked John Chisum. Nye is one of the few writers to be extremely partisan on the Murphy-Dolan side, and his story is not convincing in taking up that position.

Billy the Kid serves as the chief rascal for Nye's narrator. *Pistols for Hire* paints Billy as unalloyed blackguard. As Flick Farsom (or Nye himself) puts it, "Billy the Kid was a murderer and a thief. He would drive a bullet through a fellow's heart as lustful as he'd rape a woman; and times beyond count did both. He was a man without remorse—with regret or pity" (p. 62). The stories of a "good" Billy are nothing more than "a steamy broth of fiction." Sometimes Nye even creates a Billy that never existed, portraying him as singing lustily the hymn "Redeemed." Also, misdating the day and year of Billy's death in a "Postscript" and misusing Rio Felice and Montana for Rio Feliz and Montaño test the author's credibility. Even though Nye promises in a "Preface" that he will take no "intentional liberties" with known historical facts, he has Billy and Jessie Evans, wrongly, in a murderous conflict; he has Billy drinking; and he has him called "Billy the Kid" well before that occurred.

In short, this is a disappointing fictional portrait of Billy in the hands of a practiced novelist who should have given us something much better.

300. Ore, Rebecca. *The Illegal Rebirth of Billy the Kid*. New York: Tor Books, 1991.

For hardcore aficionados of history and biography, this book is likely to be of little interest. A work of science fiction, it relates the story of "rebirthing" a "chimera," or rebooted clone, of Billy the Kid in 2067. Simon Boyle, a CIA agent specializing in the reincarnation of characters from the past, brings a Kid figure back from the 1870s and 1880s illegally (because criminals are not to be resurrected and because he steals parts for his reconstruction).

Rebecca Ore, the penname for science fiction writer Rebecca B. Brown, plays with history, especially the final days of the Kid's life. In fact, Boyle is at times a Pat Garrett–like character set on killing off Billy and then bringing him back. Billy is lost in the present, unable to understand anything that occurred after 1881. He repeatedly asks for a pistol and a horse to solve his dilemmas. The novel's plot builds on Billy's attempts to negotiate between an enigmatic twenty-first century and an ambivalent past beset by confusing myths and legends. In a provocative "Coda" the author addresses the complexities of conflicting interpretations of Billy the Kid and advances her thoughts about the meanings of these cultural clashes.

Although Ore/Brown obviously knows a good deal about the historical Billy the Kid, this work of paranormal fiction will undoubtedly attract more science fiction fans than Old West readers.

301. Raine, William MacLeod. *The Fighting Tenderfoot*. New York: Doubleday; London: Hodder and Stoughton, 1929.

William MacLeod Raine, the British-born author of more than eighty Westerns, flooded the markets for fifty years—from 1908 to 1958—with his popular fiction. His novel *The Fighting Tenderfoot* demonstrates his ability in taking much of the Billy the Kid and Lincoln County story and adopting it for his own literary purposes. In his plot, characterizations, and bits of setting Raine reveals his indebtedness to the Kid story.

Raine's Kid-like figure is named Bob Quantrell, known also as Kid Quantrell. He is the fastest gun, haughtiest killer, and most arrogant rider in the territory of Jefferson County. Like the actual Kid, Quantrell is caught up in the vicious civil war conflict between cattle baron Wesley Steelman (John Chisum) and smaller cattlemen and merchants, who remind one of Murphy and Dolan. An Englishman named Smith-Beresford (John Tunstall) comes into the country to challenge others, and war breaks out. The hero of the novel is Garrett O'Hara, a lawyer who rides into the beset town of Concho, on edge because of a war of words gradually exploding into a gunfight. O'Hara turns out to be more of a Pat Garrett than an Alex McSween.

Raine also introduces plot elements of his own that break from the traditional Billy stories. Although Hispanics are supporters of Kid Quantrell, some of the novel's characters refer to them as "greasers," and one speaks of them as "not civilized." Plus, a romance story between young widow Barbara Steelman and Garrett O'Hara, now the sheriff, proves eventually that love wins over war. In a final scene reminiscent of the close of Owen Wister's classic novel *The Virginian*, O'Hara must do what a man's gotta do—go after bad guy Quantrell—before he and Barbara are joined in marriage.

In short, Raine derives considerable parts of his plot, character types, and action from the Kid's actual story. But his portrait of the Kid is much more the negative than the positive images of Billy that began to appear after Burns's romantic depiction of the Kid as hero in his very popular *The Saga of Billy the Kid* (103). Raine's treatment of Bob Quantrell seems more like the bad-boy Billy that emerged in the previous two generations. Along the way, the author also draws on the familiar elements of the triplex of the popular Western: hero, villain, and virtuous heroine. But in the rapid transformation of O'Hara from classic tenderfoot to a Pat Garrett–like gunman and Kid Quantrell's sudden switches back and forth in the Jefferson County war, he strains readers' credulity, especially those wanting more believable characters and plots.

302. Rhodes, Eugene Manlove. *Pasó por Aquí*. Serialized. May 27, 1926 ff., *Saturday Evening Post*. 1927. Norman: University of Oklahoma Press, 1973.

Rhodes mentions Billy only once—speaking of Pat Garrett as "the man who killed Billy the Kid" (p. 118). The novelette deals primarily with a young Billy-like Ross McEwen, who robs a bank in Belen, New Mexico, and dashes south and east to escape. He even ropes and rides a recalcitrant steer to disguise his flight. Unexpectedly, he arrives at a rundown adobe with four Mexicans—a grandfather, mother, and two youngsters—near death from diphtheria. Rather than flee from the sick Mexicans, McEwen announces "I'm here to help you." He abandons flight to endanger himself with the near-delirious family. Arriving a few days later, Pat Garrett quickly recognizes McEwen, whom he has been pursuing; perceives the good the robber has done; and looks the other way in allowing the thief to escape.

In his jaunty, rural vernacular and also his wonderfully phonetic Spanish-accented English, Rhodes tells a story of heroism, picturing a good Billy helping needy Hispanics. Also, Rhodes, a Garrett defender, paints a very positive portrait of the diligent but sympathetic sheriff. A still-appealing story nearly a century after its first appearance.

303. Vernon, John. *Lucky Billy*. Boston: Houghton Mifflin, 2008.

An obviously talented novelist, John Vernon displays his artistic mastery in this unusual novel about Billy. Through interior monologues, Vernon helps us consider, for instance, what Billy thought about his mother, his reflections on his own life shortly before his death, and what Pat Garrett was pondering as he went after Billy in 1880–1881. The author also creates numerous provocative conversations, adds imagined scenes, and conjures up a few events that, although not recorded in history, aid readers in conceiving a larger, more complex story of Billy. For example, Vernon utilizes two brief chapters to suggest what Billy's life was like as a boy in New York City, the major reliance of Billy on his mother, and the Kid's interactions with John Tunstall, Alex and Sue McSween, and his Regulator chums.

Unfortunately, Vernon's mangled handling of historical details undermines his artistic achievements. The author claims, "The details of the

Lincoln County War, and of William Bonney's participation in it, are as accurate as I could make them" (p. 291). But Vernon makes mistakes in these two areas as well as in several other facets of Billy's story.

First the factual mistakes. He has Billy's mother living several years after she died, has Wild Bill Hickok alive more than a year after his assassination, portrays Billy as a serious drinker, has Tunstall referring to Billy in his letters to his parents in London, and describes Billy as "a new leader" after the shootout at Blazer's Mill—all of which are wrong or slanted in the wrong direction.

Even more off track are Vernon's characterizations of several leading figures in the Lincoln County story. He claims to have closely followed the facts in Frederick Nolan's key book *The West of Billy the Kid* (155), but Nolan does not depict Billy as vulgar, profane, or a serious drinker. Even more skewed is Vernon's portrait of Sue McSween. His image of her is a sexually hungry woman who has not been intimate with her husband for two years and who has more recently slept with four or five other men, including an unnamed man in the McSween house on the evening of 18 July 1878, the night before the Big Kill. And Vernon has several characters, including her husband, viewing this sexual tryst.

Other miscues abound. Billy's stepfather, William Antrim, was not abusive in his treatment of the Kid—neglectful, perhaps, but not guilty of physical mistreatment. Billy is often depicted here as a young man with a piston-driving penis, leading to the pregnancy of Paulita Maxwell, raucous love-making with Celsa Gutiérrez, and references to other affairs with willing *señoritas*.

Vernon also jumps around in his chronology, dealing with events of the Lincoln County War and afterward and then retreating to Billy's supposed life in New York City and the time before he arrived in southeastern New Mexico in 1877. Undoubtedly, some of these flashbacks provide backgrounds that are helpful for a larger understanding of Billy, but they also undermine the cause-effect relationships of unfolding history. For example, chapter 5, "1878: Tunstall," deals with events immediately before and up to Tunstall's death in February 1878. The following chapter, "April 1881: Escape," treats Billy's escape from the Lincoln jail, but those important events of Billy's life, more than three years apart, disrupt and rearrange the cause-effect flow of history rather than depict how the death of Tunstall launched Billy on the path of revenge.

Finally, Vernon is often guilty of what historians call presentism, superimposing present-day ideas and attitudes on the past. His repeated references to Billy's sexual drives and Sue McSween's lust and the smutty language of the Regulators seem much more out of the twenty-first than the late nineteenth century. There is frequently in these pages a sense of the story being out of time—characters of earlier times depicted in the vernacular of more than a century later.

304. Vidal, Gore. "The Death of Billy the Kid." In *9 Modern Short Plays*, edited by David A. Sohn and Richard H. Tyre. New York: Bantam Books, 1977, pp. 3–32.

The well-known writer Gore Vidal makes numerous changes, some without apparent reason, in this script for a television drama. The author rearranges several dates, events, names, and characterizations. Some of the innovations allow Vidal to bring on scene characters who never existed and others who did not participate in events into which the author places them. For example, Pat Garrett and Saval Gutiérrez were not present when Billy shot down a drunken Joe Grant in a Fort Sumner saloon, an event that did not happen in 1878. In addition, Gov. Lew Wallace was not pardoning Billy in 1878, and a Maria Gonzalez was not the young woman to whom Billy returned after breaking out of the Lincoln jail in 1881. Why the author alters these events and characters is not clear.

On the other hand, Vidal advances provocative ideas, sometimes unique and at other times repetitious, that deserve consideration in trying to understand Billy. When Saval Gutiérrez urges the Kid to flee and tells the young desperado, "You've had your day," adding, "people are tired of killing" (p. 19), he speaks words missing from most writing about the Billy. Moreover, when Pete Maxwell also urges the Kid to abandon Lincoln County and tells him, "The country's changing, Billy. . . . It's not what it was" (p. 27), he repeats writers' conclusions about sociocultural shifts in the area dating back to Walter Noble Burns's *The Saga of Billy the Kid* (1926). Another intriguing idea is introduced when Deputy John Poe suggests that contemporaries are partially at fault since they have been guilty of launching the legends of Billy by making him larger than life.

Toward the end of his teleplay, Vidal invents a drunken character to serve as something of a chorus to comment on and direct the plot. Not only reflecting some of the author's ideas about changes reshaping New

Mexico, the drunk also represents a latter-day Judas in informing Pat Garrett of Billy's whereabouts and being paid silver coins for the stab in the back.

Had Vidal followed the known historical events more accurately rather than scrambling and distorting them, his three-act drama would have appealed even more to historically minded readers and viewers.

305. Whitlow, B. Duane. *Lincoln County Diary.* Santa Fe, N.Mex.: Sunstone Press, 1991.

The author breaks golden rules expected of top-drawer historical novelists: he not only unceasingly reimagines the events of the Lincoln County conflicts, he also rearranges the known chronology of happenings and mistakenly dates other occurrences.

First, the reshapings. The main characters are government officials and soldiers from Washington, D.C., and Fort Stanton, not the well-known figures from Lincoln County. Jimmy Dolan is the only familiar figure at the center of the story, although Gov. Lew Wallace and others play minor parts.

Billy the Kid is primarily an off-scene bit player. Whitlow tries to deal with Billy the killer as well as Billy the genial comrade, but the events of his life are so changed—even distorted—that he is not the Billy of history. For instance, Billy is captured by Pat Garrett in Stinking Spring in December 1880, but afterward he is taken to Lincoln, not to Las Vegas and Santa Fe. And there is no trial in Mesilla. Billy escapes from the Lincoln jail a few days after his capture, and Garrett guns him down another few days later. In these instances alone, about six months of Billy's life are elided and the events surrounding his last days are jumbled.

Whitlow also attempts to turn the Lincoln County conflicts into a story of government agents pursuing counterfeiters in southeastern New Mexico. In the plot focused on passing false dollars in New Mexico and Mexico, John Chisum, Alex and Sue McSween, and the Regulators are, for the most part, absent. The author also has Billy working for Jimmy Dolan, with Jessie Evans at one helm of the counterfeiting and a prominent member of the Santa Fe Ring running things from the territorial capital.

Into his narrative of numerous conflicts and murdering violence (especially the vicious actions of Jessie Evans), the author tries to incorporate romance, racial and ethnic harmony, and evocative descriptions of New Mexico landscapes and social customs. His attempts in these areas are moderately successful.

In sum, a work that sidelines Billy the Kid and undermines its authenticity through excessively imagined events and themes as well as mistakes or chronological rearrangements.

306. Willoughby, Lee Davis (Jane Toombs). *The Outlaws.* New York: Dell Publishing, 1984.

The Outlaws illustrates one trend in American popular literature from the 1960s onward. More than a few publishers, recognizing the persisting interest in things western and capitalizing on the growing fascination with violence and explicit sexual stories, combined these in a popular genre known as the "adult Western." Featuring scenes of violence and steamy sexual encounters, adult Westerns were extraordinarily popular in closing decades of the twentieth century.

Like many other adult Westerns, *The Outlaws* was written under a pseudonym, in this case by Jane Toombs writing under the pen name of Lee Davis Willoughby. The novel also appeared as the forty-ninth segment of the multivolume Making of America series. The author of dozens of books in several fictional genres, Toombs adopts the widespread technique of many historical novelists: the creation of imagined characters to accompany historical figures. Here handsome Mark Halloran from Texas, pretty Tessa Nesbitt from England (via Texas), and her younger brother Ezra Nesbitt arrive in Lincoln County and are soon entangled with Billy the Kid.

One of the first authors to employ explicit sexual encounters in a novel about Billy the Kid, Toombs nonetheless keeps Billy's sexual activities off scene. But hero Halloran (who is actually named Mark Dempsey) and heroine Tessa Nesbit engage in energetic lovemaking. And Tessa also makes love, reluctantly, with a Hispanic man and is threatened with rape on two or three other occasions. Sex plays a more prominent role than violence in this adult novel.

Toombs's Billy represents the ambivalent Kid figure who began appearing in fictional and historical accounts from the 1960s forward. He is cheerful and warm toward Tessa's younger brother Ezra and helps other persons in need. But he's also a selfish, self-absorbed killer and basely takes advantage of a young *señorita* who is hopelessly enamored with him. The negative side of Billy is featured more than his positive actions.

Toombs shows a practiced artistic hand in this story. She juxtaposes the love-and-clash scenes between Mark and Tessa, the coming-of-age actions of Ezra, and the birth of a Billy-fathered child, contrapuntally, against Billy's death in Pete Maxwell's bedroom.

For the most part, Toombs closely follows the major events of Billy's life in Lincoln County. The killings of Tunstall, Brady, and McSween are mostly accurate, as are the depictions of the happenings at the Greathouse Ranch, Stinking Spring, and Fort Sumner. Nearly always the imagined characters—e.g., Mark, Tessa, and Ezra—are on scene and participate, at least as eyewitnesses, when these events take place.

Here, the New Grey, bifurcated, or ambiguous Billy and the adult novel are combined. The result is not a first-rate novel but a reasonably accurate, provocative, and readable one on Billy the Kid.

307. Woods, Walter. "Billy the Kid." In *The Great Train Robbery and Other Recent Melodramas*, edited by Garrett H. Leverton. Princeton, N.J.: Princeton University Press, 1940, pp. 197–255.

Woods's melodrama was one of the first plays written about Billy the Kid. First registered in 1903, the drama was revised for copyright by Woods, with the aid of Joseph Santley, and opened in 1906. It was immensely popular, bringing in, one source says, six million viewers in its first six years (1906–1912) of performance. For nearly a dozen years the play drew large audiences, with one enthusiastic newspaper effusing that the Woods-Santley drama was "better than The Girl of the American West and the best melodrama I expect to see this season."

"Billy the Kid" portrayed a Kid at odds from most of the literary depictions of the early twentieth century. Billy has been driven off course by his lying, cheating, betraying father, who kills Billy's mother and stepfather. Those murderous acts send Billy reeling into a life of outlawry. But, as the dramatists make clear, Billy has a good, clear heart even if he has broken the law on several occasions (all off scene). Given an opportunity for redemption, he finally takes that path in the closing scene.

Despite all the claptrap of melodrama—several mistaken identities, fortuitous chances and circumstances, Billy dressed as a maid, and some attempts at Irish humor—the drama raises intriguing questions. Did Billy go bad because he was forced or driven in that dark direction, or was he a bad man at heart? The dramatists clearly think the former, showing that Billy prays, has a sense of God's "divine will," and realizes he can change directions, which he does in the closing lines, embracing his beloved Nellie and heading east, "where there is no trouble, sin or sorrow."

Literary Criticism

308. Etulain, Richard W. "Billy the Kid among the Dime Novelists." *Outlaw Gazette* 30 (2017): 3–6.

    This brief essay deals with a handful of the dozen or more dime novels about Billy the Kid that appeared from 1881 to about 1890. The approach is primarily that of the historian pointing out how dime novelists sometimes followed, but much more often broke from, the historical record concerning the Kid. Most of the dime novelists portrayed Billy as a villainous desperado, thus helping establish, along with negative newspaper accounts, that the Kid was largely a violent, murderous outlaw. Few of the dime novelists knew anything about the historical Billy, and nearly all were innocent of knowing anything about the American West.

309. Etulain, Richard W. "Billy the Kid among the Novelists." *New Mexico Historical Review* 93 (Winter 2018): 31–64.

    The most recent discussion of the fictional Billy the Kid, this essay is also the most extensive discussion of the subject. The piece covers fiction about the Kid from the first dime novels to what the author considers to be the best novel about Billy, Ron Hansen's *The Kid: A Novel* (287). The essay focuses, most of all, on novelists' uses of history—from the ahistorical fiction of the dime novelists to more historically oriented novelists later in the twentieth century. About thirty novels are treated in the text and footnotes.

    Etulain divides the fictional treatments of Billy into three stages. The first stage, dominated by dime novelists and buttressed by dozens of journalists, portrayed Billy as an evil and violent desperado. This negative depiction dominated works of fiction until the appearance of Walter Noble Burns's biography *The Saga of Billy the Kid* (1926), which ushered in the possibility of a second, much more positive image of the Kid. More than a few novelists followed this more positive path.

    Then, in the 1950s and 1960s, a more complex, divided Billy began to appear in novels. For increasing numbers of novelists, the Kid became a "bifurcated" Billy, that is, a young man by turns both villainous and heroic. This ambivalent figure, the New Grey Billy, has been at the center of most novels written in the past half century. Among the best of the historical novels about the Kid are Edwin Corle's *Billy the Kid: A Novel* (1953), Charles Neider's *The Authentic Death of Henry Jones* (1956), Amelia Bean's *Time for Outrage* (1967), Elizabeth Fackler's *Billy the Kid: The Legend of El Chivato*

(1995), and Ron Hansen's *The Kid* (2016). Other writers have rightly pointed to Larry McMurtry's *Anything for Billy* (1988), N. Scott Momaday's *The Ancient Child* (1989), and Johnny D. Bogg's *Law of the Land: The Trial of Billy the Kid* (2004) as intriguing works of Kid fiction.

310. Tuska, Jon. "Billy the Kid in Fiction." In *Billy the Kid: His Life and Legend*. Albuquerque: University of New Mexico Press, 1994, pp. 154–87. Revised and expanded edition of *Billy the Kid: A Bio-Bibliography*. Westport, Conn.: Greenwood Press, 1984.

This brief chapter on Billy the Kid novels combines Tuska's extensive plot summaries with his outspoken opinions about all things concerning Billy. The chapter moves chronologically from the dime novels to fiction appearing in the late 1980s. The author provides thorough discussions of what happened in more than thirty novels and short stories, but he likewise points out the "fantasies" and historical errors in nearly all the works.

Tuska considers Amelia Bean's *Time for Outrage* (1967) to be "the finest novel" (p. 178) about the Kid. He salutes her strong use of history and touts "the number of genuine insights" (p. 178) lodged in her novel. The four-page section summarizing the plot and content of Bean's historical novel runs to twice the length of the author's discussions of any other Kid novel. He concludes that Bean "correctly interpreted and reconstructed what actually did happen" (p. 181).

The chapter concludes with Tuska's conviction that novels and films are particularly important in keeping alive the story of Billy the Kid because the contents of these two mediums, cleaving more to legend than the Kid's actual life, have captured the attention of readers and viewers much more than the facts of his life. Perhaps so, although Tuska does not do much in this chapter to sustain that point.

Too much plot summary here and insufficient analysis and evaluations of these dozens of novels.

Movies
Films and Criticism

311. *Billy the Kid*. October 1930. Metro-Goldwyn-Mayer. 95 minutes. Directed by King Vidor. Johnny Mack Brown as Billy the Kid, Wallace Beery as Pat Garrett, Wyndam Standing as Tunston (Tunstall), Russell Simpson as Alex McSween, James Marcus as Donovan.

Film director King Vidor was smitten with journalist Walter Noble Burns's biography *The Saga of Billy the Kid* (103) and wanted to build a new film Western around it. Vidor's scenario follows some of the Lincoln County history and some of Burns's book, but it also revises events and characters and contributes several new wrinkles. The film opens with the Donovan character, a sheriff and community manipulator, serving as a composite Murphy-Dolan-Brady figure in dominating the Tunston (Tunstall) and McSween interests in settling and ranching in the Lincoln area. Soon Tunston is murdered, and McSween also loses his life trying to escape his burning house. The movie town reminds one, in several respects, of the actual Lincoln.

But those still living who had participated in the Lincoln County War were alienated by the movie's palpable distance from historic events. Sophie Poe, who had married one of Pat Garrett's deputies, John Poe, visited the film-in-the-making but refused to accept its positive depiction of Billy the Kid, thinking that portrait particularly ahistorical. "I knew that little bucktoothed killer," she stormed, "and he wasn't the way you are making him at all." Sue McSween was even more irate. Always conscious of her age and appearance, Sue was upset with the too-old Blanch Federici playing her. And when the film depicted her playing "The Star-Spangled Banner" as the

McSween home burned and Alex running out of the house with a Bible in hand (as Burns had in his *Saga*), she abandoned the theater, castigating the movie as "all lies."

Vidor's Billy, by and large, is depicted positively and follows a few well-established actions. When Tunston is murdered, Billy vows vengeance: "Before I die," he cries out, "I'm gonna shoot down like a dog every man that had anything to do with this." And he continues on that path of pursuit. Billy supports McSween through the lawyer's death and then sets out on a course that leads to more crimes and a sentence to hang. But the film sharply diverges from reality when Pat Garrett allows Billy to ride off free with a new sweetheart.

The two largest alterations in the film are in regard to Garrett and a romance for Billy. Pat Garrett, portrayed by Wallace Beery in a very strong performance, enters the cinematic story earlier than he did historically, and he and Billy are depicted in an untrue close friendship. In addition, the pretty Claire, who arrives as the fiancée of Tunston, transfers her love to Billy after the death of the Englishman, creating a romance that stands in for Billy's actual attractions to several *señoritas* and *señoras* as well as to Paulita Maxwell. Claire comes to love Billy. And despite his violence and sometimes distance, their love blossoms. Garrett allows Billy to ride free with Claire out of town.

Another transformation takes places among the "bad guys." Although Donovan resembles L. G. Murphy and Jimmy Dolan in the first scenes of the film, his ramrod Ballinger takes over the villain's role in the later action. It is Ballinger, resembling the bullying Bob Olinger, whom Billy shoots down in his escape from the Lincoln jail.

Although former football star Johnny Mack Brown's portrayal of Billy is, at best, mediocre, the film does follow much of the plotline in Burns's biography. Generally, the film reflects the more smiling portraits of Billy from the mid-1920s to 1960.

312. *Billy the Kid*. 1941. Metro-Goldwyn-Mayer. Robert Taylor as Billy Bonney, Brian Dunlevy as Jim Sherwood, Ian Hunter as Eric Keating, Gene Lockhart as Dan Hickey.

Historians relish seeing patterns running through time, pointing to themes, ideas, and happenings that keep actions moving down a familiar path. Unfortunately, *Billy the Kid* (1941), starring Robert Taylor as the Kid, breaks from patterns that were popular in dealing with Billy the Kid in the 1930s and 1940s more often than it follows them. Rather than portray Billy as a winsome, positive character as many Walter Noble Burns–influenced writings were, this movie depicts the Kid, at best, as thinking about reforming from his outlawing but then quickly retreating back into his violent, killing ways. In several ways, the reach of the film, particularly in its weak characterizations and faulty history, exceeds it grasp.

Billy (Taylor) comes on scene in Lincoln with an established reputation as a dangerous gunslinger bent on following his partisan, violent ways. At first signing on with a group of shootists headed up by Dan Hickey (Gene Lockhart) and reminiscent of the Murphy-Dolan contingent, Billy is challenged by an old friend from Silver City, Jim Sherwood (Brian Dunlevy), to rethink his actions and future. Billy stiff-arms such suggestions until the kindness of an Englishman, Eric Keating (Ian Hunter), and his peace-loving ways encourage Billy to reconsider. Sherwood also encourages Billy to leave the Hickey rustlers and join up with Keating. He does and experiences a new sense of comradeship—until the Hickey riders back-shoot Keating. Billy then quickly returns to his violent ways, galloping up a path of revenge and shooting down nearly six opponents in a frenzy of killing. In a final scene, Billy is jailed and challenges Sherwood to a shootout. In action unlike Garrett's killing of Billy, Sherwood bests the Kid in the gun battle. Perhaps the left-handed gunman Billy (a mistake in this movie and several others) invites his own death by switching over to his right hand and losing a quick-draw battle with Sherwood.

Taylor and most of the actors in this *Billy the Kid* are asked to perform beyond their abilities. Taylor, for instance, is asked to portray Billy's rapid moves from desperado to cowboy and back to desperado in a flurry of scenes. He is not able to convince viewers of the believability of these sudden shifts. Nor is Dunlevy up to personifying the kind but stubborn Jim Sherwood. The Murphy-Dolan bad guy, Dan Hickey, is even less authentic among the major characters.

The historical elements of this ninety-minute movie are as shaky as its leading characterizations. The film dodges much of the Kid story in Lincoln County by leaving out John Chisum, Alex and Sue McSween, the Santa Fe Ring, and the very partisan territorial and county legal officials. Even when the movie comes closest to actual history with the Tunstall and, possibly, Garrett characters, it is wide of the mark. Finally, though the physical settings are brilliantly shot in Technicolor, the faulty acting and trumped-up, distorted history sink the film. It was an inauspicious beginning for the Billy movies of the 1940s.

313. *Billy the Kid.* 2013. Lionsgate Films. 80 minutes. Produced and directed by Christopher Forbes. Cody McCarver as Leon Copper, Kimberly Campbell as Katherine Bonney (Catherine McCarty), Christopher Bowman as William Bonney (Billy the Kid).

A low-budget Western hamstrung with a weird plot, mediocre acting, and inadequate drama, this film merits the major criticism it has received. It diverges almost entirely from known history of Billy the Kid, picturing William (as he is called here), mother Katherine, and just-revealed father (Leon Copper) in actions that never occurred. The film explodes in melodrama and poorly depicted killings—on all sides.

A major failure is the character of William—not called Billy the Kid until the final moments of the film. Christopher Bowman—not up to playing the Kid believably—is weak and false. Kimberly Campbell does much better as William's mother, and Cody McCarver does equally well as his father.

The action supposedly takes place before Billy's entrance into Lincoln County. Katherine (*sic*) states she met her son's father twenty years earlier in Carson City but thought the dad was dead all these years. Hence, the movie is mistitled since it is about a time period even before Billy was called Billy Bonney let alone Billy the Kid.

Disappointing. An inferior film.

314. *Billy the Kid in Texas.* 1940. Producers Releasing Corporation. Bob Steele as Billy the Kid, Al "Fuzzy" St. John as Fuzzy Jones, Carleton Young as Gil Cooper.

The second installment in the PRC Billy the Kid series clearly abandons the historical Billy. It even includes Billy, briefly, as a town sheriff. The movie also features Billy's brother, Gil Cooper, who is nothing like the Kid's real brother, Joe McCarty Antrim. Gil at first opposes Billy and then rides with him in a typical turnabout of a major character in these films.

Billy is displayed on a $5,000 reward poster, but one of his supporters asserts that Billy was framed and is not guilty of the accused crime. Several brief conversations ensue, indicating that Billy is not outside the law, and he himself tells others that he not only abides by the law; he always upholds it. As in other movies in the PRC series, Billy is a peace bringer who stands up for the needy and opposes the malignant forces attacking the powerless.

Sidekick Fuzzy Jones furnishes a needed change of tenor, bringing comic relief through his flailing attempts to support Billy. Because the nearly incessant galloping, shooting, and fisticuffs allow for little space or time for character development, Fuzzy instills a rollicking pace in his role as stumbling, bumbling sidekick.

315. *Billy the Kid Returns.* September 1938. Republic. 53 minutes. Roy Rogers as Billy the Kid, Smiley Burnette as Frog Millhouse, Mary Hunt as Lynne Roberts, Wade Boteler as Pat Garrett.

Roy Rogers and Billy the Kid are conjoined in this curiously organized film. In the opening minutes, Rogers plays the real Kid until Pat Garrett shoots him. In the second, longer section, he plays himself, a singing, gunslinging helper of nesters. The movie reflects changes in the Kid's legends and in Rogers's career in the 1940s.

Rogers's Kid and Rogers himself fit the mold of the increasingly positive legends about Billy in the post–Walter Noble Burns era, especially from the late 1920s into the 1950s. The Kid may be a killer, often in protecting himself and others who are endangered in a vicious frontier civil war, but most of all he is upstanding in his clear efforts to aid the downtrodden. Here he stands up for small farmers who are being browbeaten by bullies resembling L. G. Murphy and Jimmy Dolan.

The movie also illustrates the rising popularity of the singing cinematic Western in the 1930s. Sound revolutionized the uses of music in popular films, first in Gene Autry and then in Roy Rogers. In this film, Rogers can be a gunman, but he also sings his way to popularity and support in the community through his musical abilities. Smiley Burnette, his sidekick, a figure often in Autry and Rogers films, also provides singing solos and humor as comic relief.

Not a major film because of its mediocre acting and so-so handling of setting and scenes, but certainly in line with the trend of a not-so-bad Billy in the 1930s. Generally, more Rogers than Billy the Kid.

316. *Billy the Kid: Showdown in Lincoln County.* 2017. ITN Movies and ForbesFilms. 80 minutes. Directed by Christopher Forbes. Christopher Bowman as William Bonney (Billy the Kid), Cody McCarver as Leon Copper.

The third of the Forbes-directed films with Cody McCarver as a main character, this film resembles the others in the series. It is a weak production in action, characterization, and its handling of history. The artistic dismissals of the film by most critics are on solid ground.

The film is set in New Mexico and moves to Lincoln County about halfway through the movie, a place dominated by Brigham Landon, an L. G.

Murphy–like character who dominates the town, trade, and banking. Several men and at least one woman—one-eyed Lilly—oppose Landon's dictatorial and murderous actions in several poorly staged shootouts.

William Bonney, becoming known as Billy the Kid, and his newly discovered biological father, Leon Copper, lead the opposition to Landon. Christopher Bowman weakly plays a curious Kid, sometimes with a weak backbone and at other times a violent shooter. An inadequate conclusion ends the film on a weak note.

Some attempts are made at history. John Tunstall is introduced and killed. Billy is on scene, and allusions are made to the Big Kill. But even the historical elements are jumbled or inaccurate.

Another unfortunate segment in the Christopher Forbes–Cody McCarver series.

317. *Billy the Kid Trapped.* 1942. Producers Releasing Corporation. 52 minutes. Buster Crabbe as Billy the Kid, Al "Fuzzy" St. John as Fuzzy Jones, Boyd McTaggart as Jeff.

This movie of just under an hour is the third in the Billy the Kid film series starring Buster Crabbe, following earlier segments in the series that featured Bob Steele. A product of Poverty Row in Hollywood and a B Western like others of the 1930s and 1940s, the movie illustrates the limitations of these low-budget, quickly produced Westerns capitalizing on the Billy the Kid name.

One should not look for accurate history in this film. There is none. True, Crabbe plays an outlaw with his two sidekicks, Fuzzy Jones and Jeff, but their actions have nothing factually to do with the actual life of Billy the Kid. Falsely accused of crimes they did not commit, which were perpetrated by others masquerading as Billy and his gang, the true guys ride, fistfight, and shoot their way to victory—and then start all over again in the final scene.

The hand-in-glove connections between Stanton, the bad guy well played by Glenn Strange, and the town judge do suggest the similar underhanded Murphy–Brady–district law officials–Santa Fe Ring combine that opposed the Tunstall-McSween-Billy forces.

Chase and pursuit, galloping horses, and incessant, rapid-fire shooting keep the movie's action-driven plot in high gear, but the acting skills and historical content are inferior, next to nil.

318. *Billy the Kid Wanted.* 1941. Producers Releasing Corporation. 64 minutes. Buster Crabbe as Billy the Kid, Al "Fuzzy" St. John as Fuzzy Jones, Dave O'Brien as Jeff.

This film is the first of the Buster Crabbe depictions of Billy in the PRC series. Crabbe took over from Bob Steele, who had tired of the repetition in the films and had signed on with Republic Pictures. Some critics think the series improved with Crabbe in the lead role, but similarity and repetition carried over more than innovation in the Crabbe roles.

Billy the Kid here is a man without complexity, a thoroughly white-hat protagonist. As critic Stephen Tatum writes, the Kid is something of a populist hero, protecting "the simple, humble common folk from exploitation." In his role, Billy serves as a foil against the L. G. Murphy–like actions of the dominating villain trying to control all of Paradise Valley. Even though the sheriff, initially, wrongly views Billy as guilty of several illegal actions, he soon changes his mind. In fact, Billy's consistent, honorable actions also win over the valley's residents.

Fuzzy, of course, is comic relief. And, as film critic Jon Tuska notes, the film features "plenty of physical action." A pinch of innovation appears in the depiction of a family of a husband, wife, and little boy as the faces of embattled settlers whom Billy upholds.

The familiar pattern of the PRC series obtains: honorable Billy; supportive roles of Fuzzy and Jeff; opposition to selfish, greedy rascals; and loads of riding, shooting, and fistfighting.

319. *Billy the Kid's Gun Justice.* December 1940. Producers Releasing Corporation. 63 minutes. Bob Steele as Billy the Kid, Al "Fuzzy" St. John as Fuzzy Jones, Carleton Young as Jeff.

The movie opens with Billy, Fuzzy, and Jeff holed up and under siege. While Billy and Jeff fire away at gun-shooting opponents, Fuzzy finds a way to dig under the back wall, helping lead the trio to safety. The subsequent action introduces a bullying rancher trying to chase a woman settler and her family off their homestead. The villain has diverted a water source and is now pressing the nesters to pay exorbitant water-rights fees or sell out to him at minimal rates.

Billy and his two buddies set out—"according to law," Billy says—to support the small farmers and crush the bullies. The jumbled plot, filled with frantic riding, shooting, and hand-to-hand battles, is not easy to follow.

Early on Billy is recognized as "Billy Bonney," but once he stands up against the villains and the false publicity about him as a criminal (a usual path of events in the PRC series), he is accepted as a stalwart hero among the settlers. In the second half of the film, Billy plays his usual upstanding role model, representing the powerless or downtrodden against the evil men. As usual in this series, the good and bad guys get the major roles, with little place for women, families, and townspeople.

320. *Billy the Kid's Range War.* 1941. Producers Releasing Corporation. 60 minutes. Bob Steele as Billy the Kid, Al "Fuzzy" St. John as Fuzzy Q. Jones, Carleton Young as Jeff.

This movie, as part of the numerous PRC series, follows a plotline similar to most other films in the group. Arriving on the scene, Billy is accused of murder, with a large reward for his capture. He is seen as guilty of several major crimes in the Lincoln area, which seems separate from the Lincoln County of New Mexico. Early on a poster indicates Billy is "Wanted for Murder."

In the opening scenes Billy laments, "I'm wanted from Maine to California, and I've never been out of the Southwest." This movie repeatedly plays on this often-stated theme in the PRC series, but the sensational actions—frantic galloping, sporadic shooting, and violent fistfights—capture more time than the emphasis on unwarranted persecution of Billy.

As per usual, Fuzzy Jones furnishes comedy in his burlesque actions, but he also provides, as sidekick partner, recurring support for Billy. St. John is a skilled clown, bringing laughter to otherwise serious if not overdone seriousness.

The evildoers here gang up on a vivacious young woman, Ellen, who is trying to build a stagecoach road. She begins as a critic of Billy's, or at least of a look-alike claiming to be Billy, and he is indeed an outlaw rascal. But in the real Billy's supportive, encouraging actions, he proves his upright ways and converts Ellen to his side.

The movie prances along, following a familiar plot devised in B Westerns. At first leading characters misread other leading characters, thinking of them as villainous rascals, but through righteous deeds the misread characters prove they are solid gold and win over the doubters. This conversion process is the lifeline of these often-utilized plots.

321. *Blazing Frontier.* September 1943. Producers Releasing Corporation. 59 minutes. Buster Crabbe as Billy the Kid, Al "Fuzzy" St. John as Fuzzy Jones.

The last of the Buster Crabbe roles in the PRC Billy series, this movie provides evidence why the series folded with this film. The usual ingredients have descended to boring stereotypes, the chief of which are the usual Billy, the hackneyed humor of Fuzzy Jones, and the good-guys-versus-bad-guys plot. Even accepting that the PRC movies were meant to imitate others in the series, the ingredients are nonetheless more alienating than appealing.

Billy is invited by a lawyer into a community riven with conflict among settlers, shysters, and the railroad. At first it looks as if the railroad and the rascals are in cahoots, but soon Billy shows that the railroad has been taken; the evildoers have pulled the wool over the eyes of the railroad's agents and leaders. The sheriff, who recognizes Billy as "Mr. Bonney," is aligned with the villains. Initially Billy seems to be working both sides until he indicates that he will make use of illegal means to bring law and order to the community.

The sameness of the series—its numerous gallops, gun wars, and fisticuffs—occupies most of the action. And Fuzzy's humorous actions descend into boring banality. The ending, too, is abrupt and ludicrous.

The nineteen quickly made and low-budget PRC films released between 1940 and 1943 reveal how difficult it is to turn out compelling, if patterned, movies about Billy the Kid. Finally, the film company—under financial pressure, losing its stars, and unable to spice up the series with bits of innovation—gave up and ended the Billy series with this film.

322. *Cattle Stampede.* August 1943. Producers Releasing Corporation. 58 minutes. Buster Crabbe as Billy the Kid, Al "Fuzzy" St. John as Fuzzy Jones, Frances Gladwin as Mary Dawson.

Toward the end of the PRC series costarring Buster Crabbe as Billy the Kid and Al St. John as Fuzzy Jones, the installments combine familiar ingredients with a few minor new ones. The hard riding, fistfighting, and frantic shooting continue apace. The upstanding white hats are clearly delineated from the rascally black hats. No complex gray hats appear in this or other installments of the Saturday matinee series.

There are two notable changes. One is the elimination of a second sidekick, usually a sturdy, strong, and upstanding rider more like Billy than the humorous Fuzzy Jones, who continues to stumble along as a laughable foil to the Kid. A second change is the introduction of a woman character, usually in a minor but nonetheless noticeable role. Here, as is often the case, Miss Mary Dawson, of a mistreated ranching family, denigrates Billy as a despicable outlaw—until his virtuous actions rescuing her and chasing off the villains change her mind. Revealingly, though violence—even murder—runs through this film, absolutely no sexual threat against the upright woman is suggested even though she is captured and held hostage by vicious killers. Murder, yes; sexual assault, not even hinted at.

The plot has Billy opposing Coulter, a crooked and avaricious land baron set on stealing small ranchers' cattle or stampeding and running off their herds so as to buy them at below-bargain rates. Billy's determined opposition to Coulter and his henchmen allows him to exhibit, repeatedly, his skilled riding, shooting, and battling. Although Billy is depicted as a wanted desperado, as he is in most of the PRC potboilers, the virtuous actions prove a dependable, upright, and masculine citizen.

Even though it is set in New Mexico, this film utilizes none of the known facts about Billy the Kid or Lincoln County.

323. *Chisum*. 1970. Warner Brothers. 111 minutes. John Wayne as Chisum, Geoffrey Deuel as Billy the Kid, Ben Johnson as James Pepper, Forrest Tucker as Lawrence Murphy, Glenn Corbett as Pat Garrett, Patrick Knowles as J. Henry Tunstall, Pamela McMyler as Sallie Chisum, Andrew Prine as Alex McSween.

By 1970, John Wayne dominated any Western film in which he appeared. Beginning with *Stagecoach* (1939) and through the next three decades, Wayne was out in front—way out in front—of other heroes in movie Westerns. If the plot was imagined, it circulated around Wayne; if it was based on history, the historical ingredients were reshaped, even distorted, to keep Wayne at the center of the story. Such is the case in *Chisum*, where actual history is redone to fit John Wayne.

Chisum includes more than a few incidents of the Lincoln County War. J. Henry Tunstall and Alex McSween, often with Chisum, take on L. G. Murphy and The House interests to control the economy of the county. That intense competition leads to the murders of Tunstall and Sheriff Brady and a fiery shootout on the main street of Lincoln. Local, regional, and territorial interests are involved in this cinematic version of the Lincoln County civil war.

Billy the Kid, already with a killer reputation in Silver City (not true, of course; it began in Arizona), first appears riding with Tunstall. The

Englishman tries to silence Billy's guns and keep him on the right side of the law, but when Murphy's men murder Tunstall, Billy swears revenge and goes on a killing rampage. Meanwhile, Billy is taken with Chisum's pretty, newly arrived niece Sallie, and a possible romance seems on the horizon until Billy's vow to wipe out Tunstall's killers sends him galloping toward death.

These historical elements are rearranged, with the revised history featuring retrofitted characters. Wayne's Chisum is much more involved in Lincoln County affairs than the Cattle King of the Pecos was historically. If the actual Chisum held back from a central role in the war, the movie Chisum leads the action, taking on The House, Murphy, and crooked law enforcement officials. And the movie Chisum wins the war rather than selling his cattle and moving away from New Mexico.

Billy the Kid also is given new clothes in his movie role. Some of the changes are minor, others major. Billy and Garrett did not become good friends during the Lincoln County War, and Garrett was not with Billy in the Big Kill days in Lincoln. Garrett and Billy did not compete for the attentions of Sallie Chisum, and they did not come together in connections with Chisum.

The movie's largest change is transforming Billy into a murderous gunslinger. Once the Kid declares vengeance for Tunstall's killing at the Englishman's funeral (Billy was not there; he was jailed during the funeral), he shoots Morton, Baker, and Sheriff Brady on sight because he sees them as murderers of Tunstall (Billy was involved in their killings, of course, but no evidence points to his being their sole killer). Before the end of the movie, Billy also kills Jessie Evans and others. There are clear differences between the two cinematic characters, Billy and Chisum: Billy wants vengeance, but Chisum desires justice. Seeing the desperado complex now driving Billy, Chisum orders the Kid off his ranch.

One final distinction frames the differences between Chisum and Billy. In actual history, John Tunstall and Alex McSween spoke out more for law and order than Chisum, although the Cattle King chose not to involve himself much in the war. But the movie Chisum becomes *the* agent of law—his own style of law. When the sheriff and territorial governor Axtell cozy up to Murphy and The House interests, which violently try to control the county, Chisum rides to bring order—order that he will control and dictate.

Billy stands in opposition to Chisum's style of order. To Billy, order will come after he employs his blazing six-guns. When Pat Garrett speaks of the smell of death, Billy accepts that he carries that smell. When Billy reads the Cain and Abel story in the Old Testament, he does not castigate Cain for murdering his brother. When Billy faces off against Murphy's men, he wants to kill them all.

Clearly, then, in its revisions of history, *Chisum* presents a largely negative portrait of Billy. He becomes a desperate killer. And in reordering Billy's historical connections with Tunstall and McSween and elevating John Wayne as new kind of John Chisum, the movie version strays far from Billy the Kid's actual experiences in New Mexico between 1877 and 1881. The cinematic Billy, unable to find a place in John Wayne's empire, rides away from Lincoln in the final scenes. Hollywood history wins again, depicting primarily the darker side of Billy the Kid.

324. *Dirty Little Billy.* 1972. WGR, Dragoti, Jack L. Warner, Columbia Pictures. 93 minutes. Michael J. Pollard as Billy, Richard Evans as Goldie, Lee Purcell as Berle.

A clear failure as an appealing film, this movie also flopped at the box office. It was patently an ahistorical, character-distorting, and mistake-riven production. The thoroughly flawed movie illustrates what can happen when a production company, director, scriptwriters, and actors sell their souls to a film that is repugnant to viewers and critics.

The plot focuses on events that did not happen historically. Most of the action takes place in Coffeyville, Kansas, where Henry/Billy; his mother, Catherine; and stepfather (not yet) William Antrim did not live in the early 1870s. The stepfather and Henry hate one another, so the young man gravitates toward Goldie, a thief, and Berle, his partner and a prostitute. They introduce Henry to cheating at cards, stealing, and having sex. Violence and death follow, with Berle shot down and Henry and Goldie fleeing west.

Director Stan Dragoti and screenwriters Charles Moss and Dragoti created a Henry McCarty far from verifiable facts. The action, setting, and characters have almost nothing to do with the historical Billy the Kid. A few of the wrong details come from Pat Garrett's 1882 (127) and Walter Noble Burns's 1926 (103) biographies, and then the director and actors spring away to follow even more bizarre paths, virtually thumbing their noses at actual history.

One of the most disappointing of all Billy the Kid films. Deserves to get lost.

325. *Four Faces West.* May 1948. Enterprise Studios, United Artists. 90 minutes. Joel McCrea as Ross McEwen, Charles Bickford as Pat Garrett, Frances Dee as Fay Hollister, Joseph Calleia as Monte Marquez.

Based on Eugene Manlove Rhodes's novella *Pasó por Aquí* (302), this heartwarming Western stars Bickford as U.S. marshal Pat Garrett in post–Billy the Kid times. Ross McEwen, a handsome young cowboy, whom many are convinced is modeled after the Kid, steals $2,000 from a bank to help his financially strapped father, and the movie plot features Garrett's diligent pursuit of McEwen through rough, arid southwestern scenes. When Garrett catches up with McEwen, the latter has endangered his escape by choosing to help a stricken Hispanic family on the verge of death, perhaps from diphtheria. When Garrett sees and understands this soft, helpful side of McEwen and learns that he has already begun to repay his stolen money, the marshal encourages the bank robber to give himself up and says he will plead for leniency for him.

Billy the Kid's name is mentioned only in introducing Garrett as the man who killed the Kid. But McEwen is depicted in Billy-like terms. He robs a bank but is a romantic gentleman in his treatment of nurse Fay Hollister (and wins her heart with his actions) and a ministering angel in his aid for the smitten Hispanics. McEwen's appeal to women and his links to Hispanics replicate numerous descriptions of Billy. And here is the nonviolent side of the young hero; even though guns are pulled on several occasions, not a single shot is fired.

Bickford is superb as Pat Garrett. Surprisingly, Johnny Boggs, in his book *Billy the Kid on Film* (337), calls Garrett "just a supporting player" in the movie when, in fact, he is one of the "four faces West," including, in addition, McEwen, Hollister, and Marquez. But Boggs is dead center in pointing out that "many film historians have suggested that the character of Ross McEwen is loosely based on Billy" (p. 158). In both Rhodes's novella and this film, the McEwen hero closely resembles the positive portraits of Billy appearing in the post–Walter Noble Burns period.

326. *Fugitive of the Plains.* April 1943. Producers Releasing Corporation. 56 minutes. Buster Crabbe as Billy the Kid, Al "Fuzzy" St. John as Fuzzy Jones, and Maxine Leslie as Kate.

A falsely accused Billy is the center pivot of this film. He is castigated as a bad man and so sets out to travel from friendly Willow Springs to chaotic

Red Rock to resuscitate his reputation and quell the rebellion there. The sheriff of Red Rock is the chief critic of Billy.

A new wrinkle is introduced in the PRC Billy series when the movie casts pretty Kate as the outlaw leader. Her actions, and her followers' and Billy's reactions to her, are increasingly unbelievable as the film tries to authenticate that this young vivacious woman is truly an outlaw. After joining her band of thugs to attempt to revive law and order in the Red Rock environs, Billy becomes well acquainted with Kate and "preaches" to her about the dangers of her actions, which include holding up a bank. She haughtily warns him to stop his preaching.

The usual frenetic riding, shooting, and fistfighting obtain, with Billy taking on the bad guys. Even Fuzzy attempts, in his cumbersome, inadequate ways, to support his buddy by participating in the hand-to-hand battles. As in all segments of the series, Billy never loses one of these fistfights.

Kate is badly wounded in the attempted bank holdup, but Billy rides to her rescue. In turn, she shoots down one of her former followers when he is on the verge of killing Billy. A snap conclusion provides an unsatisfactory ending to an increasingly unbelievable plot and disappointing acting.

326a. *The Kid from Texas*. 1950. Universal. 78 minutes. Audie Murphy as Billy the Kid, Albert Dekker as Alexander Kain (Alex McSween), Gale Storm as Irene Kain (Sue McSween), Shepperd Strudwick as Jameson (John Tunstall).

This film illustrates how much the notoriety or power of a person can shape the content and popularity of a film. The headline stories about Audie Murphy, the military hero, much influenced this movie just as the publicity of John Mack Brown and Roy Rogers did early Kid films and the notoriety of John Wayne and Clint Eastwood did in later Westerns. Audie Murphy was a much-celebrated hero of World War II and had already published his best-selling autobiography *To Hell and Back* (1949) before this movie was released. He was "the Kid from Texas," not Billy the Kid.

Even though the film and its producers claimed the movie to be more fact than fiction, the story line diverges significantly from dependable information. Billy did not kill a man in Silver City, *Colorado* (or in New Mexico), for insulting his mother. He did not fall in love with Irene Kain (Sue McSween), and Alexander Kain (Alex McSween) did not attempt to shoot Billy. Dozens of other name and event changes muddle the plot, as do mistakes in chronology.

In other ways, the movie follows, generally, acknowledged facts about Billy. Here he finds Englishman Jameson (John Tunstall) to be his friend and supporter. The Kid also opposes the equivalent of The House contingent, meets with Gov. Lew Wallace to discuss a proposed pardon, and breaks out of jail but falls before the gun of Pat Garrett on the night of 14 July 1881.

Audie Murphy, here a mediocre actor at best, nonetheless curiously paralleled Billy the Kid in several ways. Both were orphans and were often assertive and heroic. The two young men willed their way toward leadership. Murphy became a Medal of Honor recipient and a lifetime actor, Billy the chieftain of a small group of rustlers. The aura surrounding Audie Murphy and his soaring notoriety led to this movie becoming a box-office bonanza, and the magic around Billy the Kid led to his being one of the most written-about figures in the Old West. In short, Audie Murphy, "the Kid from Texas," had much in common with Billy the Kid, the New Mexican.

327. *The Kid Rides Again.* 1943. Producers Releasing Corporation. 60 minutes. Buster Crabbe as Billy the Kid, Al "Fuzzy" St. John as Fuzzy Jones, Iris Meredith as Joan Ainsley.

Not unexpectedly, this PRC film contains the familiar ingredients. Fast riding, abundant shooting, and vicious fistfighting are interspersed like clockwork. The conflict features the usual knock-down, drag-out competition between individual landowners and a set of avaricious rascals bent on stealing their land through malicious actions.

And Billy, again, is repeatedly accused of misdeeds—from the opening scenes until well into the film. In this case, Joan Ainsley, the pretty daughter of Sundown's banker, accuses Billy of multiple acts of lawbreaking, telling him the town could do without his ilk. The plot, as per usual, is the refurbishing of Billy's reputation—from false accusations to actions of benefit to the townspeople.

Repetitions occur throughout the movie. Joan repeats her verbal attacks on Billy, pursuers are outwitted when frontrunners take a quick cutoff, Fuzzy bungles his way to successes, and naive sheriffs are taken in by the villains until Billy shows them the truth.

The several killings, including some by Billy of the bad guys; the larger role for Joan Ainsley; and the place of the bank and banker provide minor innovations in an otherwise melodramatic B Western.

328. *The Last Days of Billy the Kid.* 2017. ITN Movies. 90 minutes. Cody McCarver as Pat Harrett, Jason Cash at Billy the Kid.

Although attempting to draw on the complicated, violent history of Lincoln County and the mysterious Billy the Kid family history, this movie clearly fails because of its amateurish acting, awkward plot, and inadequate scene setting. It is surprising that it was released as a movie considering its unprofessional organization and content.

In the first sections of the film, Billy lurks on the edges of the Lincoln County conflicts as a desperado whom town residents fear and bounty hunters pursue. His competing dual personality characteristics surface in his warm love for and marriage to a saloon girl but also in his quick, violent killing of opponents soon after his wife is shot.

The movie presents Billy's meeting and then conflicting with his father, about whom he has just learned. Billy's sister also appears on scene. In the closing action, the father, played by the main actor Cody McCarver, is forced to kill his son Billy, who has just slain two people and is threatening another.

A disappointing film because of its several large limitations.

329. *The Left Handed Gun.* 1958. Warner Bros. 101 minutes. Paul Newman as Billy the Kid, John Dehner as Pat Garrett, Lita Milan as Celsa, Colin Keith-Johnston as Tunstall, James Congdon as Charlie Bowdre, James Best as Tom Folliard, Hurd Hatfield as Moultrie.

Even though critics have knocked *Left Handed Gun* for its historical inaccuracies, "dead spots," and "erratic" presentation, it still may have been the best Billy the Kid film released before 1960. The acting of Paul Newman as Billy and John Dehner as Pat Garrett, the skillful direction of Arthur Penn, and the attractive, authentic scene setting are strong, appealing ingredients.

Left Handed Gun follows but also breaks from the known history of Billy the Kid and the Lincoln County War. Opening with a trudging Billy becoming part of the John Tunstall crew, the plot moves quickly through such events as the murders of Tunstall and Brady, on to the Big Kill, and then to the death of Billy at the hands of Garrett. The civil war of conflict between the Tunstall-McSween followers and the Morton (standing in for Murphy and Dolan) gang drives the film's action.

The divergences from historical fact are both major and minor. The film zips through major events, for example. In just a few minutes Brady is killed (April 1878) and the Five-Day Battle breaks out in Lincoln (July 1878). Very soon Billy escapes from the Lincoln jail (April 1881), and he is quickly shot down by Garrett (July 1881). Besides these excessively rapid events, several major happenings are also dramatically changed, including how Tunstall is murdered, how McSween dies in his house fire, and how Garrett kills Billy. The movie adds scenes, including a ludicrous, boyish attack by Billy and his boys on the military and their cartload of flour. Even more off track is the appearance of one Moultrie character, suggesting, some think, a homosexual strain in the plot.

Newman's Billy is primarily—but not entirely—on the dark side. Similar to the historical Kid, the movie Kid jump-starts a path of revenge immediately after Tunstall is assassinated. Thereafter, he is something of a psychotic killer, although never entirely bereft of sympathy and warmth for everyone in sight. A flood of relief comes—Billy says he is now "clear"—when he shoots the fourth of the quartet he believes murdered Tunstall. In his own selfishness, he seduces Celsa Gutiérrez rather than thinking about what he has done to her and her husband, Saval—in their own house. Yet Billy obviously loves his two closest chums, Tom Folliard and Charlie Bowdre. The three are the best of friends, even though in crunch time, Billy thinks more of his own safety and future than of theirs.

The Billy that Newman portrays is often compared with other cinematic juvenile heroes of the time, such as James Dean in *Rebel Without a Cause* (1955) and several youths in *Blackboard Jungle* (1955). A provocative but confining comparison. Newman's Billy is much more than one of these juvenile delinquents. He is also, in part, the Billy the Kid of the Lincoln County War in the 1870s and 1880s, trying to figure out what to do without a home, "seeing through the glass darkly" of the scriptures Tunstall bequeaths to him, and stumbling toward a shadowy, uncertain future.

A provocative, interesting Kid film. Still one of the best Billy movies.

330. *One-Eyed Jacks.* 1961. Paramount. 141 minutes. Marlon Brando as Rio (Billy), Karl Malden as Sheriff Dad Longworth, Katy Jurado as Maria Longworth, Pina Pellicer as Louisa, Ben Johnson as Bob Amory.

Based on Charles Neider's novel *The Authentic Death of Hendry Jones* (298), the movie *One-Eyed Jacks* follows parts of the novel but also adds new elements and moods. The Kid character, here named Rio, reveals his personality through his early friendship with and then hatred for Dad Longworth, who, by abandoning Rio in Mexico, leads to Rio's five horrendous years in a Mexican prison. Longworth, something of a father or big brother figure, becomes a bitter enemy, even while Rio develops a fascination for Louisa,

Longworth's stepdaughter. Once Dad fails to support Rio in Mexico, the younger man erupts in hatred, although his emerging love for Louisa complicates his emotions and decisions.

On several occasions, Rio displays his tortured background and dark temperament. Talking to a silky, elite woman, Rio tells her that his "home is anyplace where I throw my saddle down" and that he was brought up in a saloon. Rio wishes for stability, but he defeats his own dreams by allowing his grudge against Dad to drive him into violent acts. Hard-nosed and often vicious, Rio realizes sometime later that he is unable to control his emotions.

Rio exhibits little of the bright, winsome, and appealing side of the bifurcated Billy surfacing in Burns's biography and other Kid life stories in the 1950s and 1960s. Anger, vengeance, and hatred rule Rio. Even his warm feelings for Louisa cannot redeem Rio's murderous attitudes and actions: in the closing scenes, he shoots down Dad Longworth—perhaps even in the back.

Directors of *One-Eyed Jacks*—there were as many as six, Marlon Brando being the last—moved two giant steps away from the original Kid and his fictional story in Neider's novel. The movie drops all Lincoln County settings; it also omits several elements of the novelistic version. We get little sense of Monterey, California, as a community; of the second-class status of Hispanics; or of Doc, the narrator of the novel. Rather than Doc's chorus-like comments in the novel about characters and their actions, we are given little more than a few illuminating glimpses of the churning conflicts that bedevil Rio.

A provocative story with good performances from Brando, Malden, Jurado, and Johnson. Still, the California setting and the distance from Lincoln County greatly weaken the movie's links to Billy the Kid.

331. *The Outlaw.* February 1943. Hughes Productions, United Artists, RKO. 121 minutes. Jack Beutel as Billy the Kid, Thomas Mitchell as Pat Garrett, Jane Russell as Rio McDonald, Walter Huston as Doc Holliday.

The Outlaw obviously fails as a first-rate movie about Billy the Kid—and yet it is strong and more believable in most respects when compared with the nearly twenty weak movies pumped out as Saturday matinees by the Producers Releasing Corporation between 1940 and 1943. It is also a more memorable film than Robert Taylor's *Billy the Kid* (1941).

Unfortunately, the lead actors playing Billy the Kid (Jack Beutel) and Rio McDonald, the heroine (Jane Russell), deliver inferior performances in this movie early in their careers. Both are much less than outstanding—not even adequate—in these demanding roles. Beutel is too subdued, unenergetic, and flat to fulfill the dynamic Billy calls for. Russell, other than her erotic physical features, proves inadequate for her demanding role at this point in her young acting career. Conversely, Walter Huston, as a wily, idiosyncratic Doc Holliday, is outstanding. Equally of note, Thomas Mitchell, fresh from winning an Oscar for his role as the alcoholic doctor in the blockbuster *Stagecoach* (1939), portrays a seriocomic, competent Pat Garrett here. The large achievements of these two skilled character actors clearly overshadow Billy and Rio in competing roles.

The movie follows, somewhat, a few known facts of Billy's life but greatly diverges from history in most dealings with the Kid. We get some of Billy's conflicts with Pat Garrett, albeit contradictory to the facts; much of the story takes place in the Lincoln and Fort Sumner regions; and Billy's uncertainties, changes of mind, and lack of direction illustrate the historical Kid. Billy's warm attachment to horses in this film replicates, too, what is known about his actual love of horses.

Still, Hollywood history controls the movie much more than the details of Billy's life. Doc Holliday is a major character here and is depicted as a very close friend of Pat Garrett's, but in real life Garrett and Doc had no such friendship. Nor did Billy ever mention Doc Holliday. Plus, Doc is shot in this film on 13 July 1881, but the historical Doc was involved in the famous firefight at the OK Corral three months later in Tombstone, Arizona, and lived on until 1887, when he died in Colorado.

Equally off track is the role of Rio McDonald, played by the young, buxom Jane Russell. Viewers in the twenty-first century might not be upset with the sexual encounters in the film between Billy and Rio, but the mistreatment of the heroine, by both Billy and Doc, is misogyny of the most virulent kind. She competes with Red, a strawberry roan horse, for the attentions of Billy and Doc, and the horse wins most of the competitions. Howard Hughes, who bankrolled and eventually directed the movie, wanted sexual themes at its center. He wanted the ample physical features of Russell emphasized throughout the film, and Russell wrote later that he forced her to play her role topless in an alternative version of the move—for his personal viewing.

Rio rolls in the hay with Billy in their first meeting, despite knowing he has killed her brother in an earlier shootout. Later, she crawls into the Kid's bed to keep him warm as he recovers from a gunshot wound, telling her aunt

Guadalupe to call a preacher if she wants a marriage to occur. But Billy abandons Rio on a couple of occasions and even ties her up with leather thongs in still another happening. Generally, Billy doubts women—but the historic Billy loved them—and seems to agree with Doc's castigation of females. Doc says he does not "trust 'em, every one of 'em," and they "are all alike—nothing for you, or to you." Yet, at the end, Billy and Rio ride off—together.

The character of Billy depicted in *The Outlaw* is substantially more negative than his image in other Kid movies of the time. Pat Garrett summarizes the general image of Billy, as he tells Doc, "[We] never had any trouble until . . . [Billy] came along." Billy serves as a troublemaker. He claims Doc's beloved horse Red—and perhaps steals it—and, without thinking much about it, steals Doc's girlfriend Rio. The Kid's life exudes purposelessness, with no aim in sight, just following the next push he receives from transpiring or looming events.

One other facet of Billy's character becomes clear toward the end of the movie and may indeed illustrate something of the actual Billy's personality. When Garrett is upset about Billy's straining or even severing of his friendship with Doc, Billy praises Doc as "never having cold feet in his life." And in the next scene, the Kid tells Doc, "You're the only pardner I ever had." Billy perhaps seeks a father or big brother figure like Doc, who calls him "son" throughout the movie, as does Garrett. Doc fulfills that need. The threesome—Billy, Pat, and Doc—and their shifting friendships are the major theme of the plot. As Garrett puts it, "It sure is funny . . . how two or three trails can cross and get all tangled up."

Even though the mediocre acting of Beutel and Russell diminishes the aesthetic contribution of *The Outlaw*, it was a box-office bonanza. Starting slowly, sales gradually boomed and made it the biggest-grossing early Kid film. But it was not the role of Billy that drew the fans. Nor its historicity. Clearly, the Hollywood razzmatazz, and particularly the sexuality of Jane Russell, lured hundreds of thousands of viewers.

332. *Pat Garrett and Billy the Kid.* May 1973; 2005 special edition. Metro-Goldwyn-Mayer. Directed by Sam Peckinpah. Kris Kristofferson as Billy the Kid, James Coburn as Pat Garrett, Bob Dylan as Alias, Barry Sullivan as John Chisum, Jason Robards as Gov. Lew Wallace.

Several scholars have extensively discussed the directing challenges and other problems that plagued the filming and releasing of Sam Peckinpah's *Pat Garrett and Billy the Kid*. Important as these happenings are in understanding this important movie about the Kid, other facets are more significant in evaluating the film's role in developing Billy legends.

First of all, it is the premier film giving Billy (Kris Kristofferson) and Garrett (James Coburn) equal billing. In that regard, the film resembles the more recent dual biography by Mark Lee Gardner, *To Hell on a Fast Horse: Billy the Kid, Pat Garrett, and the Epic Chase to Justice in the Old West* (126). The film, structured contrapuntally, moves back and forth between the Billy and Garrett strains of the story—when they are separated. The very short opening and closing scenes are the killing of Garrett in 1908 (not in 1909, as the film indicates), with the shooting of Garrett dissolving into an earlier scene of the Kid and his chums shooting off chicken heads at Fort Sumner. The numerous fadeaways between Garrett and Kid actions, unfortunately, may often lose viewers.

Obsessions dominate segments of the film. The cinematic Pat Garrett lives on alcohol, as do several other characters. The film is obviously wrong in making Billy into an incessant drinker, which he was not, although Kristofferson—and director Peckinpah as well—loved alcohol. The scenery, frequently displayed in gray tones and devoid of appealing landscapes and sights, parallels the oppressive, depressing mood of the film and the dark sides of the major characters. The tumbledown, ramshackle homes and communities augment even more the somber tone of the film.

Garrett and Billy, of course, lead the action. Spiffily dressed and a tough customer, Garrett is also violent and lustful. He shoots without warning and, in one scene, bathes and frolics with four nude prostitutes. He warns Billy that in five days he will become sheriff and will gallop after the Kid. "Times have changed," Garrett informs Billy, who replies, "Not me." A subsequent scene features strands of barbed wire, symbolizing a Billy from an open-range West being fenced in by a newly arrived range boss, Pat Garrett.

The Billy portrayed here includes both authoritative depictions of the Kid and imagined Hollywood hoopla. A happy gunman and smiling killer, Billy also connects with Hispanics and beds down with willing *señoritas*, including one scene in which he pushes out a customer and moves into the warm, inviting bed of a pliant sex seller. In another scene, the killing of Billy's friend Paco and the rape of his wife (or daughter) dramatically transform the Kid; he abruptly ends his ride to Mexico and returns to fight the Chisum crowd, whom he thinks guilty of the murder and rape. On a few occasions, Billy turns superhero, shooting down a passel of bounty hunters. His friendship with the Bob Dylan character—Alias—is pure fabrication, perhaps allowing Dylan's musical talents to be showcased. Also contrived, early on, is the Kid's close friendship with Pat Garrett. Movie directors and historical novelists seem convinced that making Garrett a close friend and then magnifying his enmity toward the Kid allow for an increased emphasis on double-crossing, thereby augmenting the drama of their narratives.

The superb acting of Coburn and Kristofferson greatly strengthens the film. So does the depiction of the male camaraderie of the times. *Pat Garrett and Billy the Kid* remains the strongest of the Billy films, revealingly and convincingly dramatizing the persisting legends of a bifurcated Billy.

333. *Sheriff of Sage Valley.* October 1942. Producers Releasing Corporation. 57 minutes. Buster Crabbe as Billy the Kid, Al "Fuzzy" St. John as Fuzzy Jones, Tex O'Brien as Jeff, Maxine Leslie as Janet.

The plans of Billy, Fuzzy, and Jeff to rob false Wanted posters from an incoming stagecoach are thrown off track by another group of outlaws who get to the stagecoach first, hold it up, and, in an inside job, shoot the sheriff, who is riding in the coach. In the coach are Sloan and Janet, buddies who work for Kansas Ed, a vicious newcomer to Sage Valley bent on dominating the town and nearby ranches. Early on, there is mention that Ed looks enough like Billy to be his brother. Janet, played by Maxine Leslie, is an attractive young outlaw woman, a role similar to her later one in *Fugitive of the Plains* (1943).

As usual, Billy is accused of misdeeds in the area until observers realize how much Kansas Ed looks like Billy. The mayor of Sage Valley asks Billy to serve as sheriff so as to head off Sloan, Kansas Ed's chief henchman, and the other outlaws. At first Billy says no, but then he accepts the star and starts after the bad guys. Frantic rides, the usual fistfights, and Fuzzy's faltering actions appear—again and again. Finally, the mayor sorts things out after it is clear that Billy is no outlaw.

The minor innovations of making Kansas Ed into Billy's long-lost brother who followed the wrong trails and the role of the woman outlaw Janet do not save the movie from its excessive repetitions, jumbled plot, and unbelievable actions.

334. *Western Cyclone.* May 1943. Producers Releasing Corporation. 62 minutes. Buster Crabbe as Billy the Kid, Al "Fuzzy" St. John as Fuzzy Jones, Marjorie Manners as Mary Arnold (Miss Mary).

Billy once again has to prove to one and all that he is not the villainous outlaw that numerous wanted posters shout out that he is. The plot of the movie shows the Kid, partnering with the governor and sheriff after some hesitation on their part, demonstrating to a visiting senator the lawlessness of their town of Day Springs, New Mexico, and its environs.

As usual, Billy is introduced as being on the wrong side of the law—here sentenced to hanging for a murder he did not commit. When the judge says the Kid is going to hang until he is "dead, dead, dead," the moviemakers were playing on a long-held but false legend that these were the words of the judge in Mesilla, New Mexico, when the real Billy was sentenced to be hanged.

Fast galloping, frantic shooting, vicious fisticuffs, and Fuzzy Jones's clownish, acrobatic stumbling are repeated here to distraction. So are the cutoff tricks that lead riders use several times to fool pursuers. Seemingly, the director, under increased pressure to create movies on lower budgets, could not deviate from or add to familiar plot ingredients. Even the minor woman's role of Miss Mary Arnold seems stilted and out of place in a movie about "just the boys."

None of the PRC movies do much—if anything—with history, this one included. The life of the real Billy the Kid plays no role here. But one must not forget that they did much to keep Billy's name on marquees and his positive image before moviegoers.

335. *Young Guns.* August 1988. Morgan Creek, 20th Century Fox. 107 minutes. Emilio Estevez as William H. Bonney, Kiefer Sutherland as Doc Scurlock, Lou Diamond Phillips as Chávez y Chávez, Charlie Sheen as Dick Brewer, Dermot Mulroney as Dirty Steve Stephens, Casey Siemaszko as Charley Bowdre, Terence Stamp as John Tunstall, Jack Palance as Lawrence G. Murphy, Terry O'Quinn as Alex McSween, Sharon Thomas as Susan McSween, Patrick Wayne as Pat Garrett.

Young Guns is a potpourri of historical stories, contemporary sociocultural emphases, and Hollywood fantasy typical of cinematic treatments of Billy the Kid at the end of the twentieth century. The movie whetted widespread interest, largely because of its juxtaposition of these attention-gathering and alluring elements.

The largest reason for the Lincoln County War in 1878 and the surrounding years is dramatized in the opening scenes of the film. Billy the Kid, already known by that name in this movie and rumored to be a murderer, is rescued by the John Tunstall crowd from the pursuing L. G. Murphy gunmen. In the next scenes, viewers are introduced to the economic and power-motivated clashes leading to open warfare.

The moviemakers also depict well other segments of the Lincoln County area. The arid terrain, the lively town of Lincoln (several scenes of Lincoln were shot in the sleepy northern New Mexico town of Cerrillos, situated between Albuquerque and Santa Fe), and the architectural styles of the ranch and town houses are all realistic. Some of the varied strains of Native American, Hispanic, and Anglo cultures of southeastern New Mexico are also treated in believable fashion.

In several scenes, the depiction of the youthful Billy the Kid hits important targets, but it misses on others. Billy is viewed primarily as a nomadic desert rat—a "little rodent," as one competitor puts it. He is looking for a place and a people. When John Tunstall provides both, Billy seems on a new road to a new tribe, but the Murphy supporters murder Tunstall, with Billy losing his new home and leader—and then swearing revenge. But in subsequent scenes, Billy clashes with other Tunstall followers—Regulators here, including Dick Brewer and Charley Bowdre—as much as he does with their opponents. Very soon, Billy murders men, one by one and without much cause. For the most part, Billy is not heroic but is courageous and sometimes supports others, not just himself. In the second half of the movie, Billy returns to Lincoln with his handful of faithful followers to protect lawyer Alex McSween, with whom he has had a falling-out but whom he now sees as defenseless against the Murphy marauders.

In the Big Kill in Lincoln in July 1878, the longest segment of the movie, Billy is by turns a strong leader and a dubious, uncertain chieftain. He leads the handful of Regulators cornered in the burning McSween house but seems near-crazed in some thoughts and actions. As one of Billy's fellow riders points out, Billy is "like a whirlwind out there." As Billy and his supporters rush out of the fiery McSween home, a host of shooters are killed in the hailstorm of shots from both sides, including McSween, whose death was historical and verified, but not, as here in the movie, Murphy and Bowdre. The shootout at the end of the Lincoln gunfight virtually completes the movie, although a concluding voice-over speaks of Pat Garrett's shooting of an unarmed Billy.

Contemporary sociocultural emphases and Hollywood fantasies dominate several scenes. The doubtful Apache background of Billy follower Chávez y Chávez is mentioned in several instances, including one peyote-imagined scene and his monologue about a massacre of Indians in a nonexistent attack. Doc Scurlock falls for a beautiful, shy Chinese girl, a relationship that did not happen historically. In another ethnic moment, Bowdre marries a Hispanic girl, historically true, but certainly not on the first night he met her at a dance. Intriguingly, in this movie Billy shows no interest in women.

Hollywood history shows up in several emphases and in specific scenes. John Tunstall, in reality in his early to midtwenties, is depicted here as an older man, a father figure to Billy and his fellows. Here, Sue McSween is no more than a cardboard caricature, without cinematic life or meaning. L. G. Murphy, superbly played by the notable bad guy Jack Palance, was not the leader of the opponents in July 1878; Jimmy Dolan, Sheriff Peppin, and Col. N. A. M. Dudley were.

The largest distortions appear in the movie's handling of the Big Kill. McSween's side in the Lincoln shootout numbered, at first, nearly sixty men, not just the half dozen shown here in the burning McSween house. Scurlock's Chinese girlfriend took no part in the gunfight; she was not even in the Lincoln County War. Billy was not thrown down in a trunk from the second floor of the (one-story) McSween house, popping out with both guns firing and killing several opponents. The movie moguls manufactured a final, sensational scene to build to this apex of dramatic action.

In short, *Young Guns* owes as much to its times and the popular themes of that time in youthful actions, emphases on racial-ethnic themes, and Hollywood frenzy as it owes to factual history. Its importance for understanding Billy is linked more to ideas and attitudes of the late 1980s than to the historical Kid, a movie illustrating its own times more than the Kid's times.

336. *Young Guns II*. August 1990. Morgan-Creek, 20th Century-Fox. 104 minutes. Emilio Estevez as Billy the Kid/Brushy Bill Roberts, Keifer Sutherland as Doc Scurlock, Lou Diamond Phillips as Chávez y Chávez, Christian Slater as Arkansas Dave Rudabaugh, William Peterson as Pat Garrett, Jenny Wright as Jane Greathouse.

Building quickly on the immense popularity of *Young Guns* two years earlier, this sequel includes several ingredients taken from the earlier movie. The Brat Pack major actors, the nonstop violence, and the Billy-Garrett escalating conflict carry over from the prequel film. And again we get the marriage of history and movieland fantasy.

The largest innovation is the movie's seeming endorsement of the Brushy Bill Roberts claim in 1950 that he was the real Billy the Kid, who had never died and wanted the governor's pardon seventy years later. That conspiracy tale, rumored earlier but brought to center stage in C. L. Sonnichsen and William V. Morrison's book *Alias Billy the Kid* (169), provides the framework for this movie. In the opening and closing scenes, as well as in scattered voice-overs throughout the film, the Bushy Bill storyline structures this work. Although never explicitly stated, the movie seems to accept Brushy Bill's veracity—or pragmatically utilizes that rumored narrative to appeal to loyal legend believers.

Conflict, loads of it, powers this Western. Billy and Dave Rudabaugh continually bicker about who is leader of the Kid group, with Arkansas Dave unable to draw anyone to him. The Billy and Chisum gangs go after one another in imagined battles that are as contrived as the clashes between Kid followers and Garrett riders. Still another trumped-up conflict pits two lynch mobs against each other. During another conflict, Billy clarifies early on that this is rightly no range war but a "merchant war," although the film fails to show the actuality of that business civil war.

Changes and additions also illustrate Hollywood's cavalier tendency to do with history what it thinks will sell tickets. Attempting to find a woman's role in this intensely masculine story and where women are often sidelined, the movie exchanges Whiskey Jim Greathouse, a tavern keeper, for Jane Greathouse, a bordello madam, whose house of joy is burned by Garrett. Afterward, she rides out of town, Lady Godiva–like, pure naked. Another shift reveals Garrett's request that Ash Upson, even before Billy's death, accompany the sheriff, watch what happens, and write a book about the Lincoln County battles and the pursuit of Billy the Kid. Sometimes these transformations, as they do after the Kid's escape from the Lincoln jail, so jumble the plot that the story is difficult to follow.

Very little of the cheerful, helpful side of Billy appears here; this is largely the dark side of the Kid. Aware of his growing larger-than-life reputation, Billy cultivates it in his selfish, mean-spirited actions. His self-adoration is illustrated in his reading a dime novel about himself, which, by the way, had not yet been published. Following the Brushy Bill story, Billy talks his way out of a possible killing by Garrett and rides away only to reappear seeking pardon a lifetime later.

Obviously, this film grabbed viewers, even though the Billy the Kid pictured was a one-sided, negative portrait of the Kid. The distortions and slanted changes seemed not to bother the large, enthusiastic audiences.

Film Criticism

337. Boggs, Johnny D. *Billy the Kid on Film, 1911–2012.* Jefferson, N.C.: McFarland, 2013.

No volume supersedes this book as *the* source of information on films about Billy the Kid. Thorough, balanced, informative, and delightfully written, Boggs's book is the first stop for those interested in Kid movies and wanting extensive information about them. The author deals with about seventy-five Billy films, providing discussions of movie plots, historical backgrounds, actors and actresses, and evaluations of the major films and more condensed entries for less significant movies. Boggs not only utilizes the leading books on Billy, he also uses dozens upon dozens of books and essays dealing with individual films, Hollywood, and movies in general.

Boggs opens his valuable book with a brief biography of Billy and a general chapter on "Billy the Kid in Pop Culture." Then follow nine chapters, chronologically organized, tracing Kid films from the silents to the *Young Guns* films of the late 1980s and early 1990s. Four brief succeeding chapters treat the Kid in foreign films, made-for-TV films, TV series, and direct-to-video films. All chapters on the major and minor Kid films include helpful plot summaries, historical accuracies and mistakes, and comments on their Billy content.

In brief, this successful study provides an extraordinarily useful guide for historians, biographers, moviemakers, experts, and generalists alike. The beginning place for information on Kid movies. A companion volume on the Kid in fiction would be equally valuable.

338. Hutton, Paul (Andrew). "Billy the Kid as Seen in the Movies." *Frontier Times* 57 (June 1985): 24–29.

Following a well-known contention among scholars of popular thought, Hutton argues that the shifting cinematic images of Billy the Kid reflect "the changing national popular mood." For example, Billy's role in *The Left Handed Gun* (1957), starring Paul Newman, reflects the alienation of a James Dean 1950s America. In like ways, a New Grey West became popular in the 1960s and thereafter, with Billy movies such as *Dirty Little Billy* (1972) and *Pat Garrett and Billy the Kid* (1973) reflecting that unheroic West.

A helpful essay that encapsulates, early on, interpretations that Hutton advanced later in another essay (342) and that other scholars such as Stephen Tatum (171) and Jon Tuska (345) also enlarged.

339. Hutton, Paul A. "Custer as Seen in Hollywood Films." *True West* 31 (June 1984): 22–28.

This short overview of films about Custer provides helpful information for comparing cinematic treatments of the controversial general with those of Billy the Kid. Many more silent films about Custer were made than about the Kid, but the nineteen films put out by the Producers Releasing Corporation find no parallel among Custer movies. Generally speaking, the switch from a more heroic Custer to a grey-hatted general in films of the 1960s and thereafter parallels the darker and less positive Hollywood pictures of Billy in the same decades.

340. Hutton, Paul Andrew. "Dreamscape Desperado." *New Mexico Magazine* 68 (June 1990): 44–57.

This extremely well-written and heavily illustrated essay traces the rise and flowering of all-encompassing Billy the Kid legends. Hutton deals glancingly with biographies and novels written about the western outlaw, but his major focus is on the Billy movies. As Hutton notes, more movies have been made about Billy than any other western character.

Hutton's views about Billy are balanced. In addition, he's more interested in the shifting tones and content of Billy's legends than in Billy himself. Generally, this brief essay is a very helpful introduction to the mythic Billy—from his death to the late 1980s.

Drawing on the ideas and some words of Walter Noble Burns (see p. 53, #103), Hutton ends his essay with an evocative, poetic paragraph that in the subsequent quarter century has been more widely quoted than any other description of the legendary Billy:

> Bill the Kid just keeps riding across the dreamscape of our minds—silhouetted against a starlit Western sky, handsome, laughing, deadly. Shrewd as the coyote. Free as the hawk. The outlaw of our dreams—forever free, forever young, forever riding.

341. Hutton, Paul (Andrew). "Dreamscape Desperado." *True West* 54 (May 2007): 50–59.

Hutton, who has done as much as any western historian to understand the rise, flowering, and continuing interest in Billy the Kid in American popular culture, provides a capsule reading of the Kid in movies, music, fiction, and biography. His treatment of Billy movies is as extensive as the combined discussions of the other mediums.

At the time this essay was published, Hutton was serving as guest curator of a new exhibit, "Dreamscape Desperado: Billy the Kid and the Outlaws in America," at the Albuquerque Museum of Art and History. Unfortunately, the promised companion volume for the exhibit never came to fruition.

Here, Hutton is more interested in the "dreamed-up" than the historical Billy. That is, he deals entertainingly with how Hollywood, musicians, novelists, and biographers have chosen to picture Billy rather than presenting a brief historical biography of the Kid.

A brief, provocative overview, exceedingly well written.

342. Hutton, Paul Andrew. "Silver Screen Desperado: Billy the Kid in Movies." *New Mexico Historical Review* 82 (Spring 2007): 149–96.

This essay greatly expands Hutton's earlier brief essay (338).

343. Hutton, Paul Andrew, and Jason Strykowski. "Billy the Kid Filmography." *New Mexico Historical Review* 82 (Spring 2007): 197–209.

A list of sixty-six Billy films, this filmography, annotated for the most part, provides a handy guide for nearly all the Kid movies. The annotations include directors, major stars, producing companies, screenwriters, and a few other details. Most annotations also include a sentence or two of plot summary. A very useful listing. A clutch of revealing movie stills follows the filmography.

344. Seydor, Paul. *Peckinpah: The Western Films; A Reconsideration*. Urbana: University of Illinois Press, 1980, 1997.

Paul Seydor has done more than any other author to examine Sam Peckinpah's director role in the making of *Pat Garrett and Billy the Kid* (1973). In this volume Seydor devotes a long, fifty-page chapter to a close reading of the several versions of the film and Peckinpah's actions in the content and direction of the movie. Especially revealing, biographically, are Peckinpah's huge conflicts with MGM and the studio president James Aubrey as well as his difficulties with excessive drinking.

Seydor's treatment of James Coburn's Pat Garrett character is much more extensive than his discussion of Kris Kristofferson's Billy the Kid. He sees Peckinpah's identification with the Garrett character, particularly in his aging, facing change, and ending things. Conversely, Seydor views Peckinpah's Billy as a "grown-up child," a young man with no "moral sensibility or capacity for judgment," and yet in some ways a Christ figure too.

Generally, even though Peckinpah is described as a man who wanted the film his way or not at all and was sometimes drunk and contentious, Seydor salutes the director for the depth of thought and provocative content of *Pat Garrett and Billy the Kid*. The making of the film and its varied versions were a mess, and yet the movie stands as a first-rate Western in Seydor's view.

For an expansion of these ideas, see Seydor's later book *The Authentic Death and Contentious Afterlife of Pat Garrett and Billy the Kid: The Untold Story of Peckinpah's Last Western* (2015).

345. Tuska, Jon. "Billy the Kid in Film." In *Billy the Kid: His Life and Legend.* Albuquerque: University of New Mexico Press, 1994.

Tuska, a leading authority on Western films, furnished this chapter overview of Kid films as part of his longer study of the life and legends of Billy (173). Tuska opens his coverage with a discussion of King Vidor's *Billy the Kid* (1930), starring Johnny Mack Brown, and ends the chapter with *Young Guns II* (1990). Tuska includes several movie stills and a filmography listing movie titles, producing companies, directors and story writers, and actors and actresses for about forty-four of the nearly seventy-five Billy films.

Tuska rambles a bit, sometimes providing useful comments on individual films, sometimes throwing in extraneous background information. After commenting at length on the 1930 Billy film, the author covers several of the nineteen mediocre Producers Releasing Corporation's films starring Bob Steele and then Buster Crabbe. *The Outlaw* (1943), *The Kid from Texas* (1950), *Chisum* (1970), *Pat Garrett and Billy the Kid* (1973), *Young Guns* (1988), and *Young Guns II* (1990) receive considerable attention, but neither *The Left Handed Gun* (1958) nor *Dirty Little Billy* (1972) gets much space.

Tuska provides more useful plot summary than sustained, balanced evaluation. One wishes that Tuska, who knew so much about Western films, would have provided illuminating readings rather than so much summary of action.

Photographs

346. Boardman, Mark. "The Croquet Kid." *True West* 63 (February 2016): 20–31.

    A rather extensive essay for *True West*, this well-written piece furnishes helpful contexts for understanding the controversies surrounding a newly found photograph claiming to be of Billy the Kid playing croquet with his Regulator buddies, women friends, and children. In 2010 collector Randy Guijarro purchased several tintypes for two dollars in Fresno, California, and soon asserted that one of the photographs was of Billy. That claim set off a verbal civil war between those enthusiastically supporting Guijarro's assertion and those dismissing the photograph as another falsely identified Billy.

    Boardman is balanced in describing the issues and contentions dividing the two groups. His appealingly illustrated piece points to differences in views about provenance, facial identifications, and settings that divide the groups. He uses sidebars for supporting comments from advocates for and against the authenticity of the Croquet Kid photograph. The author's closing comment from historian Paul Andrew Hutton questioning the photograph suggests that Boardman sides more with the deniers than with the promoters of the photograph.

    A valuable, fair-minded overview of a revealing recent controversy about Billy.

347. Boardman, Mark. "The Holy Grail for Sale." *True West* 58 (June 2011): 24–31.

    The author provides a brief history of the only authentic Billy photo, tracing its story from its being taken in 1879–1880 in Fort Sumner to its being offered for sale by auctioneer Brian Libel. Boardman thought the tintype might sell for as much as $500,000, and Libel estimated it could bring $300,000–400,000. Others thought it might go for $1 million since the buyer would "get the 'Holy Grail' of Old West photos, perhaps the most famous tintype in U.S. history: The real Billy the Kid" (p. 27). It sold for $2.3 million to businessman William Koch in June 2011.

The essay contains interesting contextual information, tracing how the four tintypes of the only authentic photograph were made, what happened to them, and the history of the one tintype still in existence (and now owed by Koch). Added information from western photo collector par excellence Robert McCubbin, the Eastman House International Museum of Photography and Film, and a former worker for the Lincoln County Heritage Trust provides intriguing, little-known background about the famous tintype.

An informative, useful essay on the famous Kid tintype.

348. Cline, Don. "Billy the Kid Photos: The Faces, the Places, the Facts." *Old West* 22, no. 87 (Spring 1986): 46–49.

Cline considers and rejects the authenticity of about a half dozen photographs claiming to be of Billy or of persons or things associated with him. Two photos, linked to his Silver City or earlier years, show a young man with characteristics resembling the Kid in the one authentic photograph taken in 1879–1880 in Fort Sumner. Two other photographs are dismissed as unproven images of Billy's mother, Catherine Antrim. Still another is concluded not to be a photograph of the Antrim home in Silver City. Cline primarily uses his research in Silver City sources to conclude that none of these other photographs is authentic.

349. Dyer, Robert. "Billy the Kid: The Photos Face Forensics." *True West* 37 (March 1990): 26–29.

The author briefly summarizes how the Lincoln County Heritage Trust set out in 1990 to use up-to-date computer techniques to examine photographs said to be of Billy the Kid. Director Bob Hart of the Heritage Trust, in his Billy the Kid Photographic Project, hired Thomas Kyle of the Los Alamos National Laboratories and noted forensic anthropologist Dr. Clyde Snow to carry out the project. Kyle would use computer techniques to enhance the one authoritative photograph of Billy, and then Dr. Snow would examine and compare that enlarged, well-known tintype with several other photographs claimed to be of the Kid. Snow would especially focus on facial and skull comparisons. At this time, the project was beginning.

Later, the findings suggested that none of the other photographs were authentic Billys.

350. Gardner, Mark Lee. "Comparing Billy to Billy." *True West Newsletter* (online), 12 August 2014.

Gardner's brief essay compares a new carte de visite (CDV) surfacing in New Mexico in 2013 with the only authentic tintype of ca. 1880 and an earlier reprint of the tintype in a previous book *History of New Mexico* (1907). He asks viewers to decide for themselves whether the CDV "reveals more about the Kid than the tintype does." It is thought that the CDV was made in 1881, soon after the Kid escaped from the Lincoln County jail, when his legends were beginning to emerge. Others are convinced that the CDV appeared after Billy's death.

Gardner provides no answer to the question he raises for viewers but reminds them that the original tintype sold in June 2011 to William Koch for $2.3 million. A bid of $15,000 for the CDV was made in 2014, but there is no follow-up about its possible sale in this essay.

351. McCarty, Lea F. "Billy the Kid's Funeral." *True West* 8 (November–December 1960): 6–9, 62–64.

The author, an artist, claimed to have found a photograph of four men at Billy the Kid's funeral. All strong evidence casts doubt on that claim.

First, the provenance. An old-timer then operating a Fort Sumner curio shop showed the author the photograph of four men with bowed heads. One onlooker, Tom Sullivan, told the author, "Well . . . it happens to be Billy the Kid's funeral as it was on July 15, 1881" (p. 9), but he did not know the names of the four men or where the photograph came from. The author then visited the grandson of George Coe, who vouched for the authenticity of the photograph and identified the four men as later territorial governor Miguel Otero, his brother, Jesus Silva, and "Hijinio" Salazar.

But the author raises no questions about the photograph, who took it, and why there was no photograph of Billy's body, often taken first thing after a frontier killing. Nor does the author admit that Miguel Otero makes no mention of being at the funeral in Fort Sumner, but he does mention seeing Billy when the Kid was jailed in Santa Fe. Professor Robert Stahl has done careful research on those who saw Billy on 14–15 July 1881, but he does not mention Otero as an eyewitness. Finally, no one would recognize the man identified as Otero in this photograph, because he is burly and Otero was a very small man.

So, one should doubt that this is really a photograph taken at Billy's funeral.

352. McCubbin, Robert G. "The Many Faces of Billy the Kid." *True West* 54 (May 2007): 60.

This brief piece by the widely known collector of western photographs summarizes what is known about the one extant tintype taken of Billy about 1880. McCubbin speaks of the owners of the four original tintypes, what the one surviving tintype tells us about photographic techniques of the time, and the unfortunate flawed attempts by later collectors and photographers to "redo" the original, which damaged reproductions they produced. These flawed reconstructions, McCubbin writes, "look nothing at all like him" (p. 60).

The three pages following the McCubbin essay (pp. 61–63) provide copies of several of these reproductions, other early illustrations of Billy, and a few illustrated book covers and artistic renditions of the one authentic photography of Billy.

353. Weddle, Richard. "A Carte de Visite of Billy the Kid." *Wild West* 27 (October 2014): 44–45.

Weddle adds interesting information about the commercializing of the one authentic photograph taken of the Kid in 1879–1880 in Fort Sumner. The author provides backgrounds for the first reprintings of the historic photograph and then describes another carte de visite that surfaced in 2013–2014. Weddle's explanations of the carte de visite process and how copies of the authentic photograph were put into circulation add much to our visual knowledge of Billy the Kid.

354. Weddle, Richard. "Shooting Billy the Kid." *Wild West* 25 (August 2012): 56–62.

A fine piece of work on the only known photograph (tintype) of Billy the Kid, this essay provides the needed information on this notable image of the Kid. Weddle, a well-known researcher and writer on Billy topics, furnishes background material on the art of ferrotype/tintype photography, the probable steps taken to photograph Billy in 1879–1880 near Beaver Smith's saloon in Fort Sumner, and the outcome of the four plates produced by the photographer.

No one has paid closer attention to the backgrounds and makeup of this key photograph. One hopes Weddle will soon publish his book on this and related topics.

BILLY THE KID
Unfinished Business

SOME AMBITIOUS RESEARCHERS come to wrong conclusions when they hear that more than one thousand books and essays have been written about Billy the Kid and the Lincoln County squabbles. They should not become disillusioned and back away; they should not give up on researching Billy and his shifting contexts. Here's why.

Consider Abraham Lincoln and the American Civil War. Lincoln is the most written-about American, with more than sixteen thousand books published on him, and the Civil War has generated more than sixty thousand volumes. Yet every year valuable new books about Lincoln and the war appear. Publishers and readers alike still think, rightly so, that there are good subjects about Lincoln and the Civil War to be addressed—in spite of the thousands of previous publications.

So it is with Billy the Kid. There are still other subjects to be covered. Perhaps this is less so on the Kid himself than on his surrounding contexts, including people, events, and ideas influencing and shaping his life.

Yet think of Billy himself. As this author pointed out in his previous essays, unsolved mysteries engulf the Kid; several subjects still need further attention (202 and 203). We know very little about him until his name first appeared in print in 1873 in Santa Fe. More diligent research may still turn up the missing information. Recent online articles by Frederick Nolan (224) and Wayne Sanderson (252) suggest new possibilities for understanding Billy's earliest years. Neither of these interesting and provocative suggestions has been followed up. Nor has anyone checked thoroughly into the claim in the 1880 census that Billy was not born in New York but in Missouri to Missourian parents in 1855. Is that claim to be entirely dismissed? Earlier, the research findings of Waldo Koop (215), Robert Mullin (151), and Jerry (Richard) Weddle (180) showed how much diligent work could turn up new information on subjects thought to be exhausted.

Then there are the most important persons surrounding Billy early on. We have adequate information about his stepfather, William Antrim, but more research can be done on his mother, Catherine's, life up to her entry into New Mexico in 1873. The same for brother Joe; he seems to have disappeared for most of Billy's life. Even those older buddies in Silver City and Arizona seem shadowy sideline figures at this point. We should know more about Sombrero Jack and John Mackie. It would be helpful, too, to have a book providing a group portrait of "pals" or the "gang" that surrounded Billy in his years in Lincoln County, especially after the Big Kill in July 1878. These Billy "guys" include Tom O. Folliard, Charlie Bowdre, Doc Scurlock, and several others.

In New Mexico and Lincoln County, the unfinished business is even deeper and broader. At the top, we still need a biography of Alex McSween and an up-to-date, fully satisfactory life story of John Chisum. And Billy's House opponents, L. G. Murphy and Jimmy Dolan, lack anything beyond essays. Nor do we have extensive studies of Judge Warren Bristol and District Attorney William Rynerson. Books on Col. N. A. M. Dudley (140), William Brady (145), and Thomas Benton Catron (181) are satisfactory, but more probing work on them is still possible.

Consider, too, important contextual subjects meriting more consideration. We should have in-depth research and writing about Billy's important connections with women and Hispanics. Kathleen Chamberlain shows what can be done in her biography of Sue McSween (106), and Darlis Miller provides a superb overview essay of women in Lincoln County (222). No one yet has extensively traced Billy's connections with possible sweethearts. The recent research of Professor Robert Stahl (252 and 258) clears up misleading sexual legends about Billy and Paulita Maxwell, but we still have much to uncover on Billy and Paulita as well as Celsa Gutiérrez, Nasaria Yerby, and Abrana García—if not also Sallie Chisum. Paul Tsompanas (172) demonstrates what can be done in Billy-Hispanic connections in his brief biography of Hispanic leader Juan Patrón, but even more helpful would be a general overview of Billy's connections with Hispanic pals—as well as Hispanics who opposed him. Indeed, we are much in need a synthetic overview of Hispanic participation in Lincoln County history.

Think what could be done with manuscript sources that are difficult to obtain but necessary for a full understanding of Billy. Robert Barron modeled what could be done with such sources in his extensive, edited book on the Dudley hearing (98). Similar well-edited books with thorough commentary would be invaluable on the Frank Warner Angel and Azariah Wild reports.

Recent treatments of Billy the Kid and Lincoln County have included additional information on Santa Fe and Washington, D.C., connections. But those important links merit much more attention. We have placed so much emphasis on the local history—e.g., Silver City and Lincoln County—that we fail to see the immense power that Santa Fe and Washington, D.C., had in shaping the events surrounding Billy the Kid.

Johnny D. Boggs shows what can be done in singling out one venue in which Billy has been featured. Boggs's book on Billy films (337) reveals how much could be learned from book-length studies of Billy biographers and his treatment in historical fiction and in newspaper reports about him. All these venues have had major impact on the interpretations and legends that have engulfed the Kid.

So, a good deal about Billy the Kid beckons, still deserves further attention. This is not only true of new, not-yet-covered subjects and people but also for fresh overviews and reinterpretations of the Kid. The inviting, open fields lie before ambitious and diligent researchers and writers. Mount up and ride.

Index

*References to the final essay, "Billy the Kid: Unfinished Business," are to pages and are **boldfaced**. All other references are to numbered bibliographic items.*

Abarr, James, 83
Adler, Alfred, 184
adult Westerns, 306
Airy, Helen, 84, 95
Alamogordo (N.Mex.) *Times*, 70
Albuquerque Daily Journal, 52
Albuquerque Journal, 82–86, 88, 91
Albuquerque Review, 64
Alias Billy the Kid (Sonnichsen and Morrison), 110, 138, 169, 331
Alias Billy the Kid: The Man behind the Legend (Cline), 56, 107
American Mythmaker: Walter Noble Burns and the Legends of Billy the Kid, Wyatt Earp, and Joaquin Murrieta (Dworkin), 116
Anaya, A. P. "Paco," 96
Ancient Child, The (Momaday), 297
Angel, Frank Warner, 98, 216; **p. 228**
Angel Reports, 3, 98, 216
Antrim, 63
Antrim, Catherine McCarty, 16–18, 155, 191a, 199, 224, 240, 249, 250, 252; in film, 313; **p. 228**. *See also* McCarty, Catherine
Antrim, Henry, 79, 99 108, 188, 248; **p. 228**. *See also* Billy the Kid
Antrim, Joseph (Joe), 64, 153, 155, 223, 234, 239–40, 242, 249, 250; **p. 228**

Antrim, William H. (stepfather), 66, 107, 108, 121, 153, 155, 196, 215, 223, 238, 240, 250; in fiction, 283; **p. 228**
Antrim and Billy (Cline), 108
Antrim Is My Stepfather's Name: The Boyhood of Billy the Kid (J. Weddle), 180
Anything for Billy (McMurtry), 295
Apaches (Hall), 286
"Apocrypha of Billy the Kid" (Fulton), 206
Aragon, John A., 269. *See also* De Aragon, Ray John
Arizona, 19–21, 62, 73–74, 180, 197, 226, 248, 256. *See also* Cahill, Francis P. "Windy"
Arizona Citizen (Tucson), 21
Arizona Weekly Star (Tucson), 20, 188
At the End of the Santa Fe Trail (Sister Blandina), 114
Authentic Death of Hendry Jones, The (Neider), 298, 330
Authentic Life of Billy, the Kid, the Noted Desperado of the Southwest, Whose Deeds of Daring and Blood Made His Name a Terror in New Mexico, Arizona and Northern Mexico, The (Garrett), 118, 124, 127, 157, 185, 260, 265. *See also* Garrett, Pat
Autobiography, An (Wallace), 178

Baker, Frank, 22, 26
Ball, Durwood, 185
Ball, Eve, 97
Ball, Larry D., 12
Barber, Susan McSween, 222. *See also* McSween, Susan
Barlow, Billy, 135, 137–38
Barron, R. M., 3, 98
Bean, Amelia, 270, 310
Bean, Frederic, 110, 138
Bell, Bob Boze, 99, 186–88, 190–91
Bell, J. W., 48–49, 65, 198, 233, 255
Bender, Norman, 100
"Ben-Hur" Wallace: The Life of General Lew Wallace (McKee), 148
bibliographies and reference works, 12–15
Bickford, Charles, 325
"Big Art, Big Billys" (Bell), 186
"Big Haul, A!" 39
"Big Kill," 29–30, 72, 98, 176; in film, 335
Bill O'Reilly's Legends and Lies: The Real West (Fisher and O'Reilly), 122
Billy and Paulita: A Novel (Cooper; revised version of *Joy of the Birds*), 275
"Billy Bonney's Bad Bucks" (Sederwall), 266
"Billy Bonny," 52
Billy LeRoy, the Colorado Bandit; or, The King of American Highwaymen (Daggett), 279
"Billy's Bastard Child" (Stahl), 257
"Billy the Irish" (Usmar), 266
Billy the Kid, 156; bibliography of, 13–15; biographical books about, 99, 101–3, 107, 113, 121, 128–29, 133, 151, 153, 155, 158, 165, 173–76, 179–80; biographical essays about, 35, 38- 44, 66, 68–69, 75, 79–81, 161–63, 188–91, 193, 195–207, 210–12, 214–15, 218–20, 235, 237–52, 255–61, 264, 266–68; and family, 16–18, 56, 78, 108, 151, 161, 180, 199, 215, 224, 227, 230–31, 234, 240, 249–50, 252, 283, 328; in fiction, 63, 269–310; in films, 311–45; legends about, 170–71, 173, 189, 205, 250, 260; manuscript collections about, 1–6, 10–11; photographs of, 346–54; writings of, 111

"Billy the Kid" (Donan), 62
"Billy the Kid" (Fergusson), 204
Billy the Kid (Forbes), 313
Billy the Kid (Taylor), 312
Billy the Kid (Vidor), 311
"Billy the Kid" (Woods), 307
"Billy the Kid: A Case Study in Epic Origins" (Adler), 184
"Billy the Kid: A Man All 'Bad'" (Chapman), 193
Billy the Kid: A Novel (Corle), 276
Billy the Kid: A Short and Violent Life (Utley), 174
Billy the Kid: Beyond the Grave (Jameson), 135
"Billy the Kid: Faust in America" (Fishwick), 205
Billy the Kid: His Life and Legend (Tuska), 15, 173, 310, 345
"Billy the Kid—100 Years of Legend," 189
Billy the Kid: Showdown in Lincoln County (Forbes), 316
Billy the Kid: The Bibliography of a Legend (Dykes), 14
Billy the Kid: The Endless Ride (Wallis), 179
Billy the Kid: The Legend of El Chivato (Fackler), 283
Billy the Kid: The Lost Interviews (Jameson), 136
Billy the Kid, The Most Hated, the Most Loved Outlaw New Mexico Ever Produced (Brothers and Hudson), 102
"Billy the Kid: The Photos Face Forensics" (Dyer), 349
"Billy the Kid: The Subject of an Interview with H. H. Whitehill of This City [Silver City, N.Mex.]" (Whitehill), 66
"Billy the Kid: The Trail of a Kansas Legend" (Koop), 215
"Billy the Kid: The True Story of a Western 'Bad Man'" (Hough), 210
"Billy the Kid: Thunder in the West" (Etulain), 201
"Billy the Kid among the Dime Novelists" (Etulain), 308
"Billy the Kid among the Novelists" (Etulain), 309

"Billy the Kid and Pat Garrett" (Metz), 218
Billy the Kid and the Lincoln County War: A Bibliography (Chamberlain), 13
"Billy the Kid as Seen in the Movies" (Hutton), 338
"Billy the Kid Country" (Utley), 264
"Billy the Kid Filmography" (Hutton and Strykowski), 343
Billy the Kid from Frisco (Cowdrick), 278
"Billy the Kid Gets Teacher by Accident" (McGaw), 79
"Billy the Kid in Arizona" (Corle), 197
"Billy the Kid in Fiction" (Tuska), 310
"Billy the Kid in Film" (Tuska), 345
Billy the Kid in Texas (Bob Steele), 314
"Billy the Kid Model Youth in Silver City Says Boyhood Chum," 75
Billy the Kid on Film (Boggs), 337
"Billy the Kid Photos" (Cline), 348
Billy the Kid Reader, The (Nolan), 70, 156, 204, 214, 226, 260–62, 291
Billy the Kid Returns (Roy Rogers), 315
Billy the Kid Rides Again (Miller), 92
"Billy the Kid's Final Escape" (Hutton), 211
"Billy the Kid's Friend Tells for the First Time of Thrilling Incidents" (Denton), 73
"Billy the Kid's Funeral" (McCarty), 351
"Billy the Kid's Great Escape" (Peterson and Hart), 233
Billy the Kid's Gun Justice (Crabbe), 319
Billy the Kid's Kid, 1875–1964: The Hispanic Connection (Garcia), 125
Billy the Kid's Last Ride (Aragon), 269
Billy the Kid's Pretenders: Brushy Bill and John Miller (Cooper), 93, 110
Billy the Kid's Range War (Steele), 320
"Billy the Kid's Teacher Saw Him as a Fearful 'Sissy'" (McGaw), 79
Billy the Kid Still Is Causing Trouble (McGaw), 81
Billy the Kid's Writings, Words, and Wit (Cooper), 111
Billy the Kid Trapped (Crabbe), 317
Billy the Kid Wanted (Crabbe), 318
"Billy Was Just Another Brat at Silver City" (McGaw), 78
"Birth of an Outlaw, The" (Nolan), 224

Blandina, Sister, 114
Blazer, Almer, 70
Blazer's Mill, 69–70
Blazing Frontier (Crabbe), 321
Boardman, Mark, 190, 346–47
Boggs, John D., 271, 325, 337; **p. 229**
Bommersbach, Jana, 191–91a
"Bonney Brothers, The" (Rasch), 234
books and pamphlets, 95–183
Bowdre, Charlie, 38–39, 69–70, 81, 153, 241
Boyhood of Billy the Kid, The (Mullin), 151
Brady, William, 24, 26, 145, 245, 255; **p. 228**
Brando, Marlon, 330
Braun, Matt, 272
Brent, William, 101
Brewer, Dick (Richard), 26, 225
Bristol, Warren, 28, 193; **p. 228**
Brothers, Mary Hudson, 102
Brown, Johnny Mack, 311, 326a
Brown, Rebecca B., 300
Brown, Richard Maxwell, 103
"Brushy's Not Billy" (McCutcheon), 86
Buckboard Days (S. Poe), 160
"Buckshot Roberts—Fighting Man!" 232
"Building His Own Legend: Billy the Kid and the Media" (Wilson), 267
"Bullet for Billy the Kid, A" (W. Henry), 289
Burnett, W. R., 273
Burns, Walter Noble, 5, 70, 87, 103, 116, 170, 204, 205, 309, 311, 340–41

"Caballero's Way, The" (O. Henry), 288
Cahill, Francis P. "Windy," 20–21, 73, 188, 226, 248
Caldwell, Clifford R., 104, 194
Campbell, Billy, 33
Camp Grant, Ariz., 21, 201. *See also* Fort Grant
Capture of Billy the Kid, The (Earle), 119
Carrizozo, N.Mex., courthouse collections, 7
"Carte de Visite of Billy the Kid, The" (R. Weddle), 353
Catron, Thomas Benton, 105, 177, 181

Cattle Stampede (Crabbe), 322
"Caught with His Pants Down? Billy the Kid vs. Pat Garrett" (Bell), 187
census of 1880, 239, 241; **p. 227**
Chaffey, David L., 105
Chamberlain, Kathleen, 13, 106, 192
Chapman, Arthur, 193
Chapman, Huston, I, 33, 161
Charlie Siringo's West: An Interpretive Biography (Lamar), 142
Chase, Mary Richards, 79. *See also* Richards, Mary
Chasing the Santa Fe Ring: Power and Privilege in Territorial New Mexico (Chaffey), 105
Chisum, John S., 36, 40–41, 50, 163, 194, 209, 213; in fiction, 279; in films, 323; **p. 228**
Chisum, Sallie, 263; in film, 323
Chisum (Wayne), 323
"Chisum: 'Cattle King of the Pecos,'" 194
Cimarron (N.Mex.) *News and Press*, 28, 30
Cisco Kid, 288
Clark, Neil McCullough, 260
"Classic Gunfights: The Kid's First Kill; Henry Antrim vs. Windy Cahill" (Bell), 188
Cline, Donald, 56, 107, 108, 195–96, 348
Clovis (N.Mex.) *News-Journal*, 76
"Clues to the Puzzle of Billy the Kid" (Rasch), 235
Coburn, James, 332
Code of the West, The (L'Aloge), 63
Coe, Frank, 68–69, 71
Coe, George, 72, 109
Colorado, 17, 223, 252; in dime novel, 279
Colorado Springs Weekly Gazette, 53
"Comparing Billy the Kid" (Gardner), 350
Complete and Factual Life of Billy the Kid, The (Brent), 101
"Computer Enters Hunt for Kid" (McCutcheon), 85
Connor, Anthony B., 75
Coolidge, Dane, 274
Cooper, Gale, 93, 110–14, 190, 191a; as novelist, 275
Corle, Edwin, 197, 276

Cost of a Killing (Cotton), 277
Cotton, Ralph, 277
Court of Inquiry: Lieutenant Colonel N. A. M. Dudley, Fort Stanton, New Mexico May–June–July 1879 (Barron), 3, 98
Cowdrick, J. C., 278
Cozzens, Gary, 198
Crabbe, Buster, 317–18, 321–22, 326–27, 333–34
Cracking the Billy the Kid Case Hoax: The Strange Plot to Exhume Billy the Kid, Convict Sheriff Pat Garrett of Murder, and Become President of the United States (Cooper), 93, 112
Cramer, T. Dudley, 115
"Croquet Kid," 94
"Croquet Kid, The" (Boardman), 346
Curtis, John B., 199
"Custer as Seen in Hollywood Films" (Hutton), 339

Daggett, Thomas F., 279
Daily Citizen (Tucson), 73, 74
Daily Gazette (Las Vegas, N.Mex.), 53, 59
Daily New Mexican (Santa Fe), 43, 49, 54
Daily Optic (Las Vegas, N.Mex.), 39, 41, 42, 48, 50, 51, 63
"Dead Desperado, Adventures of Billy, the Kid, as Narrated by Himself," 63, 206, 280
Dead Right: The Lincoln County War (Caldwell), 104
De Aragon, Ray John, 256
DeArment, Robert K., 161–63
"Death of Alexander McSween, The" (D. Gomber), 208
"Death of Billy the Kid, The" (Metz), 219
Death of Billy the Kid, The (J. Poe), 159
"Death of Billy the Kid, The" (Vidal), 304
DellaFlora, Anthony, 91
"Deluvina Maxwell," 200.
Demise of Billy the Kid, The (P. Lewis), 293
Denton, J. Fred, 73
Detrick, Dan, 228
"Dick Brewer: The Unlikely Gunfighter" (Nolan), 225
"Digging Up Billy" (Bommersbach), 191

"Digging Up Billy the Kid's Mother" (Bommersbach), 191a
"Digging Up" controversy, 89–93, 190–91a
dime novels, 63, 278–82, 291; comments on, 308–9
"Dim Trails: The Pursuit of the McCarty Family" (Rasch and Mullin), 249
Dirty Little Billy (Dragoti), 324
"Disorder in Lincoln County: Frank Warner Angel's Reports" (McCright and Powell), 216
Dolan, James J., 24, 26, 30, 106, 153, 163, 201, 216; **p. 228**
Donan, P., 62
Don Jenardo (John Woodruff Lewis), 291
Doughty, Francis W., 281
Down at Stein's Pass, 294
Dragoti, Stan, 324
"Dreamscape Desperado" (Hutton), 212, 340–41
Dudley, Nathan Augustus Monroe Dudley, 98, 140, 161, 175, 201; in fiction, 270; **p. 228**
Dudley Court of Inquiry, 3, 98
Dworkin, Mark J., 116
Dyer, Robert, 349
Dykes, J. C. (Jeff), 14, 117, 118

Ealy, Taylor, 100
Ealy family, 5–6, 100
Earle, James H., 119
Eco del Rio Grande (Las Cruces, N.Mex.), 23
Edwards, Harold, 120
El Paso Herald-Post, 78, 79
El Paso Southwesterner, 79, 80, 81
El Paso Times, 68
"Elusive Outlaw, An" (Haederle), 87
essays and book chapters, 156–268
Estevez, Emilio, 335–36
Etulain, Richard W., 121, 168; essays by, 201–3, 308–9
Evans, Jessie (Jesse), 22, 147; in fiction, 305

Fable, Edmund, Jr., 282
Fackler, Elizabeth, 283
"Facts Regarding the Escape of Billy the Kid" (Traylor), 261

Far Southwest, 1846–1912: A Territorial History, The (Lamar), 143
Fergusson, Harvey, 204
"Few Know the Kid like the Englishman behind the Annotated Edition of Pat Garrett's 1882 Book" (Walker), 265
"Fight at Blazer's Mill, in New Mexico, The," 70
Fighting Tenderfoot, The (Raine), 301
film criticism, 337–45
films, 211, 311–45
"First Blood: Another Look at the Killing of 'Windy Cahill'" (Nolan), 226
Fisher, David, 122
Fishwick, Marshall, 205
Fitzpatrick, George, 40
Five-Day Battle, 31, 98, 176, 208; in film, 335. See also "Big Kill"
Folliard, Thomas O., 38–39, 121, 153; in fiction, 279
"Footnote to Frontier History, A" (Curtis), 199
Forbes, Christopher, 313, 316
Forgotten Frontier: The Story of Southeastern New Mexico (Larson), 144
Fort Grant, 226, 248. See also Camp Grant, Ariz.
Fort Sumner, 53–54, 88
Fort Sumner, N.Mex., courthouse manuscript collections, 8
Four Faces West (McCrea and Bickford), 325
Four Fighters of Lincoln County (Utley), 175
"Friend Comes to the Defense of Notorious Billy the Kid, A" (F. Coe), 68
Fritz, Emil, 23
Fritz insurance controversy, 236
Frontier Doctor, A (Hoyt), 132
Frontier Fighter: The Autobiography of George W. Coe, Who Fought and Rode with Billy the Kid (Coe), 109
Fugitive of the Plains (Crabbe), 326
Fulton, Maurice Garland, 5, 30, 101, 103, 123–24, 133, 159, 206, 208, 247

Gamblin' Man (Mann), 296
Garcia, Abrana, 125; in fiction, 276; **p. 228**
Garcia, Elbert A., 125
Gardner, Mark Lee, 126, 149, 207, 266, 332, 350
Garrett, Pat, 159–60, 183, 187, 192, 207, 217, 260, 265; and Billy the Kid, 51, 53–54, 61, 95, 103, 183, 187, 192, 207, 218–21; biography by, of Billy, 58, 118, 124, 127, 157, 185, 197, 205, 250, 265; biographies about, 102, 126, 137, 149, 207; essays about, 51, 53–54, 61, 64, 107, 192, 218–21; in fiction, 276, 294, 302; in film, 274, 311, 323, 325, 331–32, 344
Gildea, Gus, 73
Gomber, Drew, 208
Goodbye Billy the Kid (Edwards), 120
"Gov. Wallace," 47
Grant, Joe, 35, 42
Grant County Herald (Silver City, N.Mex.), 19, 25
"Great Escape" (M. Smith), 253
Grey, Zane, 284–85
Gunsmoke in Lincoln County (Rasch), 161
Gutiérrez, Celsa, 257; in fiction, 275; in film, 329; **p. 228**

Haederle, Michael, 87
Haley, J. Evetts, 1, 71, 200
Hall, Oakley, 286
Hamlin, William Lee, 128
Hansen, Ron, 287, 309
Hart, Louis, 233
Heart's Desire: The Story of a Contented Town (Hough), 290
Hendron, J. W., 129
Henn, Nora True, 2, 82, 130, 189
Henn-Johnson Library and Local History Archives, 2
Henry, O., 288
Henry, Will, 289
High Noon in Lincoln (Utley), 176
Hinton, Harwood, Jr., 194, 209
Hispanics, 76, 96, 125, 158, 172–73, 189, 201, 203, 251, 262; in fiction, 283, 298, 301–2; in film, 325, 330; **p. 228**

History of "Billy the Kid" (Siringo), 165
History of the Lincoln County War (Fulton), 123
Holliday, Doc, 331
"Holy Grail for Sale, The" (Boardman), 347
Hough, Emerson, 131, 205, 210, 290
House, The, 153, 163, 176, 182, 201, 236; as portrayed in fiction, 270, 299. *See also* Dolan, James J.; Murphy, Lawrence G.
"How the Lincoln County War Started" (Rasch), 236
Hoyt, Henry F., 132, 154, 167
Hudson, Bell, 102
Hughes, Howard, 331
Hunt, Frazier, 133
"Hunting of Billy the Kid, The" (Nolan), 227
"Hunting of Billy the Kid, The" (Rasch), 237
Huston, Walter, 331
Hutton, Paul Andrew, 87, 110, 112, 190, 211–12, 338–43, 346

I Buried Billy (Anaya), 96
Illegal Rebirth of Billy the Kid, The (R. Brown), 300
Illustrated Life and Times of Billy the Kid, The (Bell), 99, 186
Indiana, 66, 78
Indiana Historical Society (Indianapolis), 9, 259. *See also* William Henry Smith Memorial Library
Indianapolis World, 67
Indians, 88, 144; in fiction, 278, 286, 297
"Interview with Billy the Kid" (Fitzpatrick), 40
In the Shadow of Billy the Kid: Susan McSween and the Lincoln County War (Chamberlain), 106, 229
Inventing Billy the Kid: Visions of the Outlaw in America, 1881–1981 (Tatum), 171
"Is There Anything Else to Say about Billy the Kid?" (Etulain), 203
"Is This Man Billy the Kid?" (McCutcheon), 84

Jacobsen, Joel, 134
Jameson, W. C., 110, 135–38
Janofsky, Michael, 90
"January 1883 Marriage of Paula Maxwell to Jose Jaramillo, The" (Stahl), 258
Jaramillo, José, 257–58
Jessie Evans: Lincoln County Badman (McCright and Powell) 147
"John Simpson Chisum, 1877–84" (Hinton), 209
Jones family, 97, 208
Joy of Birds (Cooper), 275
Juan Patrón: A Fallen Star in the Days of Billy the Kid (Tsompanas), 172
Jurado, Katy, 330
Jury of Six (Braun), 272

Kadlec, Robert F., 139
Kansas, 16, 60, 215, 229; in films, 324
Kaye, E. Donald, 140
Keleher, William A., 6, 141, 185
Kelly, Ned, 177
"Kid, The," 38
Kid, The (Hansen), 287, 309
"Kid, The" (Klasner), 214
"Kid and the McCarty Name, The" (Sanderson), 252
"Kid Brother" (Mills), 223
"Kid from Texas" (Murphy), 326a
"Kid Killed, The," 51
Kid Rides Again, The (Crabbe), 327
King, David, 213
King, Scottie, 189
Klasner, Lily Casey, 214
Koop, W. E., 80, 180, 215; **p. 228**
Kristofferson, Kris, 332

Lalire, Gregory, 207, 227
L'Aloge, Bob, 63
Lamar, Howard R., 142–43
Larson, Carole, 144
Last Days of Billy the Kid (McCarver), 328
Las Vegas (N.Mex.) *Daily Gazette*, 53
Las Vegas (N.Mex.) *Gazette*, 27, 29, 31, 35, 36, 38, 40, 45, 47
Lavash, Donald R., 145, 256
Law of the Land (Boggs), 271

Law on a Wild Frontier: Four Sheriffs of Lincoln County (Dykes), 117
Left Handed Gun, The (Newman), 329
"Legacy of an Outlaw, The" (Abarr), 83
"Legendary, Mysterious Kid, The" (Etulain), 202
Lehman, Paul Evan, 292
Leonard, Ira, 36, 45, 98; in fiction, 271
LeRoy, Billy, 238; in fiction, 279
Lewis, John Woodruff (Don Jenardo), 291
Lewis, Preston, 293
Lew Wallace: Militant Romantic (Morsberger and Morsberger), 150
"Lew Wallace and the Lincoln County War" (Henn), 82
Life and Death of John Henry Tunstall, The (Nolan), 152
Lincoln, Lincoln County, and the Lincoln County War: bibliography of, 13; book histories of, 104, 106, 123, 130, 134, 141, 182, 183; essays about, 12, 82, 130, 134, 141, 143, 153, 155, 174–77, 182, 201, 236; in fiction, 287, 305; in films, 323, 329, 332, 335–36; manuscript collections, 2. *See also* Billy the Kid; Dolan, James J.; House, The; Murphy, Lawrence G.
"Lincoln County," 28
Lincoln County and Its Wars (Henn), 130
Lincoln County Diary (Whitlow), 305
Lincoln County Leader (White Oaks, N.Mex.), 65
Lincoln County War: A Documentary History, The (Nolan), 153
"Lincoln County War: An Enduring Fascination" (Ball), 12
literary criticism, 308–10
London (England) *Times*, 61
Lone Star Cowboy, A (Siringo), 166
Los Angeles Times, 87
Lost Pardon of Billy the Kid: An Analysis, The (Cooper), 113
Lucky Billy (Vernon), 303
"Lunacy of Billy the Kid, The" (Boardman), 190

Ma'am Jones of the Pecos (E. Ball), 97
"Mackyswins and the Marfes, The" (Trujillo), 262

Mann, E. B., 296
"Man Named Antrim, A" (Rasch), 238
"Many Faces of Billy the Kid, The" (McCubbin) 352
Maverick Town: The Story of Old Tascosa (McCarty), 146
Maxwell, Deluvina, 200
Maxwell, Paulita, 111, 187, 201, 219, 257–58; in fiction, 271, 275–76
Maxwell, Pete, 53–54, 57, 111, 187, 219, 261; in fiction, 271
McCarty, Catherine, 16, 17, 77, 108, 215, 224, 249–50, 252. *See also* Antrim, Catherine McCarty
McCarty, Henry. *See* Billy the Kid
McCarty, Joe, 249–50; in film, 324. *See also* Antrim, Joseph (Joe)
McCarty, John L., 146
McCarty, Lea, 351
McCarver, Cody, 313, 316, 328
McCrea, Joel, 325
McCright, Grady E., 147, 216
McCubbin, Robert G., 217, 347, 352
McCutcheon, Chuck, 84, 85
McGaw, Bill, 78, 79, 80, 81
McGeeney, P. S., 294
McKee, Irving, 148
McMurtry, Larry, 295
McSween, Alexander, 23, 25, 27–28, 103, 106, 121, 153, 163, 175–76, 201, 208, 229, 236; in fiction, 270, 275; **p. 228**; and Fritz insurance controversy, 23, 121, 153
McSween, Susan, 98, 103, 106, 121, 153, 201, 229; and Billy the Kid, 106; in fiction, 270, 275, 303; and in film, 311
Meadows, John P., 183
Merchants Guns & Money: The Story of Lincoln County and Its Wars (Wilson), 182
Mesilla (N.Mex.) *News*, 46
Mesilla (N.Mex.) *Valley Independent*, 22, 24, 26, 33
Metz, Leon C., 149, 218–21
Mi Amigo: A Novel of the Southwest (Burnett), 273
Miller, Darlis, 222

Miller, Jay, 92
Miller, John, 84, 89, 93, 95, 110, 191
Mills, William A., 223
Missionaries, Outlaws, and Indians: Taylor F. Ealy at Lincoln and Zune, 1878–1881 (Bender), 100
Missouri, 241; **pp. 227–28**
Mitchell, Thomas, 331
Momaday, N. Scott, 297
"More on the McCartys" (Rasch), 240
Morrison, William V., 110, 169, 336
Morsberger, Katharine, 150
Morsberger, Robert E., 150
Morton, William, 26
movies: films and criticism, 211, 311–45
"Much ado about Billy" (Reed), 88
"Much Misunderstood Miss Chisum" (Turk and Robert), 263
Mullin, Robert N., 1, 80, 123, 151, 180, 199, 247, 249–50; **p. 228**
Murphy, Audie, 326a
Murphy, Lawrence G., 106, 153, 161, 163, 201
"Mystery of Billy the Kid's Home, The" (Cline), 195

Nathan Augustus Monroe Dudley, 1825–1910: Rogue, Hero, or Both (Kay), 140
National Archives, Washington, D.C., 3
Native Americans. *See* Indians
"Naw, Billy the Kid Didn't Do It!" (McGaw), 80
Neider, Charles, 298, 330
Nevada (Grey), 284
"New Light on the Legend of Billy the Kid" (Rasch and Mullin), 250
Newman, Paul, 329
Newman's Semi-weekly (Las Cruces, N.Mex.), 44
New Mexico Magazine, 40, 189
New Mexico State Tribune (Albuquerque), 69, 71, 72
New Mexico State University, 10
New Southwest and Grant County Herald, The, 57, 62
newspapers, 268
newspaper articles, 16–94

newspapers and Billy the Kid photographs, 94
newspapers and the exhumation, or "digging up," controversy, 89–93
New York Times, 90
Nita Stewart Haley Memorial Library and History Center, Midland, Texas, 1, 75
No Duty to Retreat: Violence and Values in American History and Society (Brown), 103
Nolan, Frederick, 15, 70, 152–57, 165, 184, 204, 214, 224–30, 256, 265–66, 291; books by, 152–57; essays by, 224–30; p. 227
novels, other literary works, and criticism, 269–310
Nunis, Doyce B., Jr., 132
Nun Who Rode on "Billy the Kid," The (Cooper), 114
Nye, Nelson, 299

"Obituary," 55
"Of Buckets, Bullets, and Buckshot: A New Look at Billy the Kid's Escape" (Snell), 255
Old King Brady and "Billy the Kid"; or, The Great Detective's Chase (Doughty), 281
"Old Problem, New Answers" (Rasch), 241
Olinger, Bob, 48–49, 65, 255; in fiction, 276
One-Eyed Jacks (Brando and Jurado), 330
"100th Anniversary of Pat Garrett's Life, The" (McCubbin), 217
"122 Years Later, the Lawmen Are Still Chasing Billy the Kid" (Janofsky), 90
"One Word More, And" (Rasch), 239
"Only One Man Living Who Saw 'Billy the Kid' in Both Life and Death," 76
Ore, Rebecca (Brown), 300
O'Reilly, Bill, 122
Otero, Miguel Antonio, Jr., 6, 158, 351
Outlaw, The (Hughes, Mitchell, Russell, Huston), 331
Outlaws, The (Toombs), 306
"Outlaws of New Mexico: The Exploits of a Band Headed by a New York Youth," 37

Page, Jake, 231
Palance, Jack, 335
"Parting Shot: At Lincoln Historic Site, Theories Have a Way of Coming Out in the Woodwork, A" (Cozzens), 198
Partner of the Wind (Thorp and Clark), 260
Pasó por Aquí (Rhodes), 302, 325
"Pat Garrett: The Life and Death of a Great Sheriff" (Gardner), 207
Pat Garrett: The Man behind the Badge (Jameson), 137
Pat Garrett: The Story of a Western Lawman (Metz), 149
Pat Garrett and Billy the Kid (Peckinpah, Kristofferson, Coburn), 332, 344
Pat Garrett and Billy the Kid as I Knew Them: Reminiscences of John P. Meadows (Wilson), 183
"Pat Garrett Nobody Knows, The" (Metz), 220
"Patrick Floyd Garrett: 'The Man Who Shot Billy the Kid'" (Chamberlain), 192
Pawley, Eugene, 232
Peckinpah, Sam, 332, 344
Peckinpah: The Western Films; A Reconsideration (Seydor), 344
Pecos Ranchers in the Lincoln County War, The (Cramer), 115
"Pecos War, The" (King), 213
Peterson, Barbara Tucker, 223
Phillips, Lou Diamond, 335–36
photographs, 85, 94, 217, 346–54
Pistols for Hire: A Tale of the Lincoln County War and the West's Most Desperate Outlaw, William (Billy the Kid) Bonney (Nye), 299
Pistols on the Pecos, 292
Poe, John William, 61, 159, 160, 189
Poe, Sophie, 160, 311
Pomeroy's Democrat (New York City), 17
Porter, William Sydney (O. Henry), 228
Powell, James H., 147, 216
Producers Releasing Corporation, 314, 317–22, 326–27, 333–34

"Quest for Joseph Antrim, The" (Rasch), 242

Radbourne, Allan, 248
Raine, William MacLeod, 301
Rasch, Philip J., 2, 80–81, 199; books by, 161–63; essays by, 234–50
Real Billy the Kid: With New Light on the Lincoln County War, The (Otero), 158
Reed, Ollie, Jr., 88
Regulators, 26, 69, 94, 104, 232; in film, 335
Return of the Outlaw Billy the Kid, The (Jameson and Bean), 110, 138
Rhodes, Eugene Manlove, 302, 325
Riata and Spurs: The Story of a Lifetime Spent in the Saddle as Cowboy and Ranger (Siringo), 167
Richards, Mary P. (Chase), 79, 230
Richardson, Bill, 110, 112, 190
Rio Grande Republican (Las Cruces, N.Mex.), 58
Rivera, John-Michael, 158
Robert, Sallie Lynn Chisum, 263
Roberts, Andrew L. "Buckshot," 69, 232
Roberts, William Henry "Brushy Bill," 86, 93, 110–11, 135–38, 169; in film, 191, 336
Rocky Mountain Sentinel (Santa Fe, N.Mex.), 32
Rogers, Roy, 315
Rudabaugh, Dave, 39, 254, 256
Russell, Jane, 331
Rynerson, William, 105; **p. 228**

Saga of Billy the Kid, The (Burns), 5, 103, 116, 170, 311
Sánchez, Linda (Lynda), 189, 251
Sanderson, Wayne, 17, 252; **p. 227**
Santa Fe, N.Mex., collections, 4
Santa Fe (N.Mex.) *Weekly Democrat*, 55
Santa Fe New Mexican, 23
Santa Fe Ring, 105, 111, 113, 143, 181
"Search for Alexander McSween, The" (Nolan), 229
"Secret Life of Billy the Kid" (Cline), 196
Sederwall, Steve, 89, 91, 187, 190, 266
"Seeking the Creation of the Kid's Death Record" (Stahl), 29

Seydor, Paul, 344
Shadow on the Trail (Grey), 285
Sheen, Charlie, 335
Sheriff of Sage Valley (Crabbe), 333
Sheriff William Brady: Tragic Hero of the Lincoln County War (Lavash), 145
"She Taught the Kid a Lesson: The Life of Mary Richards" (Nolan), 230
"Shooting Billy the Kid" (R. Weddle), 354
"Short, Nasty Life of Dave Rudabaugh, The" (R. Smith), 254
"Sidelights on Billy the Kid" (Rasch), 243
Silver City, N.Mex., 18–19, 57, 74, 77–79, 108, 180, 195, 238
Silver City, N.Mex., library collections, 11
Silver City (N.Mex.) *Daily Press*, 77
Silver City (N.Mex.) *Enterprise*, 66, 78
Silver City (N.Mex.) *Independent*, 75
Silver City (N.Mex.) *Mining Life*, 18
"Silver Screen Desperado: Billy the Kid in Movies" (Hutton), 342
Simmons, Marc, 164
Siringo, Charles A., 142, 165–68, 205
Sister Blandina, 114
Smith, H. E. "Sorghum," 74
Smith, Mike, 253
Smith, Robert Barr, 254
Snell, Dave, 255
"So, Who was Dan Detrick" (Nolan), 228
"Some More Grist for the Mill: Has the Last Word Been Said on Billy the Kid?" (Rasch), 244
Sonnichsen, C. L., 110, 169, 336
Southwesterner, The, 79–81
Special Billy the Kid issue, 256
Stahl, Robert J., 257–58, 266, 351
Stalking Billy the Kid: Brief Sketches of a Short Life (Simmons), 164
"State Not Kidding Around: Governor Won't Mind If Probe of the Notorious 19th century N. M. Outlaw Boosts Tourism" (DellaFlora), 91
Steckmesser, Kent L., 170
Steele, Bob, 314, 319–20
Story of Billy the Kid: New Mexico's Number One Desperado, The (Hendron), 129
Story of the Cowboy, The (Hough), 131

"Story of 'Windy Cahill,' The" (Rasch and Radbourne), 248
Strykowski, Jason, 259, 343
Such Men as Billy the Kid: The Lincoln County War Reconsidered (Jacobsen), 134
Sullivan, Tom, 89, 91, 190
Sun (New York City), 37, 56
Sutherland, Kiefer, 335–36

"Tale of the University of New Mexico Libraries' Three Millionth Volume, The" (D. Ball), 185
Tascosa, Texas, 146, 154
Tascosa: Its Life and Gaudy Times (Nolan), 154
Tatum, Stephen, 103, 171, 173
Taylor, Robert, 312
"Territory Is Better for His Death, The," 53
Texas Cowboy; or, Fifteen Years on the Hurricane Deck of a Spanish Pony, A (Siringo), 168
They "Knew" Billy the Kid: Interviews with Old-Time New Mexicans (Kadlec), 139
"They Loved Billy the Kid: To Them He was 'Billito'" (Sanchez), 251
Thomas Benton Catron and His Era (Westphall), 181
Thorp, N. Howard (Jack), 260
Thunder in the West: The Life and Legends of Billy the Kid (Etulain), 121
Time for Outrage (A. Bean), 270, 310
To Hell on a Fast Horse: Billy the Kid, Pat Garrett, and the Epic Chase to Justice in the Old West (Gardner), 126, 332
Toombs, Jane, 306
Tragic Days of Billy the Kid, The (Hunt), 133
Trailing Billy the Kid (Rasch), 162, 234–35, 237–50
Traylor, Leslie, 261
"Trials of Billy the Kid, The" (Rasch), 245
True Life of Billy the Kid, The (Fable), 282
True Life of Billy the Kid, The (J. Lewis), 291)
Truesdell, Chauncey O., 77
True Story of Billy the Kid: A Tale of the Lincoln County War, The (Hamlin), 128

True West, 186
Trujillo, Francisco, 262
"Truth and Tall Tales of Pat Garrett, The" (Metz), 221
Tsompanas, Paul L., 172
Tunstall, John Henry, 24–25, 152, 163, 175–76, 225, 271; in fiction, 270, 303; in films, 323, 329, 335
Turk, David S., 263
Tuska, Jon, 15, 173, 310, 345
"Twenty-One Men He Put Bullets Through, The" (Rasch), 246

"Unholy Bargain in a Cursed Place: Lew Wallace, William Bonney, and New Mexico Territory, 1878–1881" (Strykowski), 259
University of Arizona Library, Tucson, 5
University of New Mexico, Albuquerque, 6
Upson, Marshall Ashmun "Ash," 27, 87, 101, 118, 127, 136, 157, 185, 205, 265; in film, 336
Usmar, Chuck, 266
Utley, Robert M., 15; books by, 87, 173, 174–77; essay by, 264

Vernon, John, 303
Vidal, Gore, 304
Vidor, King, 311
Violence in Lincoln County, 1869–1881 (Keleher), 141
Visions of New Mexico, 256

Walker, Dale, 265
Wallace, Lew, 9, 35–36, 46–47, 67, 82, 113, 148, 150, 175–76, 178, 259; in fiction, 279
Wallis, Michael, 179
Wanted: The Outlaw Lives of Billy the Kid and Ned Kelly (Utley), 177
War Paint (Coolidge), 274
Warriors of Lincoln County (Rasch), 163
"Was Billy the Kid a Superhero—or a Super Scoundrel?" (Page), 231
Wayne, John, 323
Weddle, Jerry (Richard), 180, 188, 256; **p. 228**

Weddle, Richard (Jerry), 180, 194, 353–54
Weekly New Mexican (Santa Fe, N.Mex.), 34
Western Cyclone (Crabbe), 334
Western Hero in History and Legend, The (Steckmesser), 170
West of Billy the Kid, The (Nolan), 155, 303
Westphall, Victor, 3, 181
Whatever Happened to Billy the Kid? (Airy), 95
"What If Everything We Know about Billy the Kid Is Wrong?" 266
Whitehill, H. H., 66, 78
Whitlow, B. Duane, 305
"Why So Much on Billy the Kid?" (Rasch), 247
Wichita, Kans., 16, 60
Wichita Tribune, 16
Wichita Weekly Eagle, 60
Wilcox, Lucius M. "Lute," 40

William Henry Smith Memorial Library, 9
Willoughby, Lee Davis, 306
Wilson, Billy, 39, 45
Wilson, John P., 182–83, 267, 268
"With His Boots Off: First Newspaper Reports on the Death of Billy the Kid" (Wilson), 268
women, 79, 97, 106, 125, 203, 222, 257, 258, 263; in fiction, 270, 279, 283, 288, 290, 303, 306; in film, 322, 326, 331, 336; **p. 228**
"Women of Lincoln County, 1860–1900, The" (D. Miller), 222
Woods, Walter, 307

Young Guns (Estevez, Sutherland, Phillips, Sheen, Palance), 335
Young Guns II (Estevez, Sutherland, Phillips), 191, 336

www.ingramcontent.com/pod-product-compliance
Lightning Source LLC
Chambersburg PA
CBHW031433160426
43195CB00010BB/718